Cathy,
hope you enjoy
the book.
Go A's!

Don

*A Family's
Long Love Affair
with One of
Baseball's Best Teams*

A Family's
Long Love Affair
with One of
Baseball's Best Teams

Donald A. Marquez Sr.

Union City Press

For further information, please contact:
don_ucpress@yahoo.com

Book design by
Arbor Books, Inc.
19 Spear Road, Suite 301
Ramsey, NJ 07446
www.arborbooks.com

Printed in the United States

Generation A's Fans:
A Family's Long Love Affair with One of Baseball's Best Teams
Donald A. Marquez Sr.

1. Title 2. Author 3. Sports/Baseball

Library of Congress Control Number: 2007921929

ISBN 10: 0-9793312-0-X
ISBN 13: 978-0-9793312-0-6

Contents

Foreword

By Tonianne (Marquez) Nemeth

I've been thinking a lot lately on how and why the A's are so important to us as a family—more so than the Raiders or other teams have been. The love and passion for them crosses gender and generations, in-laws and friends—we are connected by THIS team—the underdogs on the other side of the bay. I think Finley worked to make it a family game...Thursday was Lady's Day— Dad would take us to the game and pay $1.50 for himself, $0.75 each for the boys and the girls would get in free (bleacher seats of course)...toss in homemade goodies and he spent less than $10.00 (don't know what parking was then) to take his large group of kids to the game. And don't forget Family Nights, Farmer's Day, Camera Day, etc.—brought fans closer to the game and to the team. True we had great teams to follow but even during the lean years, the family kept going to games. It blows my mind that everyone in our family has an A's story —aunts, uncles, cousins, everyone! We can talk about the A's with anyone in the family—common ground. Pictures come to mind too...a baby in the arms of future Hall of Famers (Don with Reggie, Scott with Rickie, Patch with Stew)—whoa!!

We are a large family who grew up without many of life's extras but we thrived—the A's have always been homegrown and they thrive. As a family, we appreciate the things in life that others take for granted—that's why we can love and follow our team even when they aren't playing well. We want our kids to know what it was like to sit in the bleachers, get burnt to a crisp and beg for extra innings. We want them to go to a double-header (not even sched- uled anymore) so you get two games for the price of one and usually some kind of entertainment between games. We want them to remember when the peanuts were hot and the vendors would toss you a double pack for fifty cents. We want them to create their own memories to share with our grandkids.

The A's are important to us because we can relate to them—we share their joys and their disappointments but we are always there for them—just like we are for each other. The A's are home-made (not store-bought) like we are. They make their own prom dresses and shop at Target—they don't need $100 million dollar payroll to win a championship and we don't need $$ to be a family. They have fun and we have fun watching them—it doesn't get any better than that!

Love ya, Tone

Preface

They were no different than any other adolescent male, two young men emulating their baseball heroes on a sunny summer afternoon in 1973. And on this particular day, 15 year-old John Marquez' imitation of Oakland's Jim "Catfish" Hunter was, well, *perfect*. He and lifelong pal Tony Lopez were engaged in a typical one-on-one battle of "fast pitch," the back wall of the restroom at Cherry Grove Park serving as the catcher's area, the strike zone a poorly spray-painted box.

Typical this day with one glaring exception: today John was dealing that rarest of diamond gems, a perfect game through seven innings. Making this task even more daunting was the fact that there were no fielders behind him to bail him out. (When the real Catfish Hunter etched his name in the record books against the formidable Minnesota Twins in May 1968, he had eight gloves worth of help in the yard. To his credit, he hardly needed them.) But John, in his quest for excellence, had only his trusty left arm and over-used mitt to count on. And after retiring the side in order midway through the game, he made a not-so-subtle mention of what was transpiring to Tony.

"We'd switch each day between being the A's or the opposing team. Well on this day it was my turn to be the A's. We were going along (both announcing) when after about five innings, I realized he hadn't had a hit. Since there were no walks that meant 'Catfish,' who was on the mound that day, was pitching a perfecto. I let Tony know as I passed him on my way to the plate."

Tony, for his part, needed to hit just one fair ball past the pitcher, or in the words of Crash Davis of Bull Durham fame, "a flare, a gork, a ground ball with eyes." Up to now he had failed to do even that. As the top of the 8th inning got underway, Tony had nary a hope of catching John on the scoreboard ("I was beating him some-thing like, 12–0"). In fact, with but six chances to get a man on base, the game itself had become a foregone conclusion and the score the furthest thing from either teenagers' mind.…

A block or so away, John's youngest brother, Don, was belting out the National Anthem in his backyard, which was followed by the starting lineups for that afternoon's "game" between the Oakland A's and the Detroit Tigers. The six-year old gave the play-by-play, pitched, batted, fielded, ran the bases, and pretty much handled all the duties save for peanut vendor.

As little Don rested on the front yard lawn after his game of solitary baseball, sipping cherry flavored Kool-Aid and impatiently waiting for the sports page to be delivered, he heard Mr. King call to him from across the street.

"Don Min-yon! How'd we do today?"

"5–4, Oakland, on Reggie's dinger in the ninth," Don answered his favorite neighbor.

Mr. King grinned. "They always pull it out in the end, don't they? Now let's see Reggie do that in the real game tonight."

Inside the house, Don's oldest sister, Tonianne, sat transfixed in her bedroom, ear to her transistor radio, listening as Monte Moore got set to call the action for tonight's *real game* between the World Champion A's and the Kansas City Royals. Mom called out that dinner was not only ready; it was getting cold. But dinner could wait as far as Toni was concerned. The first pitch was only moments away and besides, Jim "Catfish" Hunter was on the mound.

Ah, yes. Catfish. The sun was beginning to set on Cherry Grove Park as John Marquez walked out to the mound to pitch the 8th inning. He was flirting ever so dangerously with "history." After retiring the first two batters, John made a diving stop on a ball for the third out, preserving the perfecto. Tony Lopez, now acting the part of the crowd, cheered wildly. (John: "I didn't even try to get a hit in the ninth and he couldn't wait to get up.")

Finally, with two outs in the final frame, Tony hit a line drive back to John who caught it for the final out. In one motion, Tony the opposing batter became Tony the ecstatic teammate as he leaped into John's waiting arms, cheering and screaming at the top of his lungs: "Catfish is Perfect! Catfish is Perfect!"

Flash forward thirty years to September 2003. The Oakland A's are in first place, desperately trying to stave off the Seattle Mariners for supremacy in the American League West, and wouldn't you know it, their closest pursuers are in for a late-season, three-game showdown that could very well decide who plays past September. Oakland's magic number to clinch a thir-teenth division crown—and fourteenth playoff berth—is down to five, and although Seattle is making things difficult, the title is still theirs for the taking. The season is drawing to a close, yet the weather has a definitive summer feel to it, very much the kind of day that six-year old Don Marquez would "play ball" in back in '73. Only now Don Marquez is thirty-six, though his boyish looks belie that number. Nothing thrills him more than a pennant race and he itches for the chance to see his team clinch at home, like they did for him in '88 and '89 and again on the final day of that incredible 2000 season. But right now it's pre-game and the goose bumps are not for the A's, but for his oldest sister, Tonianne. For today is Breast Cancer Awareness day at the Network Associates Coliseum and Tonianne and Don's Aunt Marie are stationed in cen-terfield with hundreds of other women who have been victimized by this deadly disease. Don is in the stands with his mom, Dodie, his Uncle Dan, and Tonianne's son, Patrick. As two of the bravest women he has ever known wave to him from the field, tears well up in Don's eyes. Countless memories spent in the precise vicin-ity of where he was standing, cheering on his heroes, so many of those times spent with Tonianne, and now he was cheering *her*. Saluting her. Thanking her. When Tonianne joined her not-so lit-tle brother and the rest of her family in the bleachers following the pre-game ceremony, all she could talk about was slapping five with

Miguel Tejada, the reigning American League Most Valuable Player and a fan favorite in Oakland. And once again the clock was turned back. Tonianne wasn't in her forties anymore; she was a teenager, gushing about Reggie Jackson, who too had won an MVP while wearing an "A" stitched to his uniform. There was a wonderful sense of déjà vu as she talked of "never washing her hand again," the one that touched Miguel Tejada as he passed her in the field. That the Seattle Mariners inched closer to the A's with a second consecutive convincing victory did little to dampen Don's mood. Like "Catfish" in '68 and his brother John setting down 27 in a row against his pal Tony, this day was indeed perfect.

Introduction

Almost fifteen years have passed since my Grandma Toni made the trip back Home. She died in October 1992, exactly one month before my son was born. I remember speaking at the mortuary to the multitude that she left behind, solemnly noting that such gatherings had grown too far and few between. I have now come to understand that we are victims of our own enormity. It was inevitable that a family so colossal, such as the one begot by Abel and Antonia Martinez, would set forth and multiply. And while I have serious reservations that any of us are destined to parent a dozen or so children (let alone have fifty grandkids), we have done well enough to add to the Martinez lineage—and legacy. Alas, as we have dispersed into mini-families and have scattered across this great nation, as we struggle to make-do in this fast-paced universe in which we reside, we have come to accept the fact that our only opportunity to unite is at weddings and funerals.

And sporting events, of course. Sporting events? What? Huh? Well, sure. Like when our Oakland A's kick-started the turn of this century with their first division title in eight years, more than a dozen family members and I gathered at the Coliseum that warm autumn day to celebrate the clinch. And in the recently completed 2006 season, the ebbs and flows of a baseball campaign were captured in e-mails between me and my siblings. But the games themselves, while they surely bring us together, are not the driving force to *how* we interact. Instead, it is often the *outcome* of those contests that determines our behavior. Otherwise, why is that my brother John merely shakes my hand when we happen to bump into each other, yet on that amazing afternoon in October 2000, he fought through a crowd to embrace me? (I admit I hugged him back; it had been eight years, ok?) Actually, being around John can be dangerous when our teams win. Rose has yet to completely recover from a chokehold that she received when the Raiders beat the Browns in the playoffs—*more than twenty five years ago.* (Of course, being around some family members can be even more hazardous when our teams lose. But we won't mention names).

I am not sure that a number exists for the amount of times a Martinez has set foot in the Oakland Coliseum. The players, they come and go, some memorable, some forgettable, some downright awful. Even the uniform design changes from time-to-time. And still our family represents, passed on from one generation to the next. Paintings and banners in and around the stadium remind even the most casual fan of the glory years in Oakland. Countless publications and videos further document the success stories that have taken place on the field. But wedged deep in the confines of that special place on 66th Avenue—unseen and unheard—are our memories. Memories that on occasion transcended the numbers on the scoreboard; memories that were made better still by the unmistakable sweet taste of triumph. Truly, there's nothing like being thirteen and attending a rainy doubleheader that your father flat out forbade you to go to—especially when the menu consists of the company of your oldest sister, soggy tostadas, and an A's sweep. What better way to spend a Sunday afternoon than under a steady drizzle while an upstart Oakland team kicks the Angels' butts to take over first place? And who cares that it's only April? To an A's fanatic in his teens, the sun was shining and we were winning gutchecks in the heart of a pennant race.

Moments such as these are what I cling to.

The casual fan will discover that this is far more than just another baseball book and much more than about a certain team, who for nearly forty years have been one of the Major League's most successful and colorful franchises to take part in Abner Doubleday's creation. Instead, it is about one family's infatuation with that ball club, as seen through our very eyes. Ours is a love affair that began in 1968 when Charlie Finley uprooted the A's from Kansas City to the West Coast and continues today as a fifth generation of fans has emerged. We have cheered our A's through the Swingin' years of the 70's, the Billy Ball times of the early 80's, the Bash Brothers era of the late 80's and early 90's to today's new legion of young stars. World Series and playoffs, the 1987 All-Star Game, homeruns, no-hitters, and record-setting perform-ances, we were there in some form or fashion. And some of us even integrated their success stories into our own "games." While our most cherished moments center mostly on the glory years, we look back on the dog days with a certain fondness. The constant threats of moving, 108 losses in 1979, having your choice of seat-ing every night (hey, they might even ask you to play!). In recent years, we have applauded the efforts of our low-budget team only to suffer through October heartaches and the exodus of homegrown stars.

Win or lose, we've always been there for them. Whether at the ballpark, in front of the TV, via a radio broadcast, or even on-line, the Martinez/Marquez family has had the privilege of taking part in A's Ball for nearly forty wonderful years, through the very best—and even worst—of times. We may not be lovable losers like Chicago Cub fans, or wear torment as well as the Red Sox Nation used to, but we are enamored with our A's just the same.

Many thanks to the Oakland A's for giving us so many won-derful memories since 1968. I also wish to offer my sincerest gratitude to two amazing web sites that helped fill in some of the blanks. Most of what are you about to read is from memory. But when I needed some hard, cold, and sometimes off-the-wall facts, www.BaseballLibrary.com and www.retrosheet.org were there. And, finally, a special thanks to the family that has stood by the A's all these years. It's like reading the "begats" in the Bible: Grandma Toni begat Mom, Mom begat Ernie Jr., Ernie Jr. begat Christina, and Christina begat Ethan. Five generations worth…and counting.

I hope you will enjoy reading this book as much as I enjoyed writing it. It's been a long time coming.

This is our story.

1 / A Fan in the Making

"The baseball box score is the pithiest form of written communication in America today. It is abbreviated history. It is two or three hours of complex activity, virtually inscribed on the head of a pin, yet no knowing reader suffers from eyestrain."

—Fred Schwed Jr., author of
How to Watch a Baseball Game

First off, I am not to be confused with that Red Sox fan from *Fever Pitch*. I don't have to see every single inning of every game. I do get mad when my team is playing lousy. But I will say this: every loss hurts—a little. Yeah, it's a long season but whether it's April or October, I want to win. And when we do, the sun shines a little brighter, every meal tastes a little better, and a day at the office seems a little less hectic. I'm not obsessed with the A's but I do love them. Sue me.

Come to think of it, it's safe to say that baseball was my *first* love. Maybe because back then it was safe to love baseball. In 1972, there was nary a chance of it breaking my five-year old heart. Well, that's not totally accurate; after all, the '72 season was cut short by something that is a little more common these days: the dreaded strike. And I don't mean the kind that pitchers throw.

Thankfully, baseball still got in 150 games that year, not like in '81 when the strike wiped out two months and made a mockery of the post-season, or in '94 when there was no post-season at all. Today there's as much talk of labor negotiations and revenue sharing as there is homeruns. Unless, of course, we're talking about guys on steroids who hit homeruns.

1

And although baseball has left me slightly jaded, this grand old game that I grew up on still manages to captivate and intrigue me even now. I doubt, though, that it'll ever enthrall me the way it did when I was a kid. The love of baseball came easy to a little guy like me being raised in San Leandro, California, on the outskirts of Oakland. The game hadn't yet lost its innocence, which was great because well, neither had I.

I wasn't what you'd call a gifted child, so I never really got into playing organized ball. Consequently, I paid less attention to the fundamentals and strategies, instead getting caught up in the nostalgic elements of the game. That's not to say I didn't understand the hit-and-run or the infield fly rule but what really got my attention was the aura and romance of baseball: the pomp and circumstance that surrounds Opening Day, the excitement of pennant races, the thrills that October brings. The sense that on any given day you might see something that had never been done before.

And I was thoroughly wrapped up in the game's rich history, constantly checking out books on Babe Ruth, Ted Williams, Jackie Robinson, and Roberto Clemente from the local library. While my schoolmates were playing kickball and hopscotch at recess, I was camped out in the school library, my nose in whatever baseball publication I could get my hands on. I couldn't put them down; I was completely under the spell of the author.

Hey, remember that scene in *The Natural* when sleazy sportswriter Max Mercy approached Roy Hobbs before the final game? Hobbs, who had spent 17 years just to get back into a game he so cherished, possessed little patience for a guy like Mercy (played expertly by Robert Duvall). After a brief dialogue at Hobbs' locker, the slugger (portrayed by Robert Redford) challenged Mercy's claim to having the game's best interests at heart: "You ever play ball, Max?" Mercy paused thoughtfully before he answered: "No, never have. But I make it a little more fun to watch."

I was 18 years old when that movie came out and for some reason that scene stuck with me. Maybe it's because it reminded me of when I was younger, waiting anxiously for the newspaper to crash against the front of the house. Not just so I could study stats, as I did religiously, but to read the how's and the whys of what went down at the ball yard. And I would emulate the sportscasters that I saw on the 11:00 news, years before *Sports Center* invaded our living rooms and long before the 24-hour sports and entertainment channel became the marvel that it is today. I would sneak out to the front porch on Saturday mornings before anyone else (except for Mom) had awaken and like a kid opening a present on Christmas day, I would treat the other sections of the newspaper in my hand like wrapping paper until I got to the gift; in this case, the sports pages. That section to me was the Golden Ticket in a Wonka bar. Only I was treated to one every day. Still, Saturday mornings were the best, sitting on the floor with the sports page opened to the baseball box scores, a large bowl of Trix cereal in front of me. (To this day, it is almost impossible for me to have a meal without a side order of sports, be it the newspaper, the Internet, or an old book. Mom will playfully scold me when I eat at her house: "Did you come to visit me or the sports page?") So there I sat munching on cereal made for kids and not silly rabbits, reading through the box scores as if I was John O'Reilly on *ABC News* or Monte Moore going through the out of town games on the A's wrap-up. "And in Kansas City, John Mayberry slugged his 22nd homerun to lead the Royals past the slumping White Sox, 4–2 before 22,345 rain-soaked spectators at Comiskey Park."

More than anything, Duvall's quote from *The Natural* took me back to those days in the school library, lost in a book, where word wizards like Roger Kahn (B*oys of Summer*) would transport me to an era when baseball was truly golden. In turn, I saw every book report as an opportunity to introduce my teachers to a side of the game they had not yet seen. I wanted them to be there when the Babe pointed to the grandstands at Wrigley. Or when Teddy Ballgame hit .406 in '41. To know and admire the tenacity of Robinson and the quiet compassion of Clemente. I wasn't so concerned about the grade; I just wanted to make the game of baseball "a little more fun to watch."

The game's glorious past was indeed special in its own right. Seeing history made before my very eyes was that and a whole lot more. When Hank Aaron broke Ruth's career homerun record on April 8, 1974, my friend Sherri King and I pounded on front doors up and down Gilmore Drive to let our neighbors know about it. Who cares that it was 9:00 on a school night and I was still two weeks shy of my *seventh* birthday? I spent my lunch hour—alone—in the library at Woodrow Wilson Elementary School chomping on a bologna-and-cheese sandwich the day New York's Bucky "Bleeping" Dent wrecked the Red Sox with his famous homerun over the Green Monster in the 1978 playoff. See, I didn't need to read about Hank's 715th or Dent's historic blow; I was "there," man.

As goose-bumpy as those moments were, they take a back seat to my up-close-and-personal experiences with the Oakland A's. As luck would have it, the A's won the World Series during my first three years in school, long before pro basketball coach Pat Riley introduced the phrase "three-peat" into sports lore. This is no small feat; only the New York Yankees have strung together championship seasons of three or more. Which puts the A's in pretty good company. Of course, my older brothers and sisters were the beneficiaries of that era, that is, they were old enough to actually go to playoff and World Series games. But that's not to say I don't have a few memories of my own stashed away. How could I not? My siblings and their friends would beg me to recite the entire A's lineup—player, position, uniform number and then, as if that weren't challenging enough for a first-grader, they asked me to repeat it *backwards*. I didn't mind though, in fact I'd toss in some additional tidbits for good measure, big league experience, stats from the previous season, etc. Shoot, I even knew the players' birthdays. Yes I amazed them all, but then again they were easily entertained.

The Swingin' A's were both amazing and entertaining and it all started with Charlie Finley and his uncanny ability to find— and sign—talent. But it was the sweat and sacrifice made by his players that made him the success he was. It's his players that I remember most. Reggie's commanding presence and his flair for the dramatic, the cool of Catfish in the biggest of games. Rollie's handlebar mustache and his penchant for making his manager— and fans—sweat out the ninth inning. (More often than not, he'd close the door on his opponents.) The speed of Bill North and Campy Campaneris, thieves both, the raw talent that was Vida Blue. Sal Bando's leadership, Joe Rudi's professionalism, Dick Green's glove. Finley's fireworks after homeruns and wins—there was a lot of both in those days. Reggie on crutches for the '72 Classic, Geno picking up the slack, putting on a Reggiesque performance with four home runs, Rudi's catch against the wall to rob Menke. Back-to-back in '73 featured a double-MVP from Jax and 20-win seasons from Cat, Holtzman, and Blue. Racing home as fast as my six-year old legs would carry me to catch the last few outs of Hunter's playoff-clinching shutout against the O's. Once More in '74, a Cy for Catfish, another October party. Watching the fireworks from Cherry Grove Park.

Yeah, life was pretty good back then—baseball was still the MGM of sports and the A's had a room with a spectacular view. Yet even had I tried, there was no escaping the clutches of the National Pastime.

Not when you're raised in a family of baseball fanatics.

Uncle Rick, Grandma, Uncle Dan

2 / Grandpa Abe and the Babe(s)

*"It is designed to break your heart. The game begins in
the spring, when everything else begins again, and it
blossoms in the summer, filling the afternoons and
evenings, and then as soon as the chill rains come, it
leaves you to face the fall alone."*

—The late A. Bartlett Giamatti,
from "The Green Fields of the Mind"
(The former Major League commissioner was surely
talking about his beloved baseball, but he could have also
been referring to my Grandpa Abel, who was born in the
spring—April 1909—and died in November 1980,
leaving his family to "face the fall alone.")

Our story really begins long before the A's played a single game
in the Bay Area, even before they wore uniforms with "KC" across
their chests. No, to get to the roots of this tale, we have to dig
deeper, back when the Athletics were located in Philadelphia, the
City of Brotherly Love. Thus we commence with the matrimony
of Abel Martinez and Antonia (Toni) Lovato, my grandparents on
my mom's side. Both were born and raised in southern Colorado
and it was there that they were wed. The year was 1927, a season
that would belong to the New York Yankees' Murderers Row,
widely considered the greatest team to ever set foot on a baseball
diamond. (The Philadelphia A's often felt the sting of playing in
the same league as New York; their 91 victories in '27 were only
good for second place, an astonishing 19 games behind the
Bombers.) It is right and proper to draw comparisons between my
grandparents and that legendary Yankee ball club because if I know
anything about either of them, it is that they produced in numbers

7

that boggle the mind. 1927 was more than just my grandparents exchanging vows or Ruth and Gehrig bombing their way to a second World Series title. It was the dawning of two dynasties. From that year through 1950, New York went to thirteen World Series and won twelve. Any challengers to the Yankees' throne were quickly disregarded as mere child's play. Meanwhile, there were plenty of children at play in the Martinez household. During the same time that New York's supremacy was at its peak, the couple from Colorado churned out fourteen kids, or roughly the same amount of Hall-of-Famers to wear pinstripes in that era. The Yankees have continued to rule the baseball roost—32 pennants, 22 world titles through 1980 (the year that Grandpa passed) and 39 and 26 overall. Equally impressive is the legacy left behind by Abel Martinez, one that had grown even greater by the time his wife rejoined him in 1992 and continues to blossom today (seemingly *every* day).

All in all, my grandparents raised eleven children to adulthood (three others died as infants). Still impressed by the '27 Yankees? Get a load of this lineup:

Aunt Fran...born Frances Mae on February 20, 1930... Mom's Matron-of-Honor...late husband Walter served in the Navy with my father and introduced him to Mom (says Mom with a laugh, "and I have been throwing rocks at Walt's grave ever since")...mother of the first three grandchildren born to the Martinez family—Walter James (first grandson), Carla (first granddaughter) and Brenda...also mother to the 20th grandchild (Marta)...grandmother of eight, great-grandmother of thirteen... first-born Jimmy merits special mention...born with damage to his brain, doctors recommended he be institutionalized and did not give him long to live...today Jimmy is fifty-five years old, having competed in the Special Olympics and endearing himself to all who have met him...the family left Oakland thirty-some years ago, first to the LA area, then to Oregon...but Oakland has never left them...

Uncle Donald...born Donald Eugene on May 9, 1932...my namesake...lovable—and loving—character, missed by all...married his bride Rose on the same day as my parents...made it a point to celebrate with them every June 2...family man, first and foremost…proud father of five—Donna, Marcia, Sandra, Toby, and Teresa…grandfather of fourteen, great-grandfather of two…he cherished the games…would root for the A's at the Coliseum and cheer on his son and nephews at Little League parks…did both with tremendous passion…was quick to give umpires an earful if a call went against his team…loved the Oakland ball clubs like they were family…lived and died with them—literally…as he listened to an A's broadcast at his home in May of 1983, he suffered a fatal heart attack…family was devastated by his untimely death…he was 51.…

Aunt Mac…born Ursula Maxine on April 1, 1934…my godmother…married to my godfather Sal for fifty-two years…shares Martinez record with Mom for most kids (8)—Debbie, Anita, Frannie, Sal Jr., Joe, Peter, Phil, and Amanda…grandmother of eighteen, tops among her siblings…great-grandmother of eight…as her family as grown in numbers that would make her own mother beam with pride, her zest for sports has not wavered…devoted A's and Raider fan.…

My Mom…read all about her in Chapter 3.

Aunt Sue, born Susan Marcella on April 4, 1938…Maid-of-Honor at my parents' wedding…wore yellow to go with Matron-of-Honor Fran's green…(A's colors a mere coincidence, team's move to Oakland was still twelve years away)…mother of six: Leonard, David, Theresa, Cathy, Michael and Mary…grandmother of thirteen…great-grandmother of five.…

Aunt Gloria…born Gloria Thelma on January 30, 1940…died at twenty-four after giving birth to a daughter of the same name…Grandpa Abel and Grandma Toni took to raising their granddaughter, thus cousin Gloria shared a bond with our grandparents that few had the honor of…accompanied Grandma Toni to many an A's game…gave her mother three grandchildren that she'd never know—Mariko, Louis, and Savana.…

Aunt Genie…born Belia Genevieve on July 2, 1941…last of the Martinez children to be born in Colorado…family moved to California shortly thereafter…she and Uncle Paul raised three children—Paul Jr., Anna, and Linda…loving grandmother of six…plus two great-grandchildren…she followed the games with great interest, from the Little Leagues to the pros…even later, restricted to a wheelchair, she could be found at the Coliseum cheering on the A's…another family member to leave us way too soon…she died in September 2002 at the age of 61.…

Aunt Minda…born Elena Erminda on May 16, 1945…first of the Martinez children born in Oakland (that reached adulthood)…she has faithfully supported the city's teams…married a ballplayer, Jack Stuart, a prep star coveted by a few Big League clubs…an injury cut his would-be career prematurely…shortly thereafter, Aunt Minda was left to raise her two kids—Wayne and Victoria—on her own…grandmother of five, including the first twins born to the Martinez clan.…

Uncle Rick…born Richard Aaron on January 20, 1947…the most recent to leave us (in February 2004)…died, like his brother Donald before him, in his own home…avid sports fan…allegiances stayed with Oakland even after he moved to New York…most of his calls to the West Coast went like this: "hello, how's the family, what's up with the A's and Raiders?"…last two visits to California were in 1989 and 1992 and the state was rocked by major earthquakes both times…joked about never returning…unfortunately, he didn't get the opportunity to…unbelievable character missed by all of us…left behind wife Jackie, son Christopher, and the last of the Martinez grandchildren—Kelsey and Ashley.…

Aunt Joanna, born Joanna Marie on August 9, 1948…the youngest daughter born to my grandparents…mother of three: John III, Samantha, and Emily…grandmother of eight…enjoys the gathering of family more than the sporting events themselves…has gone to tail-gate parties with no ticket to the actual game.…

Uncle Dan…born Anthony Daniel on October 13, 1950…the youngest child of Abel and Antonia Martinez…good-natured, kind-hearted, family-oriented, and one of the most sincere people you'll ever meet…also, happens to be one of my heroes…idolized him as a kid…he was Big D and I was little D…I hold him in high regard even today…married to Aunt Marie for thirty years…father of five, step-father of one, but make no mistake, they're all his: Jessica, Scott, Nick, Rebecca, Danielle, and my goddaughter Elizabeth…nine little ones call him Grandpa…his kids grew up before our very eyes, literally…the man loves his sports…probably has the widest range in the whole family...pro, college, prep, youth, you name it...A's and Raiders at the top of his list, of course....

So there you have it. For those keeping track at home, or more than likely lost track, that's fourteen children born to Abel and Antonia Martinez, forty-nine grandchildren, one-hundred great-grandchildren, thirty-three great great-grandchildren—and many more to come.

As we close this chapter and move on to the next, you'll be happy to know that no calculator will be required.

3 / Family Matters

"Will you quit hibernating in there?"
> —My dad, to whoever was in the bathroom at the time

I knew right from the start that this would be the most difficult chapter to write. It's one thing to report baseball facts as seen through every one else's eyes, but to accurately capture the personalities of my seven brothers and sisters as seen through my own is a delicate task. But these are my views and I am sticking to them. The truth is, we are not overly close-knit, but we are by no means distant, and there is a special sense of pride among us. I know that I wouldn't give them up for anything in the world. And if that's too corny for you, well, it's about to get worse.

My father Ernic and my mother Anita (better known as Dodie) were wed in Oakland in June 1956, three months before Don Larsen's World Series perfect game. Barely one year later they were parents for the first time with Mom giving birth to my oldest brother, Ernie Jr. From that day in July 1957 through March 1969, my folks put together one player short of a baseball team: eight children in twelve years. It was a tumultuous time; Mom and Dad built their family through the assassinations of two Kennedy's and one King, the tragedy at Kent State, and a war that nearly split this country in half. But through love (their marriage is at fifty years and counting), an unwavering faith, and tremendous patience, they made it through the 60's one small step at a time, just as Neil Armstrong was making one giant leap for all of us.

The Marquez clan faced its severest test, at least in terms of resourcefulness, during the school year of 1974–75. Ernie was a senior at Pacific High and my younger sister Tricia was in Kindergarten, which meant all eight of us were in school at the same time. Add my working father to the mix and it made for some interesting mornings at 1557 Gilmore Drive. All of this with one bathroom. In many ways we resembled the champion A's of that time: we fought like crazy with each other but when push came to shove (often literally), we learned to put our differences aside for the good of the team. Of course, you could say that Dad had a "hand" in keeping things in order. He had served in the Navy and there was no question this was his ship. Well, at least Mom let him think it was his.

While the A's players jousted both privately and publicly with owner Charles Finley, mostly over salaries, the kids of Ernie and Dodie understood early on that having a roof over their heads was the only luxury they'd ever need. When I would ask Dad how much I got for raking the leaves on a blustery Fall morning, his response was always the same: "You get to eat dinner tonight." I'd have an easier time picking those leaves off the lawn with a spoon than getting twenty-five cents from the dude. That's a slight exaggeration, obviously, but let's just say my siblings and I came to appreciate the simple things in life. Which does not suggest that we were deprived. Hardly. We looked forward to summertime when Dad would pile us into his brown Ford station wagon for camping trips and nights at the drive-in movies. And of course baseball games. Even before the A's moved here, Dad took Ernie Jr. and John (the second oldest of the eight kids) across the Bay to see the San Francisco Giants. But don't ever accuse them of being fans of the orange-and-black. Going to Giants' games was merely a way of passing the time, although you could do a whole lot worse than watch the likes of Willie Mays and Juan Marichal in person. It was a different story when Finley moved his team here in 1968, one year after I was born. The Marquez family immediately took to the A's, just as they had done with the Raiders eight years prior. At the very least, the A's were guaranteed nine lifelong fans (or fans-to-be) upon their arrival to the East Bay. (A tenth fan was added with the birth of Tricia in 1969.)

My dad was born Ernest Marquez on January 14, 1932, the very same day that Babe Ruth rejected a $70,000 offer from the New York Yankees. The Great Depression even had an effect on Major League Baseball as the sport vowed to cut salaries by $1 million.

The Sultan of Swat had demanded $80,000 following the '31 season, which would have surpassed the $75,000 brought in by President Hoover. When pushed for an explanation Ruth replied "I had a better year than he did." (Babe may have been correct in that assessment but his 46 homeruns and 163 RBI's in 1931 were not enough for New York to overcome the dynastic Philadelphia Athletics whose 107 wins sent them to their third consecutive World Series. Connie Mack's juggernaut fell to St. Louis in seven games, ending their two-year reign as league champions. The A's would not appear in another Fall Classic until 1972 under the name "Oakland.") Babe Ruth eventually signed for the same amount as the Prez in 1932 but there was no question who had the better year. While Franklin D. Roosevelt ousted Hoover from office in a landslide, the Bronx Bombers returned to the top of the baseball world with a sweep of the Chicago Cubs. It was in Game 3 of that Fall Classic that Ruth made his famous "called shot," which turned out to be the last of Babe's fifteen World Series homeruns.

Dad was raised in Raton, New Mexico, where he made a name for himself in both football and basketball. (Come to think of it, he has "made" a name for just about everyone else in our family. A lot of them are actual nicknames but others are because he just can't remember their real names so he picks something that sounds right to him. And it doesn't matter how many times you correct him; if he "Archie Bunkers" your name, you're stuck with it. Just ask "Bart" or "Craig") Dad grew up idolizing Stan "The Man" Musial and the St. Louis Cardinals, who won three World Series in four tries between 1942–46. If that sounds a little too convenient for you, it should. Dad epitomizes the fair-weather fan, first to cheer his team in triumph, quickest to knock the club when they're down. He's the only guy I know who will turn off a game in the first inning if things aren't going his way. He's a cynic and a hypocrite. For some reason he couldn't stand Reggie Jackson, yet when Reggie homered in his first game back with the team in 1987, there was Dad chanting with everyone else, "Reggie! Reggie! Reggie!" He dubbed Sal Bando "Rally Killer," even though few were better at bringing a guy home than Captain Sal. Whether at the game or sitting in front of the TV, Dad will often leave at the most critical moments of a game, somehow believing that he's helping his team to victory. Many times it's actually worked. Along the way, he has criticized nearly every player that has worn the green-and-gold and, in the process, has alienated his entire family. But he always made time to take us to the games— Bat Day, Cap Day, Camera Day—you name it. He would throw pieces of paper in players' cars (as they were driving away!), in hopes of getting autographs for his kids. He'd even speak broken Spanish to the Latin players, anything to gain an edge. And he always managed to come up with playoff and World Series tickets. He's still the same old fan and he always will be. I, for one, wouldn't have it any other way. Say what you will about the man, but one of the biggest reasons I am so passionate about the A's goes back to Dad.

Anita Dolores Martinez was born on July 20, 1936. Interestingly enough, there were no Major League games scheduled that day, as if baseball itself stood still for her arrival. *A Tale of Two Cities*, a Dickens classic, was nominated for Best Picture that year; coincidentally, the Bay Bridge, which connects Oakland to San Francisco, opened to traffic for the first time in 1936. The Philadelphia A's were now a shadow of their former wonderful selves, losing 100 contests and finishing 49 games behind the eventual champion Yankees.

Mom was raised in La Junta, Colorado but her family moved to Oakland when she was a young girl. She graduated from McClymonds High School (Class of '54), which is also where baseball star Frank Robinson ('53) and basketball legend Bill Russell ('52) attended. Russell, in fact, was in Mom's typing class, though she says he spent as much time servicing the typewriters as he did sitting at one. (He later found better use for his hands: defending the post for the 11-time NBA champion Boston Celtics.) To have a classmate turn pro is cool enough, but Mom went to high school with *two* future *Hall-of-Famers*, in different sports to boot. I guess the games have always been apart of her life. The same year Mom was born, Cooperstown opened its doors to the Baseball Hall-of-Fame. The world also welcomed sports notables Don Drysdale, Jim Brown, John Madden, and Wilt Chamberlain in the year 1936. And Giuseppe Paolo DiMaggio, Jr. made his big-league debut two months before my mom made her own debut onto this stage we call life. Incidentally, DiMaggio, more widely known as Joe, was born not *as* a Martinez, but *in* Martinez, not very far from where my grandparents—Abel and Antonia Martinez—would come to call home.

Mom is Dad's opposite, in nearly every fashion, which may explain why their marriage has surpassed the half-century mark. They compliment each other, even when they are taking turns driving each other up the wall. While Dad worked to keep his eight children healthy and happy, Mom, well, did everything else. Soccer moms had nothing on her. She cooked dinner, made the lunches, and baked desserts (often to fulfill a promise that one of us made to our teachers, only we didn't let her in on it until it was time for bed). She helped with homework and hemmed dresses. She took the temperatures, bandaged the cuts, and stuck that spoonful of cough syrup into our mouths. She wrote the excuse slips and met with the teachers. She played referee when the fights broke out at home and, when needed, sang that familiar phrase, "Wait 'til your father gets home." Although there was one time when I slipped up so bad (no, really) that when I begged her not to tell Dad, she replied with a glare, I wouldn't worry about what *he's* going to do." Ouch. But mostly Mom comforted and consoled. She was there for every ache, every pain, and every heartbreak. And she helped mend them all.

With Mom, everything begins and ends with prayer, although I never asked if she included the A's in her little talks with the Man Upstairs. My guess would be no; I'm certain she understands that God doesn't interfere with sporting events. It only seems that way from time to time. To Mom, the game isn't over until the final out is recorded, which is to say long after Dad has given up. And she passed that glass-is-half-full optimism on to her children and grandchildren, some of whom have sat through a rainstorm and the A's down by ten runs because well, that's what being a fan is all about. Even in something as ultimately trivial as the sport of baseball is, it helps to have an unlimited supply of faith. That's my mom.

Baseball had gone through many changes from the 1930's, when my parents were born, to the time that they began having children of their own. World War II made real-life heroes out of men who had previously been idolized for their abilities on the diamond. But for one man, perhaps it was just the opposite. Jackie Robinson served his country during the war but what he did for baseball—breaking the color barrier in 1947—may have been more significant. The relentless abuse that he was subjected to during his rookie season would not be in vain, and when Jackie retired from the game in 1957 the torch was passed to a young Hank Aaron, who would go on to hit more homeruns than anyone who has ever worn a Major League uniform. Aaron came into his own during that '57 season which saw him win his first—and only—Most Valuable Player award and World Series ring.

The year 1957 was also when Ernest Marquez Jr., was born, the oldest child of the Marquez Eight. The best of the best in the Major Leagues gathered in St. Louis that day, the ninth of July, for the 24th All-Star Game. Fitting, I suppose, since Ernie likes to think of himself as the best of the best. Stars on the A's, now in their third year in Kansas City, were hard to find, on a team that would lose 94 times in 1957, 38–1/2 games to the rear of the pennant-winning Yankees.

Ernie and his wife Yong, who he met in Korea, have been married for more than twenty-five years and they have three kids: my goddaughter Christina, Kimberly, and Ernie III. My early memories of my oldest brother are of me going through his baseball cards and hearing him scream to Mom that he was going to tear my hands off. (Thankfully, he was all talk. Would have made it a little difficult to write this book.) Ernie and I never really had a chance to be close when I was growing up; not only is he ten years my senior but he served four years in the Air Force at a time when I was barely completing Elementary School. We are also two very different people. Ernie is life-of-the-party, military background, thrives in the outdoors, and he's probably never seen a movie even remotely resembling a chick-flick, unless you count *GI Jane*. I'm, well, I'm not him. But as I got older and spent more time in his company, I discovered that we shared some similar likes, too; good conversation while seated at a poker game and drinking cold beers (poured in a glass, of course) happens to be one of those things. We also possess a passion for history, an unquenchable fondness for books, and we both agree that if a movie isn't worth quoting from, it's probably not worth watching either. And we're collectors, too, often going for those hard-to-find items. Ern may cover a wider range—war memorabilia, coins, stamps—but I can hold my own when it comes to sport collectibles. To be sure, if we ever had the time and resources to display our smorgasbord of magazines, cards, caps, bobble heads, shot glasses, and beer and soda cups (which date back to the Billy Ball days), it would make for one impressive gallery.

The most obvious thing that Ernie and I have in common is our intense devotion to the A's and Raiders. In recent years, I have attended more sporting events with him than with any of my other siblings. We are both Raider season-ticket holders and we've caught more than a few A's games over the years. To Ern, a game is not a game without a tailgate party and his, while hardly glamorous, serve their purpose nonetheless: always good eating and plenty of booze. And his spicy peanuts, timely distributed as we are making our way into the stadium, are a "guaranteed" win. Or so he thinks. You see, very few people are more superstitious than my oldest brother; he swears by Crash Davis' philosophy that you just don't "mess" with a winning streak. Even if it means wearing the same underwear for seven consecutive days. (He's actually done this. Worked out great for the Raiders. For the wife and co-workers? Not so much.) There is a certain toughness that comes with the territory of being the eldest (and he plays the part very well), but make no mistake about it: Ernie lives and dies with his teams. That is, when they lose, it hurts. Just don't expect him to show it. (That would be like admitting he cares for his sisters or something.)

Following Ernie in the Marquez lineup are John and Tonianne, who were born just ten months apart. You'll probably see more from them than anyone else in this book. If they never set foot in the Coliseum again, they'll still have enough memories to last forever. Their World Series tales alone would turn Giants' fans green (and gold) with envy. Even today the three of us will engage in day-long emails about the current state of the A's, with a dash of history sprinkled in. Comparisons are always being made—between Finley's Mustache Gang, Haas' Bash Brothers, and Beane's Moneyballers. Not surprisingly, they both agree that the championship clubs of the early 70's were head-and-shoulders above the rest. It's an opinion I trust; after all, they've been keeping tabs on the A's from Day One.

John has recently remarried, and he and his wife Jodie have a son, Xavier, and another child on the way. His daughter Carrin is from his first marriage and he also has two stepsons (one from each marriage), Aaron and Taimon. John Michael Marquez was born the fifth day of September in 1958 and baseball was bringing about more changes, changes that would ultimately have a lasting effect on the Bay Area and on this family. Heeding the words of Horace Greeley to "go west," Brooklyn's Walter O'Malley and New York's Horace Stoneham moved the Dodgers and Giants to California, eventually paving the way for the A's relocation to Oakland ten years later. (Meanwhile the Kansas City club, 4–1 losers to Detroit the day of John's birth, were on their way to a seventh-place finish.)

I don't recall too many games in particular that John and I attended together when I was a kid, but I do remember that he always seemed to catch a baseball or two. And he went to all the big games. Brought back some crazy souvenirs, too—like that patch of Coliseum turf after the '73 Series. I remember him blaring "We Are the Champions" from his car stereo after we beat the Royals to clinch the '81 division title. John was the first to hug me the day we won the AL West in 2000 and the look on his face told me that it ranked pretty high up on his long list of memorable moments. Of course, there was that Giant sweep in '89 and The Scutaro Game of '06. And I'll never, ever forget that ride on BART when I was just a kid, on our way to a Raider game. As the Coliseum came into view, John pointed to it and whispered, "There it is—The House of Thrills." Like Elton John singing about *Daniel* and his affection for Spain ("best place he's ever seen and he should know, he's been there enough"), the same can be said of John and the House of Thrills, because very few people have experienced as many thrills at The House as he.

I always looked up to John. Partly because with Ernie gone for four years in the service, he was next in line as the oldest. Our garage was like a large shed, separate from the house, and Ernie had turned it into his own bedroom and a place to hang out in private with his high school buddies. It was also where he kept his assortment of unusual pets: snakes, lizards, and tarantulas. He even had a rat-

tlesnake there for a while. But when it came time to enlist in the
Air Force, my oldest sibling closed the zoo and turned the keys over
to John. And John transformed it into a place of entertainment: he
hosted tape-recorded "newscasts" and "game shows" and best of
all, played his stereo so loud, you felt like you were at a rock concert. I would *beg* him to play his stereo while he was at work. In
the end, he always said yes. Plain in simple, John was cool. Still is.
He was cool long before Arthur Fonzarelli was cool. How cool?
Think Hendrix cool. So cool that as Mom was giving birth to him,
she sang "God Bless America." So cool that even though Mom
claims to have no favorites among her children, John is the favorite.
And we all know it and we're okay with it because he's cool. In
baseball terms, he's Crash Davis "Come on Meat, bring that weak-
ass cheese, and I'll go yard with it" cool. Of his many talents, John
is quick-witted but at the same time a great storyteller. He is old-
school in that he hails from an era long before the dawn of the
overpaid, overexposed, pampered athlete. What attracts him most
to today's A's? It's not just the winning; it's how they play the game.
With passion, with fire, with a youthful exuberance that, well,
reminds him of the A's he grew up on.

The birth of Tonianne reminds us of the calm before the storm.
The fifties were drawing to a close and perhaps with them, the age
of innocence. Not so much in the sport of baseball, mind you. That
would come later. America itself was about to enter a decade unlike
any other in its history. But before the candle burned out completely
on the fifties, Ernie and Anita brought in their third child, this time
a girl, whose existence was very much a reflection of the decade
that she would soon leave behind, of happier and simpler times.

She was born Toni Anne Marquez on July 27, 1959. The
Kansas City A's were 7–6 victors that day, their eighth consecutive win in a streak that ultimately reached eleven. (They would
endure a thirteen-game *losing* skid in September and, despite sixteen homers each by future Oakland manager Dick Williams and
soon-to-be Yankee legend Roger Maris, the A's were doomed to
another seventh-place finish.) Baseball had officially gone West
Coast that Fall when the Los Angeles Dodgers defeated the
Chicago White Sox, giving California its first Major League
championship. (Take that New York.) The oldest sister of the

Marquez clan, she is a woman of many names: Antonia, Tonianne, Toni, Tone, Tonian (ton-yawn), and the more recent, but much lesser used T-nizzle. Where would I be without Tonianne? I would not be writing this book, that's for certain. Baseball was her first love and she did not leave it (even partially) until meeting her truest love, her husband of the last quarter-century, Michael. They have one son, Patrick. Still, her heart remains as loyal to the Oakland A's as it did when she was growing up. Fiercely loyal. My dad and uncles used to love teasing Toni about the A's—and in particular Reggie Jackson—knowing full well that she was good for a debate, which was usually followed by yelling, crying, and finally, slamming her bedroom door. She'd defend her A's until the end, that was Tone. Like John, she spent much of her adolescence at the Oakland Coliseum, and like John, she saw her share of magic moments. But I think that Toni might have liked it best during the lean years of the late 70's because she didn't have to share her A's with anyone else. Well, except with me. She loved to take me with her to the games back then, so long as I didn't ask for anything to eat or drink. She'd even pay me not to ask to use the bathroom and I earned bonus money by not speaking at all. Let's just say it wasn't exactly a lucrative agreement. The A's were insanely awful on the field and the last thing a twelve-year old kid like myself wanted to do was pay attention to the game. So I asked for food, told her I had to go to the bathroom, and basically drove my sister crazy. And still she'd drag me along.

Aside from fighting with her father and uncles, I recall one particular incident that demonstrated her deep-rooted loyalty to the A's. It was in 1978. We were in the middle of a lousy season, in the midst of losing another game. Bill North, the last player remaining from the glory years was in centerfield and Toni and I were camped out in our usual spot behind Billy in the bleachers. And behind us were a few men, in their thirties, drinking heavily, cussing, and ribbing North unmercifully. I was watching my sister and I could see the anger in her nineteen year-old body building. And finally she lost it. "Shut up," she screamed in a voice I hardly recognized. The guys, well, they stopped their assault on North and looked at Toni. And I was pretty certain that we were going to die that day. Thankfully they just laughed and said things like, "Ooh, tough girl." But not another bad word about North. I always wondered how Billy would have reacted had he been told that a teenage girl shouted down a bunch of hooligans in his defense.

Tonianne was a fanatic in every sense of the word. She'd mark her calendar to count down the days from the end of the previous season until pitchers and catchers reported to Spring Training the following March. She had a notebook that logged each game with score, winning and losing pitcher, and attendance. Ticket stubs were tagged in similar fashion and she kept every single one of them. In her pocket schedules, she'd pen a "W" or "L," depending what the A's did on that particular day. She even had Tricia and I include the A's in our nightly prayers! ("God Bless Mommy, God Bless Daddy, and please, God, help Reggie break out of that awful slump of his.") And if you think that is over the top, she once made our cousin Marci cry because she accused her of being a "jinx." Toni never understood the concept of a fair-weathered fan; in fact during the three seasons that saw the team hit rock bottom, she still averaged forty to fifty games a season. So it was that when Billy Martin briefly resurrected our floundering franchise in the early 80's and the fans started to fill the stadium at an alarming rate, my sister let her disapproval be known: "Where were all you people in '79?" You know, she could be quite embarrassing from time-to-time, until I realized years later that I had become just like her. And I was totally ok with it, even if those around me weren't.

Mary Carol Marquez, the fourth branch on the family tree, was not at all like Tonianne. Indeed, Carol (as we call her) was to her older sister what Ernie Jr. was to John. If Toni reflected the innocence of the fifties, Carol more or less symbolized the radical movement of the sixties (Today that is much less the case; parenting has come to humble her, as it has most of us who've been so blessed.) She has two daughters from a previous marriage—Natalie and Stephanie—and she has been with her current husband Carlos for over a decade. It is impossible to mention Carol without first bringing up the daily ritual that we shared when I was in Kindergarten. She was in the sixth grade, her last at Wilson Elementary and every day she'd walk me home from school. Trouble was I got out a half hour before she did. So every day, I'd stand out in front of her classroom, calling her name. Now at that time I had somewhat of a speech impediment. Couldn't say my "R's" all too well. So instead of belting out "Carol" each weekday afternoon, it came out "Cawol." Then her teacher Mr. Schneider would open the door and let me in, and the next half hour was spent among my elders discussing Reggie Jackson and those upstart Oakland A's. To this day, I'm still undecided as to who looked forward to those visits more, the little kindergartener or that teacher and his sixth-grade kids.

The man most responsible for the A's success at that time— Charlie Finley—made a significant move in December 1960, when he purchased fifty-two percent of the ball club. Two days later Carol was born, just three days before Christmas. Or at least Christmas as we know it. If you had polled the citizens of Pittsburgh that year they'd have told you that Santa Claus came to town two months earlier. The backyard dreams of millions of children became Bill Mazeroski's reality when his Game-7-bottom-of-the-ninth-inning homerun made World Series champions of the underdog Pirates. Carol herself was somewhat of an underdog. Never the oldest and only able to wear "The Baby" tag for twenty months, she sort of just blended in. She was Jan to Tonianne's Marcia. In a batting order, hitting fourth meant you earned high praise for cleaning up after others; in a family of eight, born fourth still meant you cleaned up, but it was much less rewarding and nowhere near as exciting. And if we know anything about Carol is that all work and no play makes her a dull girl indeed.

As has been documented frequently in this book, being anything but an A's fan in our family was not an option. But Carol didn't mind. She enjoyed the family excursions at the ballpark, her and Tonianne attired in matching green dresses, and she basked in the glow of Oakland's success. Of course like any other girl approaching her teens, she had her crushes, too. First, it was Bert "Campy" Campaneris, whose speed on the base paths earned him the nickname, "Roadrunner." Then it was Gene Tenace. Still, there was no way that she was going to become the fanatic that was her older sister Tonianne. Quite frankly the bar had been set too high. So when Finley began to break up his championship club and it became increasingly difficult for Mom and Dad to keep treating their kids to baseball games, Carol turned to other passions. Like rock concerts. Day on the Green's brought in nearly every star imaginable and while the Mustache Gang's rebellion against the baseball establishment was sexy in its own right, there were simply no Ted Nugent's on Finley's payroll. "Toni would get so mad at me once I stopped going to games on a regular basis," says Carol who blames puberty and a driver's license on leaving her beloved baseball team behind. And so with a heavy heart, she said "goodbye A's, hello longhaired, naked men with guitars."

And in 1961…she rested. Mom delivered kids in every year from 1957–1960 but perhaps caught up in Roger Maris' pursuit of the single-season homerun record in the summer of '61, her streak came to end. So did the Babe's when ex-Athletic Maris stoked his 61st homerun on October 3rd of that year. Ruth had held the title for thirty-four seasons; Maris would hold it for even longer before another former "A" Mark McGwire went for 70 in 1998. Mom was back to having babies in 1962, the first year that a World Series was played in the Bay Area (the Yankees beat the Giants in a seven-game thriller).

Rose Elizabeth Marquez was born the 22nd of August and the Kansas City A's celebrated the occasion with a 4–2 win over Boston. But August is a month in which contenders separate themselves from pretenders and the A's of that era were a perennial pretender; they lost ninety games in '62 and finished in seventh place in the American League standings.

While the Kansas City clubs hardly sniffed a pennant race, Rose and I got a pretty good view of a team that made a habit of playing meaningful games well past the summer. She was my game partner for three magnificent seasons as we watched Tony La Russa and his ridiculously talented A's lay waste to all challengers to the American League West throne. Those A's of 1988–90 were lined with money players, guys that could smell October coming and would pick up their game a notch. Guys like Stew, Eck, Mac, and Hendu. Those were special times and Rose and I reveled in them. It wasn't just the winning; it was the indescribable feeling you had when you walked into the stadium. Like every game was a playoff game. Rose and I would pick "celebrities" out of the packed crowds, or at least ordinary people who resembled celebrities. And I'd drive her nuts by "announcing" the game live. Of course she loved the look on people's faces when I'd answer the trivia questions, even before the multiple choices popped up. It was just a fun time.

A lot more fun than the time Dad decided to treat his kids to a night at the drive-in. I was four or five at the time and Rose was dancing and singing in the front yard: "We're going to the mo-vies. We're going to the mo-vies." And then she ran back inside the house as I was heading for the door and BAM! The doorknob hit me square on the forehead. You've heard of "Dinner and a Movie" on TNT? How about "Stitches and No Movie"? (Still can't figure out why that never caught on.) Rose has more than a moderate appreciation of the film industry; in fact the family pretty much treats her collection like our very own video store. Well, before Netflix came along anyway.

Rose had a little of both Toni and Carol in her, although where Carol was high-and-fast, Rose was low-and-slow, listening to her oldies. She soon passed Carol in A's game attendance, even though on many occasions it was just an excuse to check out the homies with our cousin, Gloria. Says Glo, "I remember me and Rose use to make sure we were all dolled up when ever we went to a game, just in case there were any cute guys. We were teenagers. We watched the game but we also made a lot of trips toward the restrooms. I slowly lost interest in the games altogether but Rose gained interest in them. She couldn't help it, look where she lives." Where she lives is still at home, working as Mom's backup. She's had a hand in raising all of our nephews and nieces, as well as Uncle Dan's kids. They'd drive her crazy and chide her, some calling her "Warden" for her strict ways, but they've turned out to be pretty good kids and she deserves some credit for that.

Rose doesn't go to too many games these days but she is as in tune with the team as anyone else. In the late 80's and early 90's, she'd keep me posted of afternoon games via phone while I was at work: "Don, you have a call on Line 1. It's your sister, sounds important." (What, you're going to tell me that Canseco's walkoff *wasn't* important?) Today, she keeps me informed via e-mail, not so much of the games, but of the A's and Raider haters that write in to the local newspaper. Rose enjoys when I pull out my Jules impression from Pulp Fiction: "Well, allow me to retort!"

And since it's my goal to segue you to death in this book, "allow me to" introduce you to one of my best friends who happens to also be my third oldest brother, Joseph Abel Marquez, number six, born the ninth day of the sixth month in 1964. In January of that year, Charlie Finley signed a two-year pact to move his A's from Kansas City to Louisville, Kentucky—pending league approval. Under pressure from fellow owners, he would pen a four-year lease to remain in KC. The A's, swept in a double-header the day Abel was born, wound up losing 105 contests in '64 and finished forty-two games behind the pennant-winning Yankees (this is not a recording).

A husband to Theresa, Abel is a father of four (two from a previous marriage): my goddaughter Brittany, Jillian, Nikkole, and Vanessa—with one more on the way. He is named after both grandfathers, which I constantly rib him about, often calling him "the gringo Jose." Abel is known to everyone by his middle name (which is quite common in this family, in case that fact has escaped you). Of the eight kids, we are the furthest apart in age and there are two theories, his and mine. His is that Mom and Dad meant to stop having kids after him, mine is that masterpieces take time to create. And back and forth we go. We may be far apart in age—a whopping two years and ten months—but we are as close as two siblings can be. After all, we've spent the last fifteen years working in the same industry, often in the same office, including the last five years where I can walk fifteen feet to his cubicle. The thing is we actually enjoy working together, to the amazement of co-workers and clients alike. Of course it helps that we are able to talk sports all day long. We should have our own show.

Abel and I have so much in common, it's probably easier to list the things we don't. He's very much like Ernie in that he thrives in almost any atmosphere. There are very few conversations he feels uncomfortable in; he's seen it all, done it all, and what he lacks in life experiences, he makes up in reading. One thing I have on him is movies, which he says he has precious little time to watch, and with four daughters, I tend to believe him. But he somehow manages to catch every episode of "American Idol" and "Survivor."

The only reality shows worth watching, in my opinion, are sporting events (yeah, because their legitimacy has *never* been questioned). For all that Abel and I already have in common, sports are at the root of the bond between us. That has not always been a good thing. You do not want to sit near my brother at an important game. Meaningless regular season encounter? No problem. Playoff game against our fiercest rivals? Limit his beer consumption and strap him to his seat. He hits. Hard. Ask my cousin Nick, who left a Raider game almost as battered and bruised as the players. Hell, ask the guy who sat in front of Abel at The Scutaro Game, the guy whom Abel whacked repeatedly with one of those white towels they give away at playoff time. The funny thing is that these are games in which our teams *won!* Maybe all that pent-up "energy" stems from a childhood episode that he likes to recount to our friends over and over, although he conveniently leaves out some critical parts As I remember it, he had been teasing me about who-knows-what, to the point where I grabbed a baseball bat and threatened to hit him with it. Naturally he egged me on, practically begging me to hit him. So I did. In his kneecap. And when Mom came in and asked in not-so Catholic terms what in blazes was going on, Ernie Jr., of all people, came to my defense: "He dared him." But that didn't exactly hold up in the court of Mom and according to Abel, after she beat me (which Mom could neither confirm or deny), he finished the job. Such a nice loving family. But that was Abe, pushing and pushing until I snapped. Countless Whiffle Ball games in the back yard under his constant torture until I quit—with me in the lead—and thereby "forfeiting" the win to him. And then there were those wonderful weekday afternoons when the paperboy delivered the Daily Review to our home. Now mind you, this was way before ESPN and the Internet, so if we wanted our news, we either waited until 6pm or we beat the crap out of each other for the rights to the sports page. Being that he was older and bigger, Abel often outwrestled me for the paper and then proceeded to read off every score and every stat from the day before. I would plug my ears or move far away from him, but it didn't matter. If I wanted to read that damn paper, I'd have to get close to him and that's when he'd start up again. Hey, isn't it great how sports bring us together?

Of course, there's a tiny difference between Abel's obsession with sports and mine. I draw the line at certain sports. He watches golf, for God's sake. Bowling, billiards, poker, tiddlywinks. If you can keep score at it, he's watching. "Hey, Don, did you catch the synchronized toe-nail clipping championship at 3am this morning? Damn, some of those guys really know how to clip!" Well, at least he doesn't read the scores and stats to me anymore. Not without my permission anyway.

Abe needs no such consent when it comes to head-to-head competition. He beats me at *everything*. And it's always been that way. Whether it's Super Bowl pools, video games, Whiffle Ball, basketball, Fantasy football, finger football, cards, horseshoes, ping-pong, or even toenail clipping, he has pretty much owned me since the day I was born. He says he feels bad when he wins now, that he no longer delights in breaking my heart but I'm not buying it. Meanwhile, Dad keeps telling him that I'm going to whip him good, (he's been telling him that since I was five) to which Abel laughs heartily, but one day brother, you'll get yours, truly.

Speaking of "yours truly," I entered this world on April 21, 1967, the seventh child and youngest boy born to Mom and Dad. The A's beat the defending champion Baltimore Orioles 3–1 that day, but despite a roster loaded with future stars, Finley's club finished dead last once again, their final campaign in Kansas City. The first Super Bowl was played in 1967 (although it was called the AFL-NFL Championship at the time) and Boston's Carl Yastrzemski hit for the Triple Crown, still the last Major Leaguer to do so. While the Red Sox were on their way to an improbable Series appearance, the NBA Celtics saw their eight-season championship run come to a halt. Reginald Martinez Jackson burst onto the scene in '67, hitting the first of 563 homers on September 17. The young athlete from Philly would have a major impact on the A's, this family, and me in particular as time wore on.

Time was in short supply for Ernie and Anita Marquez as the sixties came to a close. Seven kids in ten years will do that to you. Mom bore no children in 1968, the year the A's finally made the move to Oakland. But before bidding adieu to a decade that challenged both our family and our nation, there would be one more addition to our little house on Gilmore Drive. 1969, wow, talk about putting a stamp on the sixties. Man walks on the moon, *Monday Night Football*'s debut, Woodstock, *Butch Cassidy and the Sundance Kid*, and two miracle teams from the Bronx: the World Series champion Mets and the Super Bowl winning Jets. Neither club had any right winning a title and yet it somehow made sense in a year that made little sense, culminating a decade that made even less sense. But the A's were officially ours now—and that made perfect sense—having a full season in Oakland under their belts. 1969 would see Reggie Jackson step into the spotlight with his pursuit of the homerun record (ultimately the 23-year old budding superduperstar succumbed to intense media pressure and fell well short of Ruth and Maris). In the first season of the four-division format, the A's gave a glimpse of things to come with an 88–74 record, good for second place in the AL West.

On Saint Patrick's Day of that year, Patricia Alice was born, the youngest of the Elite Eight. Poor Trish got all of the abuse from me when we were growing up because, well, I had no one else to pick on. For no reason whatsoever I used to call her "Little Man," which made her cry something awful. (Hmm, beat brother with a bat, made little sister cry, I better come up with some nice stuff soon.) Did I mention that I always looked after her? Even in high school where there was an unwritten rule forbidding older brothers to associate with younger siblings, especially sisters? But yeah, I'd make sure she'd have money for lunch and I even walked her to homeroom on her first day of school. (See, I'm not so bad.) Sadly, it was my senior year that we were last close to each other. But she'll always be my little sister. And even though I do my thing and she does hers, I know she knows I am always here for her.

I was there in the early 80's, too, when she took the torch from her oldest sister as the next great A's fan. Tricia took following the A's to a whole new level, to heights unattained by Tonianne herself. Tone counted down to Spring Training, Trish went to Spring Training. She sat in the very first row behind the A's bullpen during the Eck Era and actually became friends with some of the players. She went on the road to see the team, another family first. But although those moments surely made her giddy, she always remained so levelheaded about it. Like it was no big deal, even though clearly it was. She has followed in the footsteps of John and Tonianne into mini-retirement (she gets out to the stadium only a few times a year now), but her place in the Marquez Hall-of-Fame is secure. And still she cheers on her A's and she really believes they're hers, just like her oldest sister before her. Trish admits to liking the Raiders, but it's nowhere near how her siblings feel about them. The disparity between her devotion to the A's and her casual interest in the football team is as wide as an errant throw to first. And don't get her started on the Coliseum. The way she sees it, the Raiders left so how dare they come back and make renovations to fit *their* needs? Bad enough they tear up the field in August with their exhibition games, just as baseball's pennant races are starting to heat up. So if you dare joke about how the A's are "ruining" your Raiders' football field (as I once did) be prepared to receive a glare as cold as the winds that whip through the stadium on a night in April.

And if you really want to irritate the hell out of her, try sitting behind her without any knowledge of the game. Better yet, try mispronouncing players' names or even call a player by a completely different name. Repeatedly. On second thought, please don't. And for God's sake, if you don't know anything about the game, at least show some interest in it (quietly). My sister did not spend $25 to listen to you cry and complain about your cheating, cheapskate boyfriend for three hours. Trish doesn't let the games consume her. She goes, she cheers, she laments, game's over, she goes home, game's forgotten. She's passionate about her team but it's controlled. She's knowledgeable but she doesn't intimidate you with off-the-wall facts. When she goes to the stadium it's with the sole purpose of watching the game and rooting on the A's. There is no hidden need to be entertained. No Dot Racing for her, thank you. In another words, she's very much like Tone.

I for one appreciate the fact that Tricia sticks up for our little baseball team. Someone has to. Yeah, she's paid her dues and has since passed the season-ticket-holder baton to our goddaughter, Christina, but the Oakland A's are still as much as hers as anyone else's. Which is to say they're in very good hands.

4 / The A's Arrival (1968-1970)

"Next thing I knew, we were going to ball games, and idols and heroes were born."
—My brother, John, on his first encounter with the A's

I have an *Oakland Tribune*, dated April 14, 1968, the week the A's made their debut in the Bay Area. I don't even know where or how I got it but I do know that it stands as one of my most prized sport collectibles. The souvenir section is littered with advertisements welcoming the A's to Oakland and the area writers waxed poetic in anticipation of having the Grand Old game in their own backyard.

Ed Levitt, columnist: "Baseball is child's play but it becomes man's work for the skillful. It happens every time a kid throws a ball against the side of the building and catches it. It doesn't need fields or grass. The game can be played on asphalt, up alleys and in places where garbage is dumped. It is part of our heritage." More Levitt, on how special it was to have a team here: "There are those who ally themselves with a team and make it a personal crusade. They believe a team belongs to them and in a way it does. Soon boys from Hayward, Oakland, Berkeley, El Cerrito, and Richmond will turn into Oakland Athletic stars, to become Catfish Hunter, Rick Monday, Sal Bando, and Campy Campaneris." (How right he was!)

Bill Fiset, columnist: "All of a sudden you're a baseball nut because Oakland has a big-league team all its own, a bunch of guys whose names will become household words in a matter of weeks despite the garish uniforms and the strange drama that unfolds on a baseball field. By strange drama I mean all that stuff where the pitcher tugs at his cap, the catcher scratches himself in the most unlikely places, the third base coach takes two steps backward and it all means something."

Other articles spoke of Oakland's rich baseball tradition, the A's chances in the American League, and the stars that would soon descend on the Coliseum (Mantle, Yastrzemski). There was even a letter from owner Charles O. Finley to the fans. Meanwhile a certain California governor, who would throw out the first pitch in the A's opener, viewed the new baseball season as a much-needed diversion from the Vietnam War.

Ronald Reagan: "I am hopeful (the return of baseball) will presage a return to normalcy among our people and turn our minds to the better side of our national life. I want particularly to welcome the Athletics to California and Oakland and to wish them the best of success in their league and with their fans."

Success was not immediately apparent for our boys in those "garish" uniforms, as they lost their first game at Baltimore on April 10, and their home opener to those same Orioles one week later. But as illustrated by the 50,164 in attendance, including a future President of the United States, baseball in Oakland was here to stay. As for the town the A's left behind, well Kansas City carried a sort of "good riddance" attitude towards the man who orchestrated the move, Charles Oscar Finley.

Stuart Symington, then-Senator of Missouri: "Oakland is the luckiest city since Hiroshima."

The citizens of Oakland, for their part, smiled broadly at such good "fortune." They now had a pro baseball team and well, Kansas City didn't. Oakland, the city that author Gertrude Stein once wrote had "no there there," suddenly had the A's there. A region that had churned out such diamond notables as Joe DiMaggio, Frank Robinson, Joe Morgan, Vada Pinson, and Willie Stargell now hoped to be the place where legends not only were born, but where they prospered. But what about Senator Symington? (He first gained brownie points with Finley when he blasted him on the floor of the United States Senate, calling him "one of the most disreputable characters ever to enter the American sports scene.") Would his opinion of the A's owner—and the area to which he relocated his club—prove to be accurate? No one at the time knew or even cared. They were just happy to have a team they could call their own. Then again, some of them were too young to understand the significance of it all.

My brother, **John,** who was nine years old at the time: "My first recollection of the A's was when dad piled us in the car to go to the airport to meet and welcome the "Athletics." I had no idea we were going to meet our new baseball team. In fact, up to that point, I didn't even know we were getting a baseball team and I don't think I had ever even heard of the A's. I had read about the Philadelphia A's and knew of some of their great players, but I wasn't into baseball much yet; we had the Giants, what do you expect? And, yes I knew of Mays, McCovey, Marichal, Tito Fuentes and a few others. I don't recall knowing of a team called the Kansas City A's, however. I would learn more of the history of the team later. I asked dad where we were going and he said to meet the Athletics. I remember wondering what type of athletics he was talking about. I think I posed the question and he was a little irritated with his response, 'The baseball team! They're called the Athletics!' I remember we were up on some sort of balcony and the A's were being introduced by Finley. I'm not sure who introduced him. I remember Bando, Catfish and Rick Monday. I don't recall Reggie being introduced, but then it's hard to remember the details from thirty-five years ago." (Ancient history isn't the only thing clogging John's memory bank.) Says he: "Remember that plume of smoke that was always over the Coliseum by the fourth inning? It wasn't from cigarettes."

Tonianne: "Grandma Toni used to think that smoke was from someone burning feathers." (Baltimore Oriole feathers, perhaps?)

Well whether it was feathers or something else, um, "burning" inside the Coliseum, it wasn't enough to keep Grandma away from the ball yard. In fact nothing could; not even a flock of swallows dive-bombing spectators, herself and Tonianne included, in the second deck one afternoon. While her husband chose to follow the team on the radio or TV, she preferred the sights, sounds, and smells of the stadium. Tone remembers how Grandma would ring her cowbell after an A's homerun, a popular thing in those days. And her colossal family followed suit. Back then you were allowed to take your own food and drink to the park, so Mom and my aunts wrapped homemade burritos in aluminum foil and filled up brown paper bags with fresh popcorn, while Dad and my uncles stocked their coolers high with frosty cold brew.

Ernie: "I remember Bucket O' Beer and my uncles bringing milk gallon jugs filled with beer." (OK, hold it. To fully grasp the measure of such a beverage, picture the largest sized drink served at Jack-in-the-Box. You know, the ones that won't even fit into your car cup-holder. Now think *bigger*. Yikes, who drove these guys home?)

Tonianne points out that a day at the yard back then offered a more personable experience: "You had Abe the peanut guy, the bald beer guy who could crack open two bottles at once (both for Dad), Coke in those flimsy paper cups with the plastic wrap covers—so good on a hot day—actual hot roasted peanuts (two packs for 75 cents), hot dogs wrapped in foil, popcorn in a bread bag, Carnation Malts, and Kool-Aid in a plastic milk jug."

Brenda, cousin: "I loved those times. I remember when we all went to a double-header for Easter and we had all that good Mexican food." (Hmm, burritos and Easter eggs, there's your "plume of smoke," John.)

Yeah there was nothing like a family picnic at the "House of Thrills" and owner Charles Finley, part salesman, part showman, would conjure up any gimmick to keep families like ours coming back for more. The product on the field was full of promise, that was obvious, but Finley wasn't taking any chances. So he had animated scoreboards that showed an opposing pitcher slipping on a bar of soap after being "sent to the showers" and fireworks for when one of his players hit a homerun. (We'd run outside to the middle of the street to get a glimpse of the bombs bursting in air.) And the so-called cheap Finley had all those souvenir give-aways, much like they do today, but without the advertising.

Ernie suggests that Finley's ideas did not always have its desired effect: "Dad took us and all the neighborhood kids to Bat Day and I remember there was a real free-for-all for those bats." (Ern would agree that Bobblehead Days are less hazardous to one's health.)

Tonianne: "One year there were like 63,000 fans (a slight exaggeration) for Bat Day and Aunt Genie's kids got in and we didn't." (Let it go, Tone.)

John: "Yeah, I remember those give-away days. Bats got stolen, caps, helmets—you name it. Dad would tell us as we were walking out of the stadium to hold on tight to your bat, hat, etc. If you had something stolen, he scolded you, "I told you! Damn it!" So if you weren't crying before, you were now. The good thing was you didn't get a helmet that had Mother's Cookies printed on it or a bat sponsored by The Men's Warehouse. Of course, you could end up with a bat that had Lew Krause's signature instead of Reggie, Campy or Sal Bando."

The fun didn't end with Finley's souvenirs. There was also Harvey the Mechanical Rabbit that popped up from under home plate to provide the umpire with fresh baseballs. And of course, the team mascot of that era, Charlie O. the mule. Most people came to the conclusion that Charlie O. the man was a bigger ass than Charlie O. the beast. But he had his good days and they weren't just on Bat Days and Cap Days. Finley also knew how to attract a mature audience as demonstrated by his "Hot Pants Day" brainstorm, in which ladies in short shorts paraded around the field before the game. (I was much too young to fully benefit from such ingenious marketing.) And rather than the standard ball boys scooping up foul balls in the outfield, Finley hired attractive "ball girls." (One of the gals, Debbie Sivyer went on to become Debbie Fields of Mrs. Fields cookies fame.) He even had Ladies Day, where every Thursday home game, females got in free. Yes, Charlie O. was an equal-employment-opportunity kind of guy, even if he did have a hidden agenda.

One thing the owner had trouble hiding was the fact that he had built a pretty good baseball club and most of that talent was grown right on his own farm. In the seven seasons that Finley owned the A's prior to relocating them from Kansas City, their best record was 74–86. But from 1968–70, they finished above .500 each year, improving each season: 82 wins in '68 was followed by 88 in '69 and 89 in '70. And it didn't take long for his budding stars to make their mark. Just one month removed from his team's Oakland debut, Jim Hunter treated A's fans to one of the top all-around performances in Major League history. Always a decent hitting pitcher, "Catfish" went 3-for-4 that night in May of '68, driving in three runs in Oakland's 4–0 win over Minnesota. But Hunter's batting heroics were only a smidgen of the story as the 22-year old proceeded to toss the American League's first perfect game in forty-six years. While that feat turned out to be quite a stepping stone to a Hall-of-Fame career, two of the Cat's teammates caught the attention of the baseball world in a more lasting, if slightly less spectacular, fashion. Reggie Jackson slugged 47 homeruns in 1969 (inspiring his own rooting section, "Reggie's Regiment" in right field) and Vida Blue spun a no-hitter at the powerful Twins the following season. (Finley, who succeeded in giving Jim Hunter *his* nickname, tried to get Vida to change his first name to "True," but to no avail.)

John: "I recall the impact of Jackson and Blue vividly. I was at Vida's no-hitter so he made an instant impression on me and, being a lefty, became one of my idols. I "called" many of Reggie's homers (mostly the first half of the season of course) and followed the whole "Reggie chasing the homerun record" campaign (to use a Bill King noun) very closely. It didn't take long at all for me to become enthralled by both of these players' incredible seasons."

And through it all, the Martinez/Marquez tribe was there for the ride in some form or another. (John joined Uncle Dan and Aunt Mac in witnessing Vida's no-hitter, along with 4,281 other paying customers.)

Uncle Dan: "I had tickets but couldn't find anyone to go with. Finally, Mac and John ended up taking them. I'm glad I was there. Minnesota had a good team, too."

John: "Mom was supposed to go but decided not to, so I pinch-it. I remember it well."

(Aside from Vida's rarity on the mound, it was even more of a surprise that my uncle struggled to find any takers to a ball game in a family as large as ours.)

Aunt Minda: "Our family would literally take up rows of bleacher space on any given night; those were just special, special times."

Tonianne: "I remember stomping our feet on the metal bleachers to start a rally (even louder on Bat Day); this was before the Wave and long before the drummers in left field."

Marta, cousin: "We had neighbors when we lived on Harrington that won a calf at Farmers Day. That was quite interesting, having a calf in the city."

There were other "interesting" moments, like when some fans mistook my Uncle Paul for relief pitcher, Diego Segui. And my uncle did not disappoint the youngsters, as he signed autographs for twenty minutes.

Aunt Mac: "I loved when Mom would make that face and she'd say 'those dirty rats' if it was something against the A's or she'd shake her fist (as much of a fist as she could make). She would also get upset if the A's were losing, even if it was very early in the game. We'd tell her 'Mom, they have lots of time yet' but it still got to her. She was so funny."

Aunt Minda: "Mom would turn the game off or walk away if we were losing and I would tell her that it was only the second inning! But she didn't care."

After three consecutive winning seasons it was obvious that Charlie Finley's prospects were blossoming into young stars. The mistakes that had cost them in the standings before had been corrected, the rough edges around their overall game ironed out. Having played together for a few years now, some since their collegiate days, the A's were now ready to take their game to the next level. And Finley hired Dick Williams to manage them and to teach them a thing or two about championship baseball. Over the next five seasons, the Oakland A's would be the talk of the baseball world; sadly some of that talk would be due to their brash owner and other off-field distractions. But between the lines, the A's would execute at a level that rivals any team who has ever played this game.

Yes, the championship seasons were coming, which posed just one problem: who was Grandma Toni going to shake her fists at?

5 / Uncle Dan Fires a Kennedy

*"[Bob] Kennedy might have been the least-interviewed
manager in history. Everyone wanted to talk to
[A's coach] Joe [DiMaggio]."*

—Ron Bergman, as told to John Shea
of the *San Francisco Chronicle* on April 10, 2005,
three days after Kennedy died at 84

In *Mustache Gang*, Bergman's wonderful behind-the-scenes tale
about the 1972 World Champions, the former A's beat writer tells
of a little story that occurs at the end of the team's first year in
Oakland. He mentions that Charlie Finley visited the outfield
bleachers on the last day of that 1968 season. Bergman also states
that the owner fired his manager, Bob Kennedy, that very same
afternoon. What Mr. Bergman doesn't make known to his readers,
perhaps because he wasn't aware of it himself, is the conversation
that takes place between Finley and a certain fan—right there in
those bleachers—that may have signaled the end to Bob Kennedy's
managerial career.

The fan that Charlie O. stumbled upon that day was Dan
Martinez, my uncle. Two weeks shy of his 18th birthday, Uncle
Dan was spending that Sunday afternoon with his pal Mike, in
hopes of seeing the A's finish out a mediocre season on a high note.
Mediocre in the sense that leading up to the last game, they had
won 82 and lost 79. Their longest winning streak was four, their
longest losing skid was seven, and their highest and lowest points
of the year were five games over the .500 mark and seven games
under it. And yet there was good news: it was the A's first winning
season since 1952 when the team was still in Philadelphia, just two
years after Dan Martinez was born. And now sixteen years later

there he was sitting in the bleachers with his buddy Mike, when Finley approached the unsuspecting teenagers. According to my uncle, the owner was polite, even though his famously gruff voice often intimidated people. Belying his cheapskate status, Finley bought his young customers food and drink and before long they were engaged in a conversation about Charlie O's favorite subject (well, besides himself): the Oakland A's.

Uncle Dan: "Finley came out there and he was real nice. He said, 'would you guys like a hot dog? Coke?' Well, he had his brother-in-law with him and he (says), 'go get 'em a Coke and a hot dog.' And he comes back down with (the food) and they sat with us for about twenty minutes. So Finley (asks), 'what about these A's?' And I said, 'Ah, man I love 'em but the problem is Kennedy, he doesn't know when to change relief pitchers. He'd wait too long to bring in a pitcher or he brought them in too early and he messed the A's up by doing that because otherwise they would have won some of those games.' Thing is, I've always loved baseball, I was watching it all the time and I knew the game pretty good, so when Finley asked me that question, I just told him, 'Kennedy, he ain't got it. He doesn't know how to change his relief pitchers.' And the very next day in the paper—'Kennedy Fired.' I'm sitting there reading (Finley's reasons for releasing his manager) and I'm like, 'yeah, I told him that!'

(By the way, the A's lost that day, 4–3, after Minnesota struck for three runs in the eighth inning. Starter Jim Nash had pitched brilliantly through seven innings, but got no outs in the eighth and by the time he was relieved by Paul Lindblad, the damage was done. And no, A's fans, Jim Mecir did *not* take the loss.)

Would Charlie have given Kennedy his walking papers had he not found my Uncle Dan sitting out in those bleachers that Sunday in September 1968? More than likely. In the nine years since he had purchased the A's in 1960, Finley had employed as many managers, Kennedy being the ninth. So yeah, chances were that he was going to find himself on the wrong side of the revolving door sooner than later. Finley didn't need an excuse to remove Kennedy from his post; that much is obvious. But for some reason he felt the need to seek outside opinions and what better way to do that than by mingling with the common folk, who also happen to be knowledgeable—and paying—customers? Finley may have spoken to several fans that day but in talking to my uncle, he got a little more insight than the usual, "Kennedy is a bum" barb. No, the 17-year old really knew what he was talking about. And maybe that's a good thing. After all, what if Uncle Dan had told him, just to be nice, that Kennedy was a fine manager and worth holding on to? Would Finley have listened? It's all wasted speculation since Hank Bauer (Kennedy's replacement) won 80 games before being shown the door on the last week of the 1969 season, and *his* heir to the throne, John McNamara, received a pink slip, as reward for an 89-win campaign the year after that .

John: "I don't remember Kennedy. I remember Bauer as a decent manager but he was too soft. Johnny McNamara was fiery and was well liked by the fans. He just seemed to be missing something. I don't recall if it was how he handled the pitchers or the players in general but something was not quite right."

If the A's were to find true success, Finley was going to have to hire someone outside his general way of thinking. A manager of men, not necessarily ballplayers. A man whose sole interest in the games would be in how many he's won. He could not be counted on to make friends with either the man who signed his checks or the men under his watch, but would be keen enough to know when either one of them needed an ego massage. And he could have no interest whatsoever in the circus that often surrounded the game's greatest showman. Finley needed someone he could trust but not someone who would kiss his ass and that someone better know the difference between the two.

On October 2, 1970, Charlie Finley got his man. He didn't seek Uncle Dan's approval, but this time the owner got it right all on his own. His new manager, Dick Williams, would make Oakland the luckiest town since Kansas City. Ain't that right, Senator Symington?

.

6 / Daddy's (Oldest) Little Girl

*"I see great things in baseball. It's our game, the
American game. It will repair our losses and be a
blessing to us."*

—Susan Sarandon, quoting Walt Whitman,
in *Bull Durham*

As mentioned earlier in this book, my oldest sister often took her
support of the A's a bit too far (though not nearly as far as
Sarandon's *Bull Durham* character). Nothing came between Tone
and her team. She was this sweet, little Catholic girl, but when it
came to the G&G, all rules went out the window. Here are some
samples of that as told to me in December 2005:

"I remember one game; it was July, freezing cold as usual. I
think it was the top of the 9th and we were losing like 10–0. Dad
wanted to leave and started up the stairs. I sat there (all I had for
warmth was a crocheted poncho mom made) and I was shivering
so badly but I wouldn't leave. Dad stood at the top of stairs calling me a "stubborn woman" and saying he was going to leave. But
he got himself a cup of coffee as the bottom of the 9th started. Still
yelling down at me. And then I looked up and saw his back. He
was leaving without me! So I went after him. I don't know why
he couldn't have waited for one more out."

"I would fight with people. What was I *thinking*? At school, I
always had people telling me that the A's were going down and I'd
argue with them. Some were Giant's fans but others were just people
who thought they knew everything. At the games, it was different.
I'd yell at the fans for leaving early, asking them how they could be
so unfaithful and fair-weathered and other stupid stuff like that. One
time I was with (cousin) Frannie and she was begging me to stop

45

yelling at the departing crowd. 'Toni, please. Please stop. Please. Please.' I wasn't very fun to sit by. Nowadays I'm lucky if we stay 'til the fifth inning. It never fails too, if we leave and the A's are losing, we get to the car and the crowd roars. Something good always happens! This could be the reversed-Marcie affect, punishment for all the years I called her a jinx!"

"Another time Dad told me he was going to take me and my girlfriends to the game, but he had to go into work first. Yeah, I had turned all my friends into A's fans. But it seemed like Dad was taking forever to come home and I stood at the front window saying over and over, 'He's not coming, he's not coming.' And then Mom would call out from the kitchen, 'He'll be here! Did he say he was going to be here?' 'Yes.' 'Has he ever not shown?' 'No.' 'Then he'll be here!' And sure enough he drove up and I started jumping up and down and hugged him when he got inside and he's there wondering what the heck is going on. He had that look on his face like, 'What?' And I kept telling him over and over, 'You made it!' Of course in the car he told jokes to my friends all the way to the game and I sat there kicking myself for not taking BART."

I am forever indebted to Tonianne for many of my baseball memories, even if there were times I really didn't want to go, or times she embarrassed me, or times I worried that she was going to get us killed. But there is one game that comes to mind that she kept me from a certain danger, and took this one on all by herself. Not that I wanted her to. Even though it was late August, the 1980 season was pretty much over, with the Royals running away with the West. But brash Billy Martin and his wild brand of baseball had fans rushing to the park like shoppers to a Day-after-Thanksgiving sale. This night the Yankees were in town and 17-game winner Mike Norris was on the hill for Oakland, with another chance to sway some Cy Young votes his way. (He'd finish second.) As Tone and I made our way across the BART ramp, we were stopped by a ticket scalper. At first, we simply tried to skirt past him, but he was persistent and told us that the game was sold out. We didn't believe it; if that were the case, we would have seen fans, empty handed, coming toward us. The scalper pointed towards the ticket booths down below. There were no lines. That was enough to convince Tone and she forked over the cash for our tickets. But when we reached the ticket booth below, there were still seats available! So my sister purchases two more tickets—at regular price—and told me to go inside while she went to get her money back. I looked at her like she was crazy but she was serious. I offered to go with her, but she refused. So I went inside and stationed myself in the left-field bleachers so I could see her when she came in. I was thirteen at the time and I remember thinking "What do I do if she doesn't come back?" She might have been gone fifteen minutes but to me it felt like an hour. Finally I saw her and she was beaming. She told of how the scalper tried to give part of the money back, but she pointed to a couple of security guards nearby, and he relented. "You drive a hard bargain, lady," he told her. The kicker is, the game eventually did sell out! With the "extra" money, Tone bought me a hot dog AND a Coke and we went about our business of watching Mike Norris and the A's kick the Yankees' butts, 9–1. What a night.

By the way, I still have the ticket stub.

7 / Fall Guys (1971-1975)

"So let them say your hair's too long
'Cause I don't care, with you I can't go wrong"
— from Sonny & Cher's '70's hit, *I Got You Babe*

Dick Williams knew a thing or two about a team on a bad streak. After all, he had inherited a Boston club in 1967 that had finished in ninth place the year before and hadn't played a World Series game since 1946. One "Impossible" pennant-winning season later, the Sox were the toast of the town (even though they eventually bowed to St. Louis in the Series) and their manager, for the moment, was the city's most popular Williams. But sudden success in sports, especially for a manager or coach, can be a double-edged sword. It's like love at first sight; you sort of expect every day to be like that initial encounter. So when Williams and management begin to view things in a different light, management won out and Williams was sent packing. A year or so later he was wearing those funky green-and-gold colors of the Oakland A's.

Tonianne: "The thing that sticks most in my mind about Dick Williams is the word 'fundamentals.' I remember the first spring training, that's all he talked about; making the basic plays and playing fundamental baseball. It didn't go over right away here. The opinion was just because it worked in Boston, didn't mean it was going to work here. But we won over 100 games that first year and although we lost in the playoffs to the Orioles, we felt like we were on the verge of something big. I think he played a major part in that. He knew how to handle the team. We won with our pitching, defense and timely hitting—the fundamentals of baseball. I also remember him as a tough manager. He was the boss (in the clubhouse at least). In the end he stood up to Finley over the Mike Andrews thing. I remember feeling really bad and worried when he left. I didn't think Alvin Dark could pull it off, he was too nice. I really liked Dick Williams. I think he was the best manager the A's ever had, more like a general. I just trusted him for some reason. To think what he could have done the past five years with the Big Three, et al; does the word dynasty come to mind?"

John: I remember him getting hired and the media was very high on him. They felt that he was the type of manager the team needed to put them over the top. I remember him as a tough manager who didn't take any crap from the players, but they all loved him. He had his soft side too. The fans loved him and didn't blame him for leaving (following the 1973 season)."

For the love-fest to begin in Oakland, Dick Williams was going to have to be Houdini all over again. Giving Bostonians a chance to "dream" was one thing. Guiding the Athletics to the playoffs, even with their recent success, would be like raising Lazarus from the dead. Not since 1931—one year before my dad was born—had the A's participated in a post-season contest. Their 4–2 loss to St. Louis in that year's Fall Classic not only ended their two-year reign as league champion, it simultaneously began a four decade-long tailspin into baseball purgatory. Sox fans may have felt like their team was "cursed" (well, depending on who you talk to) but they had their '46, their '67. About all the Athletics had was a chronic case of "loseritis." Over the next thirty-nine seasons—twenty-three in Philadelphia, thirteen in Kansas City, and three in Oakland— the A's would finish with a winning record only nine times. The closest they got to first place during that time was in 1969 and 1970, when they finished nine games in back of the front-running Twins. In that same span they finished forty or more games behind the pennant winner an astonishing thirteen times, bottoming out at sixty games to the rear of the New York Giants in 1954, their last year in Philadelphia. They lost 100 or more games ten times and on thirteen *other* occasions, topped the ninety-loss mark. In baseball, hope springs eternal; in the A's organization, hope wouldn't even send a postcard.

That changed almost immediately upon the team's arrival to the Bay Area. Following an 0-fer tenure in Kansas City, in which they finished under .500 in all thirteen seasons there, the A's were two games over the break-even mark in their first year in Oakland, fourteen games to the good in 1969, and sixteen games on the plus side in 1970. Their 89 victories that year were the most since their 94-win season in 1932. So with Dick Williams bringing his Moses act to Oakland, there was reason to hope that those forty seasons wandering in the desert were about to end.

But the Promised Land, the new manager would tell you, was made easier to reach with Vida Blue's left arm firing bullets at American League hitters. Fresh off a stirring September the year before, which included a no-hitter against the heavy-hitting Twins, Blue turned baseball on its collective ear in 1971. And the A's rode him all the way to the Western Division title. Oh, he had some help, of course. Catfish Hunter came into his own, winning 21 games against 11 defeats. Reggie Jackson hit 32 taters and Sal Bando drove home 94 runs. But it was Vida who left opponents feeling, well, blue. He pitched a shutout on April 9 to get Oakland in the win column after an 0–3 start and from there he and the A's took off and never looked back. They jumped into first place the day before my fourth birthday (behind another shutout, this time by Hunter) and stayed there until season's end. Meanwhile Blue blew his heater past AL hitters at a blistering pace and piled up the wins en route to an astonishing 17–3 first half. Talk of him reaching the magic 30 may have worn on the young star, just as the pressure wore on his teammate Reggie Jackson as he pursued the home run record two years prior. But make no mistake, 1971 belonged to Vida Blue. The numbers alone don't tell the whole story which is saying a lot considering that the numbers were quite gaudy in their own right. 24 wins against 8 defeats, which did not include his triumph in the All-Star Game, his league's only such win between 1962 and 1983. A microscopic ERA of 1.82. 301 strikeouts. Eight shutouts. He struck out 17 Angels in 11 shutout innings on July 9 (eventually won by Oakland 1–0 in 20 innings). He tossed a one-hitter at Detroit for his 18th win and got his 20th victory on August 7th (!) with a 1–0 shutout of Chicago. If ESPN's Stuart Scott were to describe him today, he'd say "dude was sick." And that dude, Blue, walked off with the MVP *and* the Cy Young Award for his efforts. But it wasn't just the amazing numbers (which included large crowds to see him pitch); it was his style, his exuberance. The way he'd run off the mound after retiring the side. The Year of Vida eventually would top the Year of Reggie, and not just in the season-end awards department. Behind Blue, Dick Williams' club won 101 games (the best number of them all) and the American League West title.

But alas all good things must come to an end, and the A's, novices at the post-season party, were swept three straight by the defending champion Baltimore Orioles. But while they didn't quite make it through the World Series door, there was surely a key waiting for them under the mat. And this time the manager was going to stick around to finish what he started.

Tonianne, recalling the first home playoff game in Oakland A's history: "I can even remember what I was wearing that day. The weather was so hot, total smog alert. It was the third game, we were swept of course, but no one acted like we lost. It was almost as if people knew what was to come. Two hours after the game ended the parking lot was still full, people didn't want to leave! You could feel this sense of being on the verge of something great. I will never forget that—it was awesome!"

John: "If I remember correctly, 1971 was a lot like this past season (2005)—a team on the verge of greatness. There were guys who had no fear—Bando, Campy, Green, Rudi, Holtzman, Hunter, Blue, Linblad, Knowles, Rollie. The current team sports Ellis, Swisher, Kendall, Johnson, Payton, Kotsay, Blanton, Harden, Calero, Street. All of those had or have a certain fire in their eyes. The '71 team was a little overwhelmed by the playoffs as were the fans (or at least I was). I remember being in this big crowd of people in the first deck for game three. I was used to sitting in the bleachers with much smaller crowds. It was strange to see this many people at a game and so many in business attire. The game seemed liked it lasted twenty minutes. I had no idea of the magnitude at that time. It started out with big roars on every pitch and it stayed loud until the end. I can't recall a single play by either team that stuck with me. It was all a blur and like I said a quick end to our first taste of the post season. However, this taste was all they needed, as this team would never again be overwhelmed or intimidated by anyone or anything."

But first, there was this little matter of actually getting the 1972 season underway. With the focus centering on health and pension benefits, the players decided to strike on April 1st (no foolin'), canceling the scheduled start of the season for the first time in history. Twelve days later the strike was over and the defending division champion A's christened the season with a 4–3, 11-inning victory over the Minnesota Twins. Perhaps more significantly, Reggie Jackson sported a mustache in that game, the first player to wear facial hair since Wally Schang in 1914. Schang, despite hitting five-hundred and four less homeruns in his career than Jackson, actually had more in common with the star right fielder than just some hair on his upper lip. Like Mr. October, Schang began in his career in an A's uniform and won World Series' with both the A's and the Yankees. And like Jackson, he too was involved in a fight or two with teammates before he and those same teammates took the field to beat up on their opponents. He also played with the Boston Red Sox during their World Series winning season in 1918. Talk about a guy being at the right place at the right time.

After a salary dispute with Charlie Finley, Vida Blue was wishing he could go back in time, to that magical ride of one year before. As he had done to Reggie Jackson In 1970, Finley broke Vida's spirit and the star pitcher, like Jackson, struggled mightily because of it. After holding out, Blue signed on May 2 for $63,000. ($63,000!) That's just wrong. But not nearly as bad as this: the left-handed Blue won his MVP and Cy Young awards on a paltry $14,750 salary. Vida won only six games in 1972, but would be heard from again come October. One of his ten losses during the regular season featured the kind of useless stat that baseball fanatics live for. Angel's pitcher Don Rose (how's that for a name?) bested the A's on May 24 with his arm (getting the win) and his bat (homering in his first-ever plate appearance, off starter Diego Segui). Rose would not win another game or hit another homerun in his short major league career. Twenty-three years later, I attended a high-school football game and upon a trip to the bathroom, suddenly realized that the man in the urinal beside me was Vida Blue. It was the first and only time that I ever relieved myself next to a guy who once appeared on the cover of *Time* magazine. Now *that's* some useless info.

Meanwhile, Finley, ever the showman took to this whole mustache thing and offered $300 to any player who would grow one. For the cash-deprived A's it was a no-brainer. Or in this case, a no-shaver. Already dressed in colorful uniforms and white shoes, the long-haired and mustachioed A's took another swing at the Establishment. Which no doubt pleased Charlie Finley, who would go on to earn *Sporting News* Man of the Year in 1972. Thus the Mustache Gang was born. Amidst the mustaches and meddling from the owner, the revolving door of players and the bizarre game of musical second-basemen, the A's somehow found time to play some pretty good baseball.

Tonianne: "That whole year was very interesting; like we knew our destiny (sounds corny but really true). There was no doubt in my mind we were going to the Series. After losing three straight the year before, we somehow knew it was our turn!"

The A's were in first place from May 27 through August 11, and then alternated between the top spot and second until August 29, when they regained the lead for good. The Chicago White Sox stayed on their heels for most of the final month, but the A's, as was their style throughout their three-year championship run, won the games they had to. You wondered how they did it, what with their modest offensive numbers (Joe Rudi led the team with a .305 average, Mike Epstein launched a club-best 26 homeruns, and Sal Bando's 77 RBI's were the most among his teammates.) But somehow, they always got the big hit when they needed it. Oh, and they pitched pretty well, too. Catfish Hunter (21–7), Cub castoff Ken Holtzman (19–11) and John "Blue Moon" Odom (15–6) made up a pretty decent trio and with a guy named Rollie Fingers coming out of the pen, the A's were tough to cross the plate against. On September 28, they stormed back from a 7–0 deficit to stun Minnesota 8–7, with Captain Sal Bando scoring the winning run in the bottom of the ninth to clinch the American League West. It was playoff time again and the A's had some unfinished business to attend to. Next up, Billy Martin's Detroit Tigers.

The A's scored two runs in the final frame to win a 3–2 thriller in Game 1, their first post-season victory since 1932. Gonzalo Marquez provided the key hit and Gene Tenace scored on Al Kaline's error to send the Oakland fans (all 29,000 of them) into a frenzy. Both "Uncle Gonzalo" (as we Marquez' called him) and Geno would be heard from time and time again as the playoffs progressed but they would take a back seat to the Campy Campaneris drama that unfolded in Game 2. And poor John Odom, who pitched a stirring 5–0 three-hit shutout, got overlooked, too. Campaneris had already gone 3-for-3 in the game when he was hit by a pitch by Lerrin LaGrow. Taking exception to what he deemed an intentional throw, the Cuban shortstop did some throwing of his own, flinging his bat at the Tiger reliever. Bedlam on the field ensued and both the batter and the pitcher were tossed out of the game. Meanwhile, Martin challenged the A's to a fight they saw no point of getting involved in. But Martin did achieve one aim: he fired up his club enough to win the next two games at home and even the series. The finale would be played in Detroit, too, but the A's didn't seem to mind. It was a game they had to win and they were going to find a way to win it. With the Tigers in front 1–0, Reggie stole home as part of a double steal to tie the game. It proved costly, as my hero tore his hamstring before my very eyes and was lost for the remainder of the playoffs.

Rose: "When Reggie got hurt, I thought we'd never win without him and I remember crying about it. As most people who cling to one player and think they don't have a chance to win without him, that's how I felt about Reggie:"

Thankfully the crying didn't last long as good ol' Geno provided a portent of things to come, driving in George Hendrick with the lead run in the fourth inning. Vida Blue, much maligned throughout the regular season, came in to relieve Odom, and would not need (nor get) any more run support from his mates. When Hendrick caught the final out, the A's were off to the World Series.

Abel: "I was listening to the game on my transistor radio with the speaker cord running inside my shirt up to my ear so the teacher wouldn't know I was listening. The problem was all my friends were gathered around my desk asking 'What's going on? Who's winning?' Good thing Mrs. Silverman was an A's fan!"

John: "I'm huddled around a radio with six or seven other guys (and a couple of teachers) in the John Muir school library. The crowd noise, even over the radio, is deafening. The tension is unbelievable as the game moves to two outs in the bottom of the ninth. The final out is recorded and we're all screaming and high-fiving each other. After we settle down you hear this low roar that gradually grows louder and louder. I step out of the library to see what's going on. It's pandemonium. Students and teachers are running through the halls screaming and hugging each other. The whole school is going bonkers. It's one thing to be at the game with a huge crowd. This was totally unexpected and a scene I'll never forget."

Tonianne: "Loved the pressure of the playoffs (a stomach ache like no other). I remember listening to the playoffs in school, and the roar that echoed through the halls of John Muir when we beat Detroit. I had my radio in a lunch bag and held up to my ear. Mr. Thane was the lunch-duty teacher. Any other time he would have snatched it away in a heartbeat. He slowly walked towards me, stopped in front of me, stared a minute and then walked away. As he did, he asked me how my "lunch" was doing! I was in Mr. Walker's Algebra class (at the game's conclusion) and he wouldn't let us listen. When we heard the roar, we all ran out of the classroom. I get chills to this day thinking about that sound."

The sound coming out of the Swingin' A's locker room was well, swinging. It was Game 5 starter (Odom) versus Game 5 closer (Blue). Seems that Blue accused Odom of not having the "nerve" to close out a ball game. Odom didn't take kindly to that accusation and went after Blue. Look out Big Red Machine, here come the Angry A's. Game 1 was played in Cincinnati, where the Reds, losers of the 1970 World Series, were the overwhelming favorites to beat the Reggie-less A's. The Classic was dubbed "The Hairs versus The Squares," the A's with their overflowing locks against the Reds and their clean-shaven look. The Hairs, behind an unlikely source, drew first blood in the Series with a 3–2 victory. Gene Tenace, he of the five homeruns during the regular season, became the first player ever to hit two long balls in his first two

Series at-bats, an effort that left one fan (if not the Reds themselves) thoroughly impressed.

Uncle Dan: "Man, my eyes almost popped out of my head when Tenace hit those home runs. He wasn't even our regular catcher during the season."

Game 2 brought two new stars, this time Catfish Hunter, who worked eight stellar innings and also drove in a run and Joe Rudi, who homered to give Oakland a 1–0 lead and whose spectacular catch in the ninth inning preserved the 2–1 victory. The A's, with their superstar on crutches, were heading home up two games to none.

Uncle Dan, of Rudi's glove work: "a great, great catch. I'll never forget it."

The Big Red Machine, whose lineup boasted of four future Hall-of-Famers—Pete Rose, Joe Morgan, Johnny Bench, and Tony Perez—suddenly forgot how to hit. (Just like I forgot that Rose isn't really in the Hall.) Three runs in two games were not exactly the stuff of legends. And they hardly broke out against Odom in Game 3, scoring one lousy run, but it was enough as the A's bats took the night off. Cincinnati took a 2–1 lead going into the last half of the ninth of Game 4, three outs from a tied series. But the Mustache Gang, led by That Man Tenace, rallied back. ("Gene" no longer sufficed for Tenace, who hit his third homer of the series earlier in the game.) "Uncle Gonzalo" hit a one-out single in the ninth and "That Man" followed with a base hit of his own. Don Mincher, the second pinch-hitter of the inning, drove home pinch-runner Alan Lewis with another single. On the very next pitch, Angel Manguel (Dick Williams' record third pinch-hitter in the ninth), dribbled a ball past Morgan, and Tenace, arms raised in triumph, jumped on home plate with the winning run. Manguel was mobbed by his mates, fireworks filled the sky, and the A's were one game away from a World Series title.

Pete Rose made sure that the celebration waited at least another day, connecting for a homerun on Game 5's first pitch and driving in the lead run in the ninth. Even That Man Tenace, who hit a record-tying fourth homerun of the series (a three-run job that had given the A's a 3–1 lead) wasn't enough to win it for the home folks; Dad, Tone, and John among them.

John: "I remember going back to school the day after that game. I had with me an 'excuse' for missing school. No one really fell for it though. When Mr. Butler was taking roll call in P.E. and I said 'here,' he looked at me and asked, 'how was the game?'"

Tonianne: "When we missed school for day games, we had to show our tickets in the office before we were able to leave. The first year they didn't record tickets so some people were able to leave by showing the same tickets as their friends (or brothers in some cases). They caught on by the second Series. The secretary would record and compare tickets to the ones already listed just to make sure that students without actual game tickets weren't just using them so they could go home and watch it on TV. As if anyone would do such a thing (hehe). Anyway, Dad took me to game five of our first Series; we sat in section 112 behind the Reds dugout. Pete Rose's (first) wife had a Big Red Machine t-shirt under her sweater and she kept turning around and lifting her sweater to show everyone. I remember that Dad booed her the loudest but I think I was able to keep him from throwing something at her!" (Rumor has it that Pete Rose "lost" his wife in this Series; he had the Reds in six.)

A betting man would surely have wagered on Cincinnati heading into Game 7, as the Squares squared the series at three games apiece with an 8–1 romp over Blue and company. This was the only contest that was not decided by one run and clearly put the momentum on the Reds' side. But the A's had That Man Tenace on their side and in the final game he delivered an RBI single in the first and drove in another run with a two-bagger in the sixth. Sal Bando's double drove in pinch runner Alan Lewis, giving Oakland a 3–1 lead they would never relinquish. The Reds tacked on a run in their half of the eighth to draw within 3–2 but Rollie Fingers, making his sixth appearance of the Series, closed it out in the ninth. In the words of NBC's Curt Gowdy: "And as the final out of the 1972 World Series settles in Joe Rudi's glove, the Oakland A's are the World Champions of baseball."

Dad: "I was at the Coliseum for a Raider game against the Broncos. When they announced over the PA system that the A's had won, the place went crazy."

When the newly crowned champs touched down in the East Bay, thousands of fans were there to greet them including the

Marquez,' the same family that had greeted the A's upon their arrival to the Bay Area in 1968.

Tonianne: "I remember all of us going to the airport to welcome the A's home from Cincinnati. I think we practically walked from home; couldn't get close to the place. I also remember Mom trying to keep Trish and Don from getting crushed in the crowd. She was up against the windows on the second floor trying to create a pocket of air."

Rose: "I recall after winning the Series, we were all at the airport and I got pushed up to the front by myself. It was so crowded and someone said, 'Let the kid in, she can't see.' I was scared, because I got away from the family, but the crowed pushed me up front so I could see better."

After the Series, an album came out titled *Finley's Heroes,* full of recorded highlights of that championship season. I think everyone in the Marquez household had that thing memorized. (And, yes, I still have the record.)

The A's would go about generating more highlights for their fans minus a couple of players who had played key roles in the club's previous championship run. First basemen Mike Epstein, who led the team with 26 homeruns the previous season, was shipped to Texas and catcher Dave Duncan was traded (along with George Hendrick) to Cleveland (for former All-Star Ray Fosse, who was most remembered for his collision with Pete Rose in the 1970 Midsummer Classic). Both Epstein and Duncan had clashed with upper management and were thereby deemed expendable. But for one particular 10-year old fan, losing Duncan was like seeing her first crush move to another school.

Rose: "For some odd reason, I had a thing for the catchers; don't know if it was the mask or the black stuff they put under their eyes that made them more attractive to me. I remember being crazy for Dave Duncan (and later Mike Heath) but didn't feel that way about Ray Fosse. As the years went on, some of the other catchers we had were always my favorite players."

The 1973 A's happened to be one of my favorite teams and it had everything to do with one Reginald Martinez Jackson, who took

MVP honors after missing the previous World Series. Reggie was a unanimous choice among voters as he led the league in homeruns, RBI's, and runs scored, while sporting a .293 average. The A's won one more game than the '72 version and, coincidentally, conquered their division by one more game than the year before. On paper, they were a far better team than that tiny margin suggests. Besides their right-fielder's heroics, Sal Bando regained his power stroke with 29 homers and 98 RBI's and starters Catfish Hunter, Ken Holtzman, and Vida Blue all won 20 games (the A's are the last club to boast such a trio). Oakland started slow; the team was 28–28 on June 9 and was no-hit by Texas' Jim Bibby on July 30. I clearly remember Dad and Tonianne going to the Bibby game and leaving me at home, even though I *begged* for them to take me. As the game wore on, I actually rooted for the no-hitter just to spite them.

John, responding to an e-mail thirty years after that game in which I scolded Tone for leaving her kid brother at home: "Maybe you should have asked me (to take you), because if memory serves me correctly, and I'm not *that* old, I was at the game when Bibby pitched his no-no. I remember it rather vividly. It was a warm summer night, with a slight breeze blowing in off the bay. There was a small group of us with our usual brought-from-home food: hotdogs wrapped in foil, which made the bun super moist and caused it to stick to the dog; popcorn in a brown paper shopping bag, with grease stains around the bottom; Kool-Aid in a Tupperware container, with ice now nearly melted; and of course, some homemade cookies, still warm from the oven. I don't recall who of us were there, but I know I was there, Toni and Dad. In fact Dad, fair weather fan that he already was, even thirty years ago, was angry that the A's weren't hitting and making this youngster look like Cy Young. (He still says that about every no-name pitcher who is having a good game against the A's.) I managed to send him over the top when I said, rather innocently after the end of the sixth inning, 'Hey dad! This guy is pitching a no-hitter!' Dad grumbled something about me becoming a Texas Ranger fan, and then stomped off to have a smoke, banging the lower metal portion of the bleachers like a gong, with each step he took. As the game went along and the fans began to turn the attention more on the no-hitter and less on the A's winning, Dad became even more restless and frustrated. I guess that's who we learned our appreciation for the National Pastime from."

The A's gained momentum in August (with a club record nine straight wins) leaving pesky Kansas City in the dust. A rivalry that began brewing in May when centerfielder Bill North used pitcher Doug Bird's face as a punching bag would escalate in the years to come as the Royals became the A's fiercest challengers for supremacy in the AL West. Behind Blue's 20th win, Oakland clinched its third division crown on September 23rd. Waiting in the wings in the American League playoffs were the Baltimore Orioles, the same club that had made short work of Dick Williams' squad two seasons before and took Game 1 of this series by a 6–0 count. Captain Sal Bando slugged two homeruns to draw the A's even and they took the series lead when Campy Campaneris decided to use his bat for swinging rather than throwing; his 11th inning homer made a winner out of Holtzman. Given a chance to close out the ALCS, Vida blew a 4–0 lead and the Orioles headed into the fifth and final game flying sky high. But Catfish Hunter has a way of bringing teams back to earth and the A's earned a second consecutive trip to the World Series with a tidy 3–0 win. I ran home from school to catch the last few outs and they had to stop the game a few times to escort fans who had prematurely wandered onto the field. Sadly, there were less than 25,000 on hand to see the champs clinch, a sure sign that the paying customers had become a little blasé about their A's.

A little bit of everything was in store for the World Series, something you came to expect from a team owned by Charles Oscar Finley. Oakland faced the New York Mets, who were looking for an encore to their 1969 Miracle season. Yogi Berra's bunch strolled in with 82 wins to their name plus three more against the favored Reds in the NLCS. The A's, favorites themselves, did enough of the little things to record a 2–1 victory in Game 1. But if we knew anything about our boys, it was their uncanny knack of doing things the hard way. Game 2 served up an extra dose of audacity (on the part of the aforementioned owner) and ugliness (on the part of almost everyone in uniform that day). An unforgiving sun turned anyone with a mitt—including the aging Willie Mays—clueless.

The Mets finally won the four-hour contest in 12 innings, 12–7, thanks to second baseman Mike Andrews' two costly errors in the deciding frame. Afterwards, Finley convinced Andrews to admit that he was ill and could no longer participate in the World Series, which infuriated the A's, particularly Dick Williams, who told his team that he was quitting after the Classic came to its conclusion. Commissioner Bowie Kuhn, a long time nemesis of Finley, vetoed Andrews' "resignation."

John: "I don't have any detailed memories (of the Game Two fiasco), just that they were sad chapters in an otherwise glorious period. The Mike Andrews incident really turned the tide for Finley. Most of baseball already didn't like him, and this deal turned the Oakland fans against him as well. I know everyone was pulling for Mike even the opponent's fans. Seeing Marcus Allen standing on the sidelines (for the Raiders) all those years reminded me of the Andrews fiasco. It was ugly, plain and simple. I didn't really understand and even see any problems with Finley until Dick Williams called it quits. Charlie had a lot of good ideas but he, like Al Davis, began to take the control thing too far and the Mike Andrews incident, Dick Williams, and even (designated runner) Herb Washington were the beginning of the end."

The Series switched to the Big Apple for Game 3 and the Mustache Gang racked up another must-win, a 3–2 eleven-inning thriller. Mike Andrews drew most of the attention and was given a standing ovation when he came to bat. His ground-out to short was his last at-bat in the majors, perhaps the most famous of Finley's casualties. Meanwhile, Campaneris' single in the 11th drove in Ted Kubiak with the game-winner. Undeterred, the hosts beat the champs with some filthy pitching: Jon Matlack and Jerry Koosman held the A's to a single run in Games 4 and 5 combined. The mustachioed ones returned home down three games to two and having to face Tom Seaver in the mother of must wins. Reggie Jackson once said of the Mets' ace: "Blind men go to games to hear him pitch." Seaver must have wished Reggie had vision difficulties after the MVP lit him up for two run-scoring doubles that lifted the A's into a series tie. Turned out Seaver was done in by *two* Hall-of-Famers-to-be this afternoon, as Big Game Hunter was again at his high-stakes best in the 3–1 victory. One more for all the marbles and the poor Mets didn't have a chance. Campy and Reggie connected for two-run homers in a four-run fourth and the A's went on to a 5–2 triumph. Watching his teammates on crutches just twelve months prior, a vindicated Jackson took MVP honors in the Series and staked his claim as baseball's best. A claim that the Swingin' A's could make for a second straight season. How about Once More in '74?

John, on the celebration that ensued after the World Series: "I had a choice of going to either game six or game seven. I didn't even consider that there might not be a game seven. I just said I'll wait because I want to run on the field when they win it. There was no tension, no nail biting during the game. I was just waiting for the last out. Running on the field was a blur. I didn't know which direction to go. I finally made it to the dugouts and only was able to grab a matchbook. I remember running onto the field after the game and taking some infield dirt. I can't believe I actually planned for it by bringing baggies with me to stuff dirt in. One of the ushers was trying to keep second base from being taken by fans. He was lying on the ground with his arms wrapped around it, crying as he was getting the pulp beat out of him. The pitching rubber and home plate were dug up as well. Joe Perez (cousin) made off with some turf and Uncle Dan got a couple of towels from the Mets dugout. I also tore a chunk of sod from the A's bullpen area. People were taking pieces off of it as I exited the stadium. Others who had followed suit were caught by security guards and had theirs taken away before making it out of the stadium so I hid the turf under my shirt. The Mets' John Milburn, who was a big dude, had his hat taken by a fan at the end and he took his hat back by force. I also recall Reggie getting his hat taken by a fan who ran onto the field prematurely, thinking that the ground ball that was hit was going to be fielded for the final out. Reggie tackled the guy, got his hat back, and then "helped" the guy over the right-centerfield wall."

The A's, it seemed, would need some help entering the 1974 season, now that Dick Williams had called it quits. But my brother knew better, even as he waxed iconic in his salute to arguably the best manager ever to wear the green and gold.

John: "Dick Williams leaving was akin to the breakup of the Beatles. They were starting their solo careers and the music was still good, but it wasn't the same. The A's in fact, didn't need a manager anymore. They knew they were the best team and nobody could knock them off the top of the hill. Injuries, owner's distractions, in-fighting, were like flies. They were pesky, but they couldn't harm them. They were so talented and so confident that they could laugh when they were booed at the All-Star games, even in American League parks. Their uniforms were not in conformity with the rest of the league, they looked like hippies and their fans were nasty. They were the Raiders, only in baseball uniforms. They were hated and they reveled in it."

My brother was right; heck, *he* could have managed the 1974 A's. Even when they got off to another slow start under the watchful eye of manager Alvin Dark; no eyebrows were raised, no panic buttons pushed. The cream always rises to the top. Sometimes it rises in July. Cleveland's Gaylord Perry strode into Oakland on a rainy night with a 16-game winning streak and a full house on hand to watch. Playoff atmosphere, only the lowly Indians weren't accustomed to such pressure. Oh, they were game; they even took a late lead thanks to Dave Duncan's homerun off of Blue. But the A's rallied back to win in extra innings on 19-year old Claudell Washington's single to score Rudi. Rare as it was for the home team to show off its post-season form in July, it was rarer still that no Marquez was among the partisan crowd to witness it. Which my oldest sister still steams about when the topic comes up.

Tonianne: "It had rained all day long but stopped well before game time but I still had to wait for Dad to get home. And he just kept saying that they weren't going to play so he wouldn't take me and I said they were going to play. That they *had* to play. But he insisted. And I was so mad that I vowed never to talk to him again or anyone else or listen to the game. I ended up putting the game on, with the volume turned way down. And when it started, I ran out of my room and yelled at Dad. 'I told you they were going to play!' I mean if my son had yelled at me like that…but Dad, he just sat there. I don't even think he looked up from what he was doing. But I was heartbroken because Dad never let me down. Ever! So I listened to the game. I could barely hear it; the volume was

so low. The only time I'd turn it up was when I'd hear the roar of
the crowd. And then to win it like that, I was so mad. The
announcers didn't even pronounce Claudell's name right. It was
more like Claw-dull."

So how long did you go without talking to Dad?

"I'm sure I talked to him the next day. There was another game
that night and I wanted to make sure I could go."

Alas the A's turned back into their uninterested selves that July,
even falling victim to a no-hitter for the second straight season.
(Cleveland's Dick Bosman turned the trick.) But no worries.
Everyone in the East Bay knew that when summer turned to fall,
the magic switch would go on and the season would end as it always
did. Take the A's for granted? That in itself became an annual thing.

John: "I didn't know any better once we became champions.
I just thought every October was supposed to be like that. The A's
would win the Series, I'd run on the field, we'd go to the parade."

An all too familiar pastime in Oakland, one that surely had the
rest of the baseball world shaking their collective heads. Ah, but
familiarity, we are reminded, breeds contempt. And this band of
brothers on the baseball field sometimes behaved, well, like brothers off of it. Reggie and Bill North had already done some
squabbling at the dawn of the '74 season due to a ground ball that
the reigning MVP took as dogging it by the speedy North. But that
was merely an undercard to the main event in June when the two
outfielders went toe-to-toe, with Jackson injuring his shoulder
(slowing him down for good after a sizzling start). But catcher Ray
Fosse got the worst of the deal; he crushed a disk in his neck trying to break up the fight and was done for the regular season. In
most other clubhouses, such dissension would doom a team, but
the A's thrived off of it. This was the original "Fight Club" and who
doesn't love a fight? On most teams, managers give inspirational
speeches to kick their players into gear; in Oakland, the players
fought among themselves to get fired up. That's how it is in a family; brothers fight all the time. But if someone outside the family
messes with one of them, that someone better know a very good
doctor. This was never more evident during the team's three-year
reign than late in the 1974 season when the playoffs loomed and

the A's were serving notice that no one messes with the champ. Especially in the champ's backyard.

John: "The A's and Royals were neck and neck in the race for the AL West title in September. KC was coming to town for a four game showdown highlighted by a twi-night double header on a Monday Family Night. I don't know if you remember those Family Nights, but calling it 'Family' Night is like calling Ozzie Osbourne a pop singer. There were more fights in the bleachers than there are in an NHL game. Raider fans were even afraid to attend these "Family Night" games. If you took your kids and sat in the bleachers, they left scarred for life. There wasn't a fan in attendance that night that wasn't absolutely positive what the outcome was going to be and no team wearing "baby blue" was going to come into our house and have a sniff of a chance at changing anyone's mind. The party began early and ended late and it wasn't limited to the bleachers. About midway through the first game the fans near the Royals' bullpen began calling their players out and were actually reaching in and trying to pummel them. In those days, and especially on these raucous Family Nights, you didn't boo fans for behaving like that, you cheered them on. The Royals had to clear their team off the field until order was restored and that was the beginning of the end for them. The house was rockin' and the A's went on to sweep the series (behind shutouts by Catfish and Blue) and never looked back on their way to a third straight championship."

Tonianne: "I remember all it took was for two people to stand up and look toward the left-field bleachers…then the whole section would stand up and look that way…craning their necks and standing on toes to see the fight in the next section! And, if there wasn't a fight already going, one would start!"

A's fans, it seemed, were no different than the team they adored: they beat up fans of other teams and sometimes each other, too! And they celebrated together. In the ESPN era, where players' private lives crawl across the bottom of your TV screen, even as they are protected more than ever from Joe Fan, there will never be another team quite like those 70's A's. On or off the field. And with heightened security in today's ball parks, there will never be crowds quite like the ones that cheered those A's on. During the regular season, it wasn't quite as obvious, what with barely a million fans attending games each year. But when those October lights came on, the Swingin' A's and their fans were at their swingin'-est. Bad was never so good.

Rose recalls a moment that further illustrates the effect that those A's had on their fans, particularly our family: "It was after a game and we piled up in the station wagon to go home and were headed for the freeway. All of a sudden we saw Rollie Fingers and his wife in the car behind us. We started screaming and Dad started honking the horn even though Rollie could see us without him honking. We must have waved and waved until our hands broke off. Rollie kept waving back and smiling and I knew he must have gotten tired of it, but we were kids and he just obliged. It was such a thrill to us."

After that little formality known as the regular season (the A's "celebrated" their fourth consecutive division title by taking the champagne home rather than spraying it), the bell rang for the play-offs to begin. Baltimore again. I finally got to go to my first post-season game and Catfish was on the mound to boot! Or it was someone that *looked* like Catfish because he sure didn't *pitch* like Catfish—the Orioles lit him up for three homeruns en route to a 6–3 win. Unfazed, the A's won the next three games, giving up one; check that, ONE run in the process. Kenny and Vida tossed shutouts in Games 2 and 3 and Catfish (the real Catfish) and Rollie held the O's to a ninth-inning run in Game 4. The A's walked 11 times and got one hit—a tie-breaking double by Reggie to clinch it. The A's were, yawn, off to, ho-hum, another World Series, this time against the upstart Los Angeles Dodgers. How to get up for the young and cocky Dodgers? Cue the *Rocky* music and call the "Let's Get Ready to Rumble" dude. Or maybe we should bring in Rod Serling instead. In a three-day span that was whacko even by A's standards, former second basemen Mike Andrews sued Finley for 2.5 million (for the '73 Series mess), Catfish charged the owner with a breach of contract, and, oh by the way, Fingers and Odom brawled on the eve of Game 1 of the 1974 Series. Which, naturally, was won by the A's, who by now treated any sort of adversity with a simple shrug of the shoulders. Reggie homered in that first game (normal stuff) and Hunter relieved Fingers (not so much) to save the win. The Dodgers won Game 2 by the Game 1 score of

3–2 and the two teams headed north for the next three contests. And that's all the A's would allow LA to play in this Fall Classic. Another 3–2 win (pitched by Cy, I mean, Catfish) was followed by a 5–2 affair won by Holtzman, who also homered in the game (so much for the DH, huh?). Dick Green, who was an absolute magician throughout the Series at second base, ended the game on his belly as he flipped the ball to Campaneris, triggering a mind-blowing double play and setting off Finley's fireworks at the same time. That put Blue on the mound against the Dodger Blue for the finale but it was Blue Moon who got the victory in relief; a role reversal from the last game of the 1972 playoffs, only this time no post-game fisticuffs ensued. With the score tied at two in the seventh inning, the game was halted as fans littered the field with debris. Their target? Young Bill Buckner. Yes, *that* Bill Buckner. Billy had won the ire of the A's and their fans by suggesting that only two Oakland players were fit to play on the Dodgers: Reggie and Campy. Billy forgot about pitching. And, um, defense. (But we already know that story, don't we?) So while the umps cleaned up the mess on the field, ultra arrogant reliever Mike Marshall opted not to warm up. When play resumed, batter Joe Rudi figured the heater was coming, and as champions do, he not only guessed right, he deposited Marshall's offering somewhere in Fruitvale.

John: "It was loud as the umps cleared the field and it just kept getting louder as Rudi stepped up to the plate and then BOOM! Game, set, match. Loudest sound I've ever heard."

A's fans proceeded to spend the next two innings or so celebrating the inevitable. And Billy Buckner added to the festivities as he led off the eighth. His single got past North in centerfield so Billy Buck headed for second with an unhesitating eye on third. But there was Reggie backing up his brother and Reggie rifled a bullet to Green who wheeled and threw to Bando, who applied a hard tag on poor Buckner. Like I said Billy; *defense*. The play epitomized the dynasty that was the 70's A's. Picking a teammate up. Positioning. Symmetry. Fluid. Not having to think, just doing. Trusting. And ultimately unnoticed amid Finley's Freak Show. The Series ended with Rollie on the mound, as he was in '72. Von Joshua grounded meekly to Fingers who jumped and ran towards first before finally throwing to Tenace for the final out. The three-peat was complete. And I watched the fireworks from Cherry Grove Park around the corner from my house. Some family members had a much better view of the Mustache Gang's final World Series.

Tonianne: "I just remember sitting in the dugout after we won. For someone accustomed to the bleachers just being in the first deck felt different. But to be on the field, it was a larger than life experience. It was like, too much for me to handle."

John: "In '74 it was even more of a sure thing. I went to game five knowing it was over. It was just a formality as to the final score. Toni and I moved from our bleacher seats to the first deck in the top of the ninth. When the final out was recorded, (Rollie jumping up and down) we were down near third base in a crowd of people standing near the gate that opens up to the field. The security guard opened the gate and was actually helping people on to the field. The parades were, as I recall, anti-climatic but I guess they usually are. It was still fun to go and celebrate with the team one more time though."

The A's motto for the next year was to "Keep it Alive in '75." But Finley's magic was about to run out, on and off the field. Jim "Catfish" Hunter, perhaps the greatest pitcher to ever don an Oakland uniform, won his claim against Finley in December and was declared a free agent due to breach of contract. On New Year's Eve of 1974, Hunter signed a $3.75 million contract with the Yankees, which tripled every other salary in all of baseball. Somehow the A's managed to win more games (98) without Hunter in 1975 than in any of the previous three seasons with him. But where his departure hurt the champs was in the post-season and the A's three-year reign ended on the very field that had been home to so many celebrations. Boston, like Baltimore in '71, swept Oakland three straight. Back then they were on the verge of something magnificent; this time it was the end of the road. Gene Tenace, so much a part of the greatness of the A's, didn't hesitate to lose the one thing that symbolized the uniqueness of Finley's Heroes: immediately after the game, Geno shaved off his mustache.

Tonianne: "Losing in '75 was hard because of school (big sis was starting her junior year). Even before the season started, people were telling me how the A's weren't going to win again. And then when we lost, they were mean about it. Someone even left a note in my locker that said, 'told you the A's were going to lose!' I just told them that we had won three straight World Series and when was the last time someone did that?"

John: "It wasn't a great surprise when they bowed out in '75. It was inevitable. The wind had been taken out of our sails. Soon we would have our hearts ripped out and witness the destruction of one of the greatest baseball teams of all time by the very man who created it. Charlie "O" had become what he once described Bowie Kuhn as—"The Village Idiot." He let the power go to his head. I never did hate him though. He gave us the greatest thrills of our lives and he knew what he was doing when it came to assembling talent. I remember trying to emulate all of the players. Me, Tony Lopez, Armando etc. knew all of their batting stances and would mimic them when we played Whiffle Ball in the backyard. I even recorded the National Anthems played at different ballparks. We would play the tape and stand at attention before starting a game. Seeing your heroes sold off or traded was gut-wrenching. Unfortunately, it was something Oakland fans would become all too accustomed to. It wasn't just the Reggies, Bandos, Hunters and Rollies that departed. They begat the Rickys, McGwires, Cansecos, Giambis and Tejadas."

Tonianne: "To me (the player's departures) were different then, not like when Jason (Giambi) left. When he left, I blamed him. When it happened with our World Series teams, I blamed Finley."

8 / Power Trip

"Chicks dig the long ball."
— Atlanta Brave pitcher Greg Maddux to fellow hurler
Tom Glavine in a 1999 Nike shoe commercial

Reginald Martinez Jackson was my first hero. (You might know him better as Reggie.) Took a picture with him on Camera Day when I was three, got his autograph when I turned seven. Wrote my very first book report on him. Second one, too. He was like a member of the family. And since his middle name was Martinez, some of us took that sentiment literally.

Tonianne: "I told them he was our cousin on Grandpa Abel's side. I was convinced of it, too."

Rose: "I told people he was our uncle. I really thought he was related to us. I think we called him 'Uncle Reggie' until he went to the Yankees!"

Rose even had a cat named after him. And Mom crocheted a green and gold hat that Tone gave to him on his birthday. (He was my sister's baseball crush.) Reg thanked her and told her that was the only gift he got that day, before tossing the hat into his trunk. Tonianne figures he didn't want to mess up his 'fro by wearing it. There was another time when she wanted to give him a rabbit's foot for good luck, so John threw it to him from the bleachers! Reg called time out while trying to link the charm to his mitt. Rose recalls that he struggled with it before finally putting it in his back pocket.

Yep, Reggie Jackson. Mr. October. The Yankee who smashed three consecutive World Series homeruns. The Straw that Stirred New York's drink. Had a candy bar named after him. Went to the Hall of Fame with "NY" on his cap. Well, not exactly *that*

71

Reggie Jackson. The Reggie I am referring to made his mark in Oakland. He didn't need the Big Apple to win a championship. New York needed *him*. Reggie himself admitted as much when he said, "I didn't come to New York to be a star. I'm bringing my star with me."

Reggie won his only Most Valuable Player award in Green and Gold. Unanimous decision at that. I can still remember his license plate: "MVP 73," a personal memento to a monster season. As I mentioned previously in this book, I didn't say my "R's" very well when I was growing up. But that hardly stopped me from cheering on my favorite player whenever he came to bat. "Hit the ball, Weggie," I'd shout to him. And that Weggie, er Reggie, could hit it a ton. I mean, he'd knock the crap out of that ball. And he was the first guy to really admire a homerun. Just stand there and watch it for a second or two before rounding the bases, ever so slowly, as if to soak it all in. It was as if the game came to a halt whenever Reggie hit one of those long taters.

I remember in 1974, when he got off to a blazing start, the world couldn't get enough of Reggie. He was on the cover of *Sports Illustrated*, *Sport*, and even *Time*. The headline in *Sports Illustrated* turned off some people a bit: "Everyone is Helpless and in Awe." But not me. I couldn't agree more. When "Buck" was at the dish, the opposing pitcher was helpless and the rest of us were in awe. And that was the case whether he belted one into the stands or struck out swinging. Which he happened to do both of with tremendous frequency.

Still, even his own teammates found him hard to stomach at times. Said Catfish Hunter of the free-swinging right fielder: "Reggie would give you the shirt off his back. Of course, he'd call a press conference first." This from reliever Darold Knowles: "There's not enough mustard in the whole world for that hot dog."

Yeah, Reggie's big mouth often accompanied his big stick. But while he talked the talk, he also walked the walk. I was one month into Kindergarten when the A's met the Detroit Tigers in the 1972 playoffs. Being that I was a "late-bird" (as they called it in those days), I was fortunate to catch some of the deciding ball game. I will never forget Reggie stealing home to tie the score, then lying on the field in agony. He had helped propel us to our first World

Series, but our leader was forced to watch from the dugout on crutches. Reggie returned in 1973 on a mission, hitting 32 homers and driving in 117 runs. With the A's facing elimination in that year's World Series, he put his teammates upon his broad shoulders, and carried them to a second consecutive title. In Game 6, he roped a pair of RBI-doubles off Tom Seaver, as Oakland triumphed, 3–1. Then in the clincher, he stroked a two-run homer off Jon Matlack to spark a 5–2 win. The headlines read: "World Champions Still."

So you see, Yankee fans, "Mr. October" was born in Oakland, not New York.

Reggie's double-MVP performance in 1973 only strengthened his status as my favorite "A" and when I received an autograph book for my seventh birthday, I knew I wouldn't be happy until Number 9 had signed it. To top it off, the champs were in town that April afternoon in 1974 and Dad had one more surprise in store for his youngest son: first deck tickets at the Coliseum. Afterwards, we'd see about getting some signatures for my book. As I waited anxiously for Reggie to make his grand entrance into the parking lot following the game, my cousin Paul and I tracked down some of the other players on the A's and the visiting California Angels. (Back in those days, you could just walk right up to the players—almost as if they were real people!) But little did I know how tough this autograph business was. We approached a young Bobby Valentine, who was signing amid a modest crowd of kids. Seeing me decked out in my brand new green and gold A's cap, Bobby V. decided to have a little fun. "Oh, I don't sign for A's fans," he said to me. Demoralized, I began to walk away when I felt a hand on my shoulder. It was Valentine. "Hey," he said, beaming, "I was just horsing around!" And he signed. But if you've ever wondered why there are no World Series rings on his fingers, well, now you know. Karma, baby. There are just some things you don't do to a kid on his seventh birthday.

I don't remember what other ball players left their signatures in my book that day, because truth is, I didn't keep any of the autographs I collected. Except one. A crowd of youngsters waited by Reggie's black Grand Prix, hoping to get a glimpse of the reigning MVP. I wasn't taking any chances. Book in hand, I camped out in front of the driver side door of Reggie's car. (Actually my body was planted so tight against the vehicle, you'd have sworn I was a car ornament.) Which Mr. Jackson took great exception to. "Away from the car," his voice boomed, even louder than the sound of my heart pounding through my A's shirt. I remained steady, not budging from my spot. Or maybe I was so petrified that I couldn't move, but I certainly wasn't going to tell Reggie that. That is, if my mouth were able to actually form words. My hero of heroes asked me, in a not so gentle tone, if I had heard him correctly, and I replied with my best deer-caught-in-the-headlights pose. Surely Reg was in no mood for this, having seen his teammates blow an eighth-inning lead. He looked around for some possible help, maybe a family member that this seemingly deaf and dumb kid belonged to. Bad enough that I had completely sucked the last ounce of patience from Reggie Jackson, but I could feel the weight of one hundred eyes staring at me. It was then that Dad saved the day. "Tell him what you want." Reggie turned back to me. Nothing. Then to my father, again. "Does he talk?" Now the old man was laughing. "Yeah, he talks. Today's his birthday and he wants your autograph." Once again I was face-to-face with this mammoth of a man. He wasn't satisfied with my Dad's request, he wanted to hear me say it. I mumbled, in what surely sounded to him like a different language, that it was indeed my birthday and I wanted him to sign my book. Reggie took it from my trembling hands and wrote, "Happy B'Day Don. Reggie Jackson" And then he pro-ceeded to tell me, a little more politely this time, to get away from his vehicle. Able to move finally, I managed to peel myself away from his car. Reggie signed a few more autographs (for those that actually stuck around), then he climbed into that black Grand Prix with the "MVP '73" plates and was gone.

Two years later Reginald Martinez Jackson was gone for good. Shipped out to Baltimore, the birthplace of Babe Ruth. After just one uneventful season with the O's (and thank goodness—he looked downright *weird* in those orange digs), Jackson joined Catfish Hunter in a city more widely associated with The Babe—New York. Which brings to mind one more Reggie Moment.

And I am not referring to Game 6 of the 1977 World Series. I admit, that one is up there. Way up there. As much as it pained me to see my hero in pinstripes, I couldn't help but cheer as an awed Reggie rounded the bases after his third homerun of the game—and his record fifth of the Fall Classic—clinched the title for the Yankees. Only one man had homered three times in one Series game—there's that name again—Babe Ruth. And Reggie did it on the first offering from three different pitchers. Three pitches, three swings, three blasts into the crisp autumn night.

A magic evening to be sure, but three years later, Jackson, in my mind, topped even that. The stakes weren't nearly as high and the game itself didn't call for Reggie's uncanny flair for the dramatic. Thus it may not be a highlight worthy of *ESPN Classic*. But I was there when it happened and it's something that I'll never forget.

A full house greeted Reggie and his Bronx cohorts on a June afternoon in 1980. In his first three seasons with New York, the presence of Jackson alone was enough to put butts in the seats, even for an Oakland team that was drowning in obscurity. But on this day there was a different feel among the masses, if only because some of the fans in attendance were actually rooting for the home team!

And with good reason. The A's were winning again, thanks to Reggie's ex-manager—and former antagonist—Berkeley's own, Billy Martin. Martin was up to his usual tricks of reviving a floundering franchise. He had found similar success in previous stops to Minnesota, Detroit, and Texas. And there was a certain swagger about his young A's players, a swagger more often seen on the other side of the diamond. Yes, the newfound rivalry between the upstart A's and the despised Yankees was dripping with drama. Reggie was in town visiting his old stomping grounds to face a team that had suddenly learned to do some stomping of its own.

The A's opened the four-game series in fine fashion, defeating lefty Ron Guidry, 4–3, on the front end of a Friday twi-night doubleheader (remember those?). But the Yankees came back to win the next two games, which seemed to suck the life out of the Oakland ball club (the latter defeat was exceptionally painful as Bobby Murcer crushed a two-run homer with two outs in the ninth to give the Yanks a stunning 2–1 victory). On Sunday, Jackson—who was on his way to perhaps his best overall season (.300 batting average, 41 homers and 111 RBI's)—took over to keep the A's from salvaging a split of the series.

I was camped out in my usual seat in the center-field bleachers that afternoon, a 13-year old sharing space with 47,000 other spectators. In those days the Coliseum was configured in such a way that there was a gap between the outfield fence and the elevated stands. If a homerun landed in that gap, fans in pursuit of a souvenir would have to run downstairs to get to the ball. Many times, fans would wait at the rail, unsure if the ball was going into that gap or if it was going to clear it and land in the bleachers. Standing at the rail gave them plenty of time to react to either scenario while the ball was still in flight.

Reggie had already sent a rocket into the right field seats in the first inning, a two-run shot off starter Steve McCatty, and as he came to bat for the final time of this four-game set, his team ahead 7–2, literally hundreds of kids picked up their gloves and rushed to the rails of each bleacher section. This before the first pitch was even thrown! So sure were these youngsters that Reggie would deliver a parting keepsake to one lucky soul.

I myself was in the company of adults that day, hanging out with the famed "Bleacher Bums" of that era. A couple of them turned to me and scoffed, "Those idiots! They actually think he's going to hit another one!" I just nodded and smiled, and then smiled some more as Reggie sent an otherwise meaningless ninth inning blast well past those glove-wielding kids, and into my memory bank for all time.

9 / Dynasty Dead (1976)

"Oh, where are the A's of the good old days?
That's the cry of the fan.
All that's left are the legal briefs,
For they took the money and ran."
—from Sports Illustrated, 1977

The day that Charlie Finley traded Reggie Jackson to the Baltimore Orioles was one of the most painful days of my nine-year old life.

That's saying a mouthful considering I had endured some pretty nasty stuff up to that point: appendicitis, a scarred forehead, and stitches on my tongue. (Don't ask.)

Having already lost Catfish Hunter to the "evil empire," more accurately known as the New York Yankees, Finley was intent on getting something in return for the other soon-to-be-free-agents on his roster. So on April 2, 1976, just a few days before Opening Day, Finley traded Reggie Jackson and ace southpaw Kenny Holtzman for right-hander Mike Torrez and future MVP Don Baylor. It affected all of us.

John: "The biggest disappointment and most devastating event of my young life was the day Reggie was traded. I was in shock for a few weeks, maybe longer. Reggie was the face, the force, the tenacity, the voice and the heart and soul of the Oakland A's. His presence on the field or in the clubhouse, in uniform or on crutches, at the plate or on the bases, made the opposition quake in their boots. He was a strikeout king, a homerun king and king of the baseball world in his time, not unlike the last player to bring the same type of persona to the sport, namely one George Herman Ruth. Reggie had power, speed and a great arm but he also used his head (sometimes for the opposition) and got into the heads of opposing players. He would do whatever it took to win. He was a fighter. He fought the opposing players, his teammates, his managers and his owners, but not because he was a Prima Donna (he was), a hot dog (he was) or a hot head (he was). He fought because Reggie was above all a winner, a fierce competitor, who would shine the brightest on baseball's biggest stage. But he wasn't just "Mr. October." He was Mr. April, May, June, July etc. as well. He may have alienated himself from his teammates at times but he was also the glue that held them together. He made those around him better like many great players do and pushed the more talented players to an even higher level. He was my hero, your hero, one of Finley's Heroes and I'm sure the hero of many others. He made the A's the A's and when he was traded, for all the talent that still existed, the Oakland A's, Finley's A's, Reggie's A's, our A's, would never be the same."

Tonianne: "That was one of my darkest days as an A's fan, the day all of the illusions of the 'game' went out the window, the day I first saw baseball as a business, the day the magic disappeared, the day the music died. If Reggie could be traded, what then?"

A year later, the floodgates opened, and gone were Captain Sal, Geno, Rudi, Campy, and Rollie. Joining them in the great escape were two guys who had barely gotten their feet wet in Oakland: Mike Torrez and Don Baylor. And that was the swift and stunning end of Oakland's once-proud dynasty. Coincidentally, it was the start of New York's three-year reign atop the American League.

You might recognize some of the guys that helped the Yankees get there: Reggie, Catfish, Holtzman, even Mike Torrez. The other A's scattered across the land: Bando to Milwaukee, Rudi to the Angels, Campaneris to Texas, Geno and Rollie to San Diego. Only Fingers, the most famed mustache of the Mustache Gang, had any kind of success outside of Oakland.

Without Reggie and Kenny in '76, the A's somehow marched on, just as they did without Catfish the year before. (The Billy Beane A's would too learn how to cope without their greatest stars.) Chuck Tanner took over for the departed Alvin Dark and coaxed 87 wins out of his squad. Not since 1970 had the Green and Gold not won at least 90 games, and consequently the A's were left on the outside looking in the Playoff Window. The Kansas City Royals ended the champs' five-year stranglehold on the American League West. Tanner, for his admirable work in a strenuous situation, was given—surprise!—his walking papers. Bad enough he was dealt a bad hand, poor Chuck was still expected to throw down a royal flush, not get flushed by the Royals. How Tanner didn't quit is a bigger surprise, what with that crazy night in June, when a desperate Finley "sold" Vida to New York and Rollie and Rudi to Boston, who happened to be in town when the fire sale took place. The two newest Red Sox actually donned the enemy uniforms but saw no action. Once again Commissioner Kuhn stepped in, vetoing the moves in "the best interests of baseball." At the end of the season, everyone but Vida and Bill North (who both had a year left) were gone anyway, celebrating their freedom with champagne as if they were toasting another title. But this time the man who was responsible for the exodus would get not a single penny of compensation for his players' departures.

The destruction of the A's dynasty happened so fast, especially to a young boy like myself. One minute I'm awing over Finley's fireworks in the park, the next I'm watching Catfish in a Yankees hat on the evening news. I was there in July 1976 when Reggie came home, in a Baltimore uniform. I'll never forget listening to the radio in my mom's room as my heroes announced their signings with other ball clubs. Sal Bando compared leaving Oakland to the passengers who had survived the sinking of the Titanic. A perfect analogy, to be sure, considering the once-proud A's were considered unsinkable.

And now they were gone, and it would be thirteen long years before our A's returned to the top of the baseball world.

10 / LaHon's Lament (1977-1979)

"Can anyone here play this game?"

> —Legendary manager Casey Stengel asked this
> of his 1962 New York Mets, who apparently had no one
> that could. The team lost a record 120 games.

George LaHon was the first fantasy baseball player ever. And if you're thinking, "who's he?" Well, that's the point. That's because George LaHon came from the world of make-believe, conjured up by the talented, not quite demented, mind of my brother John. Back before video games stripped a generation of having any kind of imagination, John and my cousin Paul would entertain themselves with nothing but a tape recorder and their God-given wit. And it was during one of their staged nightly news broadcasts that George LaHon was "born." John introduced him as the "Who's-He Kid." A far cry from the "Say-Hey Kid," for Willie Mays, he was not.

LaHon once made 63 errors in one week. In short, he'd have fit right in with the Oakland A's of the late 70's. It took three short seasons for the A's to go from the class of the league to class clowns. From a list of "Who's Who" to "Who's He?" Out were players whose first names only need apply—Geno, Campy and Rollie; in were Dave Revering, Rob Piccolo and Bob Lacey. Even with a scorecard, you'd have difficulty recognizing these guys. I could have placed George LaHon in that group and it wouldn't have made any difference. In fact he's probably more known in my family than the actual players who made their living in the purgatory known as Oakland.

There was a precedent of course for what was happening to our A's. Connie Mack had done similar dismemberment to his

81

1910–1915 dynasty and then again with the 1929–31 teams. It would take forty years and two moves for the A's to find success again, but fans in Oakland, having witnessed nine consecutive seasons of over .500 ball, would not be so patient. They barely made it out to the Coliseum when the A's were putting on parades in the fall; they were not about to fork over money for a team with, well, "no there, there."

Jack McKeon followed Chuck Tanner as A's manager, still 26 years away from leading the Florida Marlins to an upset win over the Yankees in the 2003 World Series. Poor Jack barely got his feet wet with the depleted roster; he was 26–27 when Finley replaced him with Bobby Winkles. Winkles proceeded to lose 71 of the 108 he managed as Oakland finished 63–98, easily its worst showing since 1967, and good for last place in the American League West. The A's even slipped behind the expansion Seattle Mariners. Somehow Winkles, who had managed Reggie Jackson at Arizona State, kept his job for 1978. Meanwhile his most famous former player was earning candy bar status in New York.

A month before the 1978 season started, Finley traded Vida Blue to the Giants for seven players and some cash; another championship member sent away. But the A's started the season well, winning 24 of their first 39 games. John made me a shirt that said "Amazing" only he inserted "A's" in place of the "z" so that it read "AmaA'sing." The camera folks in the centerfield bleachers thought enough of it to put me and the shirt on TV. My fifteen seconds of fame.

Bobby Winkles, it turned out, lasted only a little longer than that, but it was his own doing. Tired of Finley's meddling (imagine that), the manager resigned his post. In the back door came McKeon, who fared considerably worse this time around: 45 wins, 78 losses. A 1–16 stretch to close out August was the beginning of the end for the 69–93 A's. And once again McKeon was fired. If anyone had thought that the mess in Oakland couldn't get any worse, they were dead wrong.

Jim Marshall was next in line for the stumbling, bumbling A's. 1979 saw the dawning of ESPN and the birth of my oldest niece (and goddaughter) Christina. She would one day take the torch from Tonianne and Tricia but these A's were still Tonianne's. In fact on certain days they were *only* Tonianne's. In the club's worst showing since 1916, the once-proud A's hit rock bottom at 54–108, 34 games behind the front-running Angels. Not that anyone noticed (not even ESPN, I'm sure). 306,000 fans watched the A's in Oakland that year. By contrast, the 1979 World Series drew over 360,000 spectators—in 75 less games. On April 17 against the Mariners, only 653 people showed up. 653! I've seen more fans get *arrested* at Raider games. Teasing, only teasing.

Abel: "I believe that Tonianne and I were at this game. Talk about lonely, buy hey, at least we won."

Tonianne remembers a different time: "That wasn't the only time we had less than 700 folks in the stands that year. John and I went to a game with Uncle Rick, Pat, and Christopher in July. It was freezing that night. I think the official attendance was 687. (Tone may have meant September 18 when there were 750 fans rumored to be in attendance.) There were more ushers and security folks than there were fans. I remember most games that year you could yell across the field from the bleachers to someone in the first deck and they could hear you, loud and clear!"

John: "We could actually count the number of people in the bleachers. I think there were eighteen. The paper the next day listed the names of the people in attendance instead of the number. They also had the bullpen pitchers sit in the stands to make it look like more people were there."

I wanted to end this chapter on a good note and I'd be remiss if I left out my best friend for the past twenty-seven years. I met Terry Hoback in September 1979, as the A's were finishing their worst three-year stretch in Oakland history. Orientation at John Muir Junior High. Two guys who couldn't have been any less alike. I was the nice guy from the east side of Davis Street; he was the homie on the west side. OK, so he was white and I was Latino, but you wouldn't have known that by the company we kept. I was the kid with his nose in a book; Hoback was the kid who'd break your nose if you didn't give him the answers. Through the years, we both learned a little from each other. Today I'm still that nice kid, but with an edge, and he's still that tough guy, but refined. I don't remember our first game together; I'm guessing 1981. I *do* remember our last; Game 2 of the 2006 ALCS. That's baseball some twenty-five years apart. In the years between, we've consumed a mountain of nachos and a river of soft drinks. (And one or two beers.) We've seen the exciting, the mediocre, and the dominant. Hobe was at Mom's with us the night we won our last Series in '89. We've watched the A's from nearly every angle of the Coliseum, through three or four different bleacher configurations. Bashes, high-fives, and hugs. (Man Law: OK for two men to embrace if a player named Scutaro hits a bases-loaded double in a playoff game with the capacity crowd already chanting his name.) Hoback, who in case you haven't caught on does not like to be called by his first name, likes to give little predictions before and during the games. It's amazing how many times he's been right. Now if he'd call Gail Smith like he promised, we'd be alright. Hobe was my Best Man at my wedding, and even if we went a whole year without talking, he'd still be my first phone call if I were ever in trouble.

Or if I had playoff tickets.

11 / Bleacher Teachers

"People will come, Ray...they'll pass over the money
without even thinking about it. And they'll walk out to
the bleachers; sit in shirtsleeves on a perfect afternoon."
—James Earl Jones, in *The Field of Dreams*

The Marquez/Martinez clan started out watching the ball games
from the right-field bleachers. Surely a guy named Reggie had
something to do with our seating selection. But at some point we
made our way to the center-field bleachers. Though no one remembers exactly when, **Tonianne** clued me in to the why: "Reggie
played a few games there so we followed." Well, duh. Now for the
shocker—when Number 9 moved back to his normal slot in right,
the family stayed put because, as my oldest sister put it, "we liked
center better."

Nick, cousin: I don't remember my first A's game but my ear-
liest memories of the A's and the Coliseum have to be those
awesome wooden bleachers and those metal stairs that sounded
great when you stomped on them during a rally. My favorite childhood memory has to be a perfect sunny day by the bay sitting in
the centerfield bleachers right behind my favorite player, #21, The
Murph. I can remember how lucky I was that my dad was taking
me to see the A's and we got to see two games in one day, something they never do anymore. I remember the Bash years, Canseco,
and the brawl with Cleveland. And of course, Destiny's first
game. We dominated the Yanks on Mother's Day."

Speaking of mothers, **Mom** recalls that in the early years, we'd
go to as many games as we could afford to. "Back then tickets were
a dollar each so even with a big family like ours, we still made it
work," she said. "Especially when we were able to bring in our own

85

food. We literally planned our Easter Sunday picnics at the Coliseum. We always told the kids, 'We brought food so don't ask us to buy anything at the concession stands.' But (my uncle) Donald's kids always asked anyway and their father would buy whatever they wanted so the other would kids would start to ask for Malt ice creams and stuff like that. Drove me crazy."

The bleachers in those days were, as Nick pointed out, indeed wooden benches, marked for assigned seating but seldom used in such a manner for baseball games. They were bad on the back because, well, the benches had no back. But with the sparse crowds, we were often able to lean on the bench behind us and enjoy the ball game. Thus "bleacher back" was born, that red mark left across one's back for enduring nine or more innings of leaning against a wooden bench. For some reason we didn't mind. In the late 70's when the team struggled to win ball games and the crowds were not crowds at all, we often found other ways to entertain ourselves at the ball yard. Abel and I would play finger football across the benches or I would run to the top of the steps and roll Kool-Aid cups down the stairs. (Where do you think the Dot Racing creators got their idea?) Goofy Grape was a big winner in those days. We also did stupid stuff like placing snacks or beverages on the seats in hopes of getting a relative or friend to land on a popcorn or a soda. Sometimes that ploy would come back to haunt me; my behind once had an untimely meeting with a cup of hot cocoa. Often we begged the centerfield camera man to put us on TV for the family back home. And sometimes he'd oblige, like in 1980 when Scott was decked out in his A's uniform and Grandpa Abel was in the hospital. Tonianne held up her godson, hoping that Grandpa was in his bed watching the game. He was. And he turned to the nurse and said, "Hey, there's my granddaughter."

Poor Scott had some interesting moments out in those bleachers. There was the time that Tony Armas crushed a 14th-inning, walk-off, grand slam to beat Baltimore. I was holding Scott, who was a couple of weeks past his third birthday. The minute Armas swung, I knew it was gone and I immediately started jumping up and down on the bench I was standing on, all the while squeezing the life out of my little cousin. Tonianne says she had taken her godson to another extra-inning affair and he was *begging* to go home. "One more inning," she kept telling him. Finally when the A's pulled out the win, Tone threw Scott up in the air and barely caught him on the way down. And of course there was the time that we lost him. Well, almost. Me, Abe, Trish, and Jess took Scott with us to a weekend afternoon game and when it was over, the girls went to the bathroom while we waited for them. All except little Scotty, who kept walking towards the exit. When the girls came out, we all looked at each other, like "Where's Scott?" Me and Abel ran and caught up to him just as he was about to reach the exit gate. When we got hold of him, he looked at us with worried eyes and uttered those famous words, "Where was you guys?" Aside from those traumatizing episodes, Scott still talks to us. He and Nick were Tone's constant companions during the summers in the late 70's when school prevented me from hanging out with her.

One luxury I enjoyed in the bleachers was the walkway behind the seats where people hung out, drank their beers, smoked their cigarettes, and even watched the game once in a while. In the late 80's when the Bash Brothers were terrorizing opposing pitchers, the walkway was one big bash in itself. There was magic on the field and in the stands. One time the opposing team had a man on first with one out and some annoying fan who obviously had been to the beer stand way too many times started shouting from his seat, "Let's Go A's, double play, double play!" Over and over again. And the fans standing directly behind him looked up from their beers and conversations to laugh at the dude. That is until the A's pitcher induced an inning-ending double play, to which the fans went from teasing the poor guy to slapping him on the back in celebration. It was an unbelievable scene.

The bleachers were also a place to collect batting practice or live game souvenirs.

John: "I remember catching my first baseball at a game against Detroit. Jim Nettles hit a homerun and we were sitting in the bleachers with a large extended family gathering. The ball bounced below at the bottom of the stairs then popped up right to me. I had my Carl

Yaztremski mitt and caught it. The whole family started cheering and we got some weird looks from the fans around us."

NOTE: Nettles' three-run job off Catfish Hunter on that August evening in 1974 was just the thirteenth of sixteen home-runs that he would hit in his short career—and the last one he'd hit wearing a road uniform. As for the "weird looks," his tater in the seventh inning put the Tigers in front 4–3 and they went on to win 5–3. Back to you, John.

"I remember getting a ball from Hank Aaron during batting practice. I also remember entering the stadium at the left field bleacher side and looking up and seeing a ball headed toward me! I think George Scott hit it. I caught it just underneath the ice plants. One of the more memorable ones was at the last game of the '74 regular season. Bill North caught the last out and I called out to him. He turned and threw it right to me. This was before players threw balls into the stands on a regular basis. He was another one of my idols so it was special."

Abel: "My most memorable souvenir was a homerun hit by Bo Jackson while he was playing for the Royals. 'The Ex' and I were sitting in the left field bleachers, a rarity for us. I can only guess we were sitting there because of Bo. I had caught a batting practice homer earlier that night. We were sitting in the top half (the cement half as opposed to the metal half) of the bleachers when Bo hit a line shot that was headed towards our section. For whatever reason, my 'state of mind' was able to track the ball very well. I stood up, took four or five steps down the stairs, watched as the ball hit the lower metal portion of the bleachers in front of me, reached my hands out and caught the ball after one bounce. I walked back to my seat as if I had done that a million times before. I'm pretty sure that was the only live-game homerun I ever caught."

John: "Lenny caught Hank Aaron's 750th homerun and pre-sented it to Hank for an autograph as he sat on the team bus. Mr. Aaron tells Lenny that it is sort of a milestone and offers another ball. Lenny wanted a bat but was turned down. Hank did autograph the ball with the number "750" on it. He also signed the batting practice homerun ball that I got from him on the same day. I don't know what happened to either of those baseballs. And don't for-get Sal Jr. catching Joe Rudi's first grand slam. He went to get it autographed after the game and Joe Rudi asked for the ball. He promised Sal that he would give him two autographed balls the next time he saw him. We went to about four or five games with Sal and talked to Rudi each time and each time he didn't have a ball. Finally, he gave Sal one of those cheap souvenir baseballs, the ones they sold in the stands." (Ah, the influence of Finley!)

As John mentioned, my cousin **Lenny** hit a similar negotiating snag with Baseball's Home Run King upon handing him the ball that was Number 750: "I guess my greatest memory is one that happened in the year of the Bicentennial, and actually isn't an A's memory, but a baseball memory. Hank Aaron only had ten home runs in the baseball calendar year of 1976. I still can recall seeing Hank on TV as he strode around the bases after breaking the Babe's record in 1974. I was sixteen when I sat in the bleachers with Johnny and saw the 750th home run come off the bat of Hammering' Hank. It rose and fell so quick most fans remained stuck to those wooden planks they called bleachers. But Johnny and I were up in an instant as we saw the angle that the ball came off Henry's bat. Paul, David, John and I always knew when the ball had a chance! Being bleacher fans (gave us an advantage over) those who sat in Section 114, who stood every time a bat made that distinctive whack that signaled a long one. From our view we knew if we should run for the stairs or pour another beer from our milk jug as we watched another long out. But this was different and Johnny and I both knew it. We hit the stairs down to the area behind the center field fence and watched the rope come screaming at us. It hit fast on the concrete that used to separate left and right. I saw it all as it hit a bleacher upright and bounced straight into my hands. I clutched that ball as another twenty guys looked at me with envy and desire. This was before the million dollar baseball suits that ensued in later years, but at that moment I knew what the guy at Pac-Bell Park felt when he held that famously litigated ball. They turned at me and showed their teeth. I, in turn, showed them mine. As they advanced, my always sound-thinking cousin John grabbed me by the shoulders and backed us away from the pack.

We waited that night for Hank to load into his bus. When he did, he opened the window and began to sign autographs. John and I waited and when we got our chance I thrust the ball at Hank and told him this ball was home run number 750. He laughingly said he'd signed ten of them already. I told him this was the real one and Johnny told him the same. He chuckled and signed my ball '#750 Hank Aaron.' It's been over thirty years but I still have that ball. The letters have all faded but you can see still see the scuff marks on that yellow baseball that were made as it hit the concrete there between our beloved bleachers, long since gone. Every once in awhile my stupid cat decides to knock that ball off it's esteemed place where it resides in our home. As I put it back into its cup, I bless everyday I have ever spent in the Oakland Coliseum watching my beloved boys of summer."

At times, other team's fans have invaded our territory. During the 2000 Division Playoffs, a Yankee fan, in all his smugness told me, "You're in my seat." To which, I replied, "You're in my *stadium*." He got a laugh out of that. But there was nothing particularly funny about seeing Yankee and Red Sox fans come out in large numbers in the late 70's and again in recent years. What fascinated me was how arrogant Sox fans were, even before they won the 2004 World Series. I mean, you expected it from Yankee followers, but their team had the titles to back it up. I might have felt sorry for Bostonians had they not reveled in their misery. They thrived on it. And because of that, it was almost scripted; they wore despair and hopelessness on their faces like Raider fans in skulls and cross-bones. But why should I hate them anymore than I do Yankee fans? They're both obnoxious. It just pissed me off that after the Sox won, people talked about it being so life altering. *Sports Illustrated*, in honoring the club as Sportsmen of the Year, even posted letters from their long-suffering fans to the team. I mean, did the Red Sox cure cancer and bring world peace when I wasn't looking? Yeah, they made a great story and maybe they were deserving of that funny looking trophy that SI gives away. But let's stop making them out to be conquerors of the universe. The Red Sox forked over good coin for the pitching that was suited for a post-season run. Their fans? Please. Bad enough we had to see their downtrodden faces over and over again all those years, as if the sky was about to fall on them. Now we had to read about them being "freed"?   There are millions who are just as passionate about their teams and some who have "suffered" just as long. Forgive us if we don't pull off the woe-is-me act as well as they do. If anything, winning the World Series ended decades of chronic whining, and that being the case, seeing the Sox hoist the trophy was worth it. But I didn't dare go see them when they came to Oakland in 2005. If their fans were loathsome before they won, I wasn't about to find out how they'd act afterwards. But not all of them are bad. Ernie Jr. has friends who root for the Red Sox (hello, Brian and Jill), and during the 2003 ALDS I got a few laughs out of the guy in front of me—at his team's expense. Not that we exchanged phone numbers afterwards or anything like that. Dude's a Sox fan. And yes, I'm still bitter about them beating us that year and winning it all the next; they actually get more write-up in this book than I had intended. Or that they deserve.

Some A's "fans" liked to ride our own players. Billy North bore the brunt of many frustrated spectators during the 1977 season, but Glenn Burke who replaced North in centerfield, got it worse than that. According to John, there was one game where it had become public knowledge that Burke was a homosexual. "There was a fan taunting him through the whole game," recalls **John.** "At the end of the game, Burke told the fan to meet him in the parking lot. I don't think the fan thought he'd show. Burke was going to kill him until a bunch of us fans intervened and told him it wasn't worth it. Soon after that, he kind of disappeared from baseball."

Thankfully, there were plenty of A's fans that, well, cheered on the A's. I think my fondest bleacher memories are of a bunch of guys who made losing in the late '70's a little more bearable. They were the Bleacher Bums, a collection of pot-smoking hippies in their late 20's, early 30's, who found their way into a ten-year old boy's world. Dave was sort of the leader—he and his cohorts even got some write-ups in the local papers—and he was easily the loudest. And man could he hold a note. "BOOOOOOOOOOOOOOOOOOOOOO," he'd shout at the opposing team's center-fielder, for more than a decade. To keep his voice from going out on him, he moistened it with orange juice and vodka, which he kept in an old Aunt Jemima syrup bottle. There was also Fritz, Kevin, John, and Greg. Others joined in later but that was the main group. Fritz' voice was really deep and almost always hoarse. Kevin hardly did any yelling but had this real squeaky laugh and he'd nod and laugh when one of the other Bums got off a good one. John was black and not one of the originals and he actually sat in the next section over but he and his booming voice belong in this group. He actually reminded me of Reggie a little bit. Greg was the silent one, often coming late and leaving early but he was one of them, no doubt. And they took to Tonianne and I because we were the only ones nutty enough to watch the A's lose game after game after game and still come back for more. Dave even took to my sister's tune of "Where were you people in '79" when the Billy Ball crowds invaded our inner circle. Even after Tone got married in '83, leaving me to carry the baton, the Bums, Dave and Kevin in particular, would ask how she was doing.

They were hardly original or even terribly witty but they were unrelenting and loud and got on the player's nerves like no hecklers I've ever seen. Sometimes Dave showed up fashionably late in the bottom of the first inning just so he could yell out behind the opposing center-fielder: "TIME OUT! TIME OUT! THERE'S NOBODY IN CENTER FIEEEEELLLLD!" And you'd look at the other bums, and they'd wipe their brows, thanking the heavens that Dave was there to save the day. On more than one occasion, I could hear him, ever so faintly, on a radio broadcast. The guy was unreal. If a player was having a particularly bad game, Dave delighted in letting the player know just how bad. "Hey, Fred, you know what you are today? You're 0-for-3! Zero! (Others chiming in) Zero! ZEROOOOOO!!" It was even more fun when the center-fielder went 0-for-the-series. And even more satisfying when said center-fielder responded with the bird. Victory for the Bums. Their favorite targets, in no particular order were, Amos Otis, Fred Lynn, Gorman Thomas (who they dubbed "Pizza Face") and Willie Wilson. They actually played over a boom box the last out of the 1980 World Series, which ended with Wilson striking out for a record twelfth time. And when Willie was suspended for cocaine use, Dave didn't miss a beat upon the Royal center-fielder's return to action. As Wilson turned to take first base on what he thought was ball four, only to be returned to home plate by the umpire, Dave belted out, "That's just like you, Willie. Always trying to get a free…base!" Aside from that low, um, "blow," the Bums usually kept things clean and fun:

> Dave: "What's the matter with Gorman?"
> Chorus: "He's a bum!"
> Fritz: "The last time I saw something that looked like you, I had to flush it!
> Chorus: "TWICE"
> Fritz: "You bum!"
> John: "I hope your dog dies!"
> Fritz: "You bum!"
> Kevin: "You couldn't hit water if you fell out of a boat!"
> Chorus: "You bum!"
> Greg: "I've seen better swings at a playground!"
> Chorus: "You bum!"
> (Gorman grounds out weakly to short.)
> Dave: "Ninety feet and take a seat!"
> Chorus: "You bum!!"
> (Gorman runs out to center field.)
> Dave: "Hey, Gorman! You know what you are in this series? You're 0-for-12!" Zero! Zero.…"
> (Uh-oh, Gorman's getting closer to the fence!)

As much as the Bums rode the opposing center-fielder, they absolutely adored ours. (**John** recalls them as fans of Billy North; "the guys who wore t-shirts that said 'The F'in' A's,' instead of 'The Swingin' A's.") But they were, uh, especially supportive when Dwayne Murphy roamed the outfield. "Alright, Murph! Doing it all, Captain Dwayne!" And Murphy, who quickly became a favorite of mine, loved us right back, often tipping his hat to us at the start of games. It helped greatly that Murph was a magician in the field, earning six consecutive Gold Gloves during his tenure in Oakland. But it was on a rainy Sunday in April 1980 that really demonstrated the bond between Number 21 and his fans. Billy Ball had just started turning heads when the defending division cham-pion Angels came to town for a four-game set. The A's won on Friday night and Saturday and would go for the kill in Sunday's double-header. A steady drizzle threatened to "rain" on Oakland's parade but the games would be played. So the only thing left to spoil matters was Dad, who on his way to Mass forbade Tonianne and I from going to the Coliseum. Well, Tonianne had learned from her Claudell experience in 1974 so she packed some leftover tostadas in a plastic bread bag, the fixings wrapped in aluminum foil, and headed out, with me right behind her, to the BART station. Having disobeyed Dad's direct orders, my 13-year old mind figured the rain would come down hard enough to cancel the action, or we would lose both games. I'm a karma kind of guy. But the A's kicked karma to the curb and, forgive me Lord, the Angel's asses in the process. I swear the only fans in the bleachers that day were the Bums, my sister, and me. And when the top-of-the-ninth came, we took to celebrating the four-game sweep with chants of "First place A's! First place A's!" To which Captain Dwayne Murphy responded with an enthusiastic "yeah" and a raised fist as his adoring fans cheered heartily. Hell, it was worth Dad being pissed off at us, which he really wasn't, seeing that the A's swept.

As the 80's drew to a close, the Bums' stay in the bleachers was in jeopardy. Tickets to see Tony La Russa's juggernaut were a hot commodity indeed. I myself, now twenty-one years of age, had moved over to the—for shame!—first deck. But there was still one moment of glory with the least known of the Bleacher Bums in the fall of '88. The night the A's went for the clincher of the American League West crown, their first non-strike division title in thirteen years, this ten-year old punk-turned-twenty-one, seemingly overnight, drank beers with Kevin and Greg. And when the last out was recorded and the playoffs a certainty, two gentlemen who had such an impact on my youth, turned to me and shook my hand. There were tears in their eyes. Of joy, definitely, but of sorrow, too. For it was a handshake of triumph and of gratitude (for sticking with the team through some agonizing times). It was also a handshake of closure, for I would never see the Bums again. Only on that night, I didn't yet know it.

12 / Billy Comes Home (1980-1982)

"Nothing worries me about this team. I refuse to be negative about any part of it. We can beat California. They've got the superstars, but we can beat them."

—The late Billy Martin to the late Ralph Wiley of the *Oakland Tribune*, March 23, 1980

"The A's are a kind of exhilaration not because of a man, but because of an attitude. Billy Ball. If it were a fever, the A's would be an epidemic. There's another name for it. Confidence."

—Ralph Wiley, in the same *Tribune* column, coining the phrase for the A's style of baseball that is still recognized in these parts today.

The Charlie Finley Era was at its end. The owner sold the club to Walter Haas, his son Wally Jr., and Roy Eisendhardt. But before he said goodbye to a sport that he had a hand in dramatically altering, Finley hired a manager who specialized in dramatically altering the fortunes of every team who called upon him. This was not a Dick Williams situation of taking a solid team to the next level; this was a rescue mission of the highest order. And as he had done in previous stops to Minnesota, Detroit, Texas, and New York, Alfred Manuel Martin was intensely up to the task. Yes, Billy Martin was home and baseball in Oakland would never be the same. Both Williams and Martin were students of Baseball Fundamentals 101 but whereas General Dick demanded it, Billy, for all his passion and fire, *taught* it. Something of which he truly enjoyed. Acquiring a rag-tag ball club that had lost 291 games in its previous three seasons was baseball's equivalent to MTV's *Pimp My*

Ride. But as we all know, Billy was *the* Pimp. And in 1980, he resurrected the A's in a way that rivaled the other sports miracle of
the year: USA's Olympic triumph over the USSR in Lake Placid.
From 108 defeats to 83 wins in the matter of one jaw-dropping season. Take a closer look and you'll see that Charlie Finley had a little
magic left before he called it a career. More homegrown talent like
Rickey Henderson, Mike Norris, and Dwayne Murphy meshed well
with others brought in via trades, most notably Tony Armas and
Rick Langford. The seeds had been planted for a Renaissance in
Oakland and no one sowed seeds like Billy Martin.

No manager or player could rest when the Oakland A's were
in the other dugout. Hit-and-run, double steals, suicide squeeze,
the A's epitomized the element of surprise. They were Forest
Gump's box of chocolates; you never knew what you were going
to get from Billy's boys. In fact, they were very much the opposite of Billy's (Beane) boys of today except for the fact that many
of the 1980 A's were so adept at drawing walks. Trouble was, they
hardly stayed put once they reached first base. Trouble for the
opposing teams, anyway. And it wasn't just Rickey Henderson, who
on his way to becoming history's greatest leadoff hitter and base
thief, swiped an American League record 100 bases. (I was in the
bleachers the day Rickey stole his 96th base, which pulled him even
for the league mark previously held by some guy named Cobb. One
of the bleacher bums cleverly saluted Henderson by yelling, "Nice
to see you tie Cobb!" Get it, *tie* Cobb? *Ty* Cobb? Never mind.)
Martin had everyone's wheels in motions, even slow, white guys
like Wayne Gross and Jeff Newman, both of whom stole home a
la Jackie Robinson during the season. But you win games with
pitching and these A's were armed for success: Norris won 22
games, followed closely by Langford (19) and Matt Keough (16).
It's a joke that Keough didn't win the AL Comeback Player of the
Year. He went 2–17 in 1979 with an ERA over five, only to turn
it all around under Martin. Along with Steve McCatty and Brian
Kingman, Oakland's starters often finished what they started; they
recorded an are-you-kidding-me 94 complete games. (Ultimately
the long days at the office would spell doom for the young hurlers,
but why be a party-pooper, right?) And yes, there was plenty of

partying going on in Oakland, with Kool and the Gang leading the *Celebration* after every A's home win.

After one of the most exciting baseball seasons in Oakland history, the Martinez family lost its patriarch. Grandpa Abel passed away on November 11, 1980.

The A's were back on the map and, following a 29-game improvement in the standings, the Haas family set out to upgrade the Coliseum, where crazed fans would fill the stands for an encore of Billy Ball. The seats were all painted the same color, not like that grotesque mixture of green and orange that was as bad on the eyes as the team was in the late 70's. The club also installed a Diamond Vision screen and a state-of-the-art sound system that the *Oakland Tribune*'s Dave Newhouse wrote "could be heard in San Jose!"

The baseball team was about to make some beautiful noise that would be heard all across the land. They opened the 1981 season on the road, as renovations continued back home. Four games in Minnesota, four wins. Four games in Anaheim, same song different verse. In the seventh game of the season, Tony Armas greeted television viewers with an eighth-inning, three-run moon shot that brought Oakland back from a 3–0 hole. I was watching that game from the floor of Mom and Dad's living room, thinking how 6–1 was still a lofty start. But Armas not only wowed his teammates— I remember how loud it was in the A's dugout—but he convinced this 14-year old that anything was possible. After beating the Angels the next night to go to 8–0, Billy's boys came home to find that their Coliseum debut was sold out.

Oakland was a happening place to be on April 17, 1981, maybe more so than in anytime in club history—even during the glory years. 50,255 Athletic supporters applauded like mad for their conquering heroes as they were introduced before the game against Seattle. We cheered on Steve McCatty as he set the Mariners down in order in the first. And we shouted and screamed as the A's put a five-spot on the board in the bottom of the inning. Captain Murph and Cliff Johnson hit back-to-back homers and the rout was on. Rickey went deep in the third and Armas hit a two-run shot in the fourth, which ended with the A's in front 10–1. By the time the 7th inning stretch came around, I felt like I was in Fantasyland. The sound system was blaring John Denver's *Thank God I'm a Country Boy* and I turned around to see my brother John waving his A's cowboy hat, while fans of every color danced in the aisles. The entire night was like living in a cartoon and just when I thought it couldn't get any loonier, the A's exploded for six runs in the seventh, with Armas putting a stamp on the inning—and a 16–1 win—by jacking his second homer of the night and sixth in nine games. With the throng yelling "Tony, Tony," the right-fielder came out to not one, but *two* curtain calls, something that even Reggie Himself could not lay claim to. As I waited for that moment for Mom to wake me up from this dream, I turned to my cousin Wayne and we just started laughing. Clapping and cheering no longer made sense. Hell, the whole night didn't make any sense. So we just laughed as if tons of money had been dropped from the skies above. But it wasn't just me and Wayne; everyone had that weird, incredulous look on their faces. I ran into a schoolmate after the game and he was talking all fast and his words were running into each other; that's what that night in April did to all of us.

The A's had to play another game the next day and while the baseball world waited for the inevitable letdown, Billy's juggernaut rolled on—8–0—for a record-tying tenth straight win to start the season. Mike Norris took the mound for the front-end of an Easter Sunday double-header and me, Abe, John, and Tone got first-deck seats for the record-breaker. The A's didn't disappoint, winning 6–1 before losing their first game of the season in the nightcap. It's rare for a team to get a standing ovation after a loss, but that's what those young upstarts had earned from us that day. They also earned cover action from some major publications: Billy's face adorned *TIME* and his pitching staff graced the cover of *Sports Illustrated*. After going 17–3 in April, the A's hit a bump in the road, thanks to a brutal East Coast swing. When the Yankees came to town in the second week of May, I bore witness to yet another phenomenon. I arrived a little late to a Sunday afternoon game, only to be treated to an uprising in the 3rd deck. One section after another rose up and then down again, as if it were a tidal wave. And there was Crazy George in the corner of the third deck orchestrating the whole thing. Soon this Wave made its way down to the other two decks below and finally to the bleachers, fifty thousand fans in unison, all feeding off a balding white guy with a drum. Only in America.

America's Pastime was about to lose its grip on her faithful following as the players went on strike on June 10. The A's finished as the "first-half champions" of the American League West, which would give them an automatic playoff berth if and when the regular season resumed. Ironically, it was a future "A" that helped keep Oakland in first place on the last day before the strike. I was in the second deck with Uncle Dan and his family for this one. One strike from defeat, Armas played Houdini again, this time with a game-tying, two-run homerun that electrified the crowd. The Boston starter who served up the gopher ball? Dennis Eckersely. Two innings later, Doin' It All Dwayne cleared the fences off reliever Mark Clear to win it. When the strike ended in early August, the wind had been taken out of Oakland's sails a bit. But the A's played well down the stretch and in a first-ever Divisional Playoff Series, swept the defending league champion Royals in three straight games, the clincher coming before the home folks. Up next was Billy's old team, the Yankees. The young A's, like ten years before, did not stand a chance against a more experienced foe and bowed out in three games. Still, as I watched the Bombers celebrate on my field, there was that same feeling of a decade before; that we were on the verge of something great. The way I saw it, my own glory years were right in front of me. Boy was I mistaken.

The 1982 season turned out to be Billy's last in Oakland, and only a record-setting season by Rickey Henderson made Martin's exit year even remotely bearable to watch. The starting pitchers, surely weary from all those innings pitched, all took turns on the disabled list. This was not the Mustache Gang reincarnated; it was the horror of the late 70's all over again. As was his wont, Billy tore down a team as fast as he built it. In the end, he did just about everything to get himself fired, as if 94 losses wasn't enough reason. Rickey, meanwhile, stole 130 bases, shattering Lou Brock's record of 118. No one in the history of the game caused more havoc on the base paths than the Oakland Tech High graduate. He was a "walking double," they said. Like Levi Strauss manufactured blue jeans, Rickey manufactured runs. The "Rickey Run," they called it. And he did it with the kind of flair not seen since a guy named Reggie.

Rose: "Rickey always had a way of making things happen. I remember one game that went into extra innings. We were already cold and tired and we wanted to go home. When Rickey came up, we chanted 'walk like a man.' We didn't care how they scored as long as they scored. And of course he walked, and stole second and third, and then scored to give us the win."

But the A's as a whole had lost its Midas touch. Their leader was fired on the same day that St. Louis and Milwaukee took the field for Game 7 of the World Series. Replacing him was Steve Boros. From Billy Ball to Boros Ball. Meanwhile, Armas, another right-field hero of mine, was traded to Boston in December. For A's fans it was like, "Here we go again."

Tricia: "I'm *still* trying to get over the Tony Armas trade! I don't know why that one hit me so hard but I remember when Abel walked into the kitchen and told me he was traded. I didn't believe him." (I felt compelled to remind her that the player we got in return was some guy named Carney Lansford.) "I didn't remember that we got Carney in the trade. I do remember that I didn't like him at first. I was holding a grudge."

While the Billy Martin Era turned out *not* to be the Second Coming of the Dick Williams Era, and as Tricia's grudge carried through the mid-'80's, the Armas trade eventually paid off. Carney Lansford would be, as **Abel** put it, "the cornerstone of many great A's teams." You can say he put the "Carn" in Oakland's reincarnation. But that was down the road.

For the next five seasons, the A's would not bring home any "A's" on their report card.

More like a C– average.

13 / Mediocre Times (1983–1987)

"No one wants to be Average Joe or Average Jane. They're plain, un-special, they're average. But I ask you, what's wrong with average?"
— Brian Fletcher, author of *Second Chances*

At first glance, there was nothing particularly endearing about this period of A's baseball. While there were no championships to boast of, there were no last-place finishes to cry over either. The A's were sort of just there, like cork floating in a bottle of wine, half of it above the surface, half of it below. The first two managers of the post-Billy regime—Steve Boros and Jackie Moore—were stick figures compared to their dirt-kicking predecessor. Their winning percentage over those five seasons was .475, and they placed fourth, fourth, fifth, fourth, and third. Plain as can be.

The remarkable thing is that I went to a boatload of games during these Mediocre Times. I was barely sixteen when the 1983 season started, and twenty when the 1987 campaign ended. So by then I was going to the Coliseum alone or with my high school friends. Abel, Rose, and Tricia were there a lot, too.

On one hand the 1983 A's did pretty well with Billy Martin's hand-me-downs. They won six more games than the season before and actually finished ahead of the defending champion Angels. On the other hand, they finished 25 games behind this year's winners, the Chicago White Sox, who were making their first trip to the postseason since the year Tonianne was born. Their return, sparked by a manager named Tony La Russa, coincided this time with Tonianne's wedding.

My recollections of the '83 season are few considering that I attended 66 of our 81 home games. Then again, twenty-three years

101

will do that to you. I do remember three straight shutouts by the pitching staff in August, that wonderful stretch when Steve McCatty, Gorman Heimueller, and Chris Codiroli made like the '63 Dodgers. Allowing 14 runs in three games would have been decent enough, but the A's gave up a total of 14 *hits* during that span.

The night that rookie pitcher Mike Warren outshone them all, I wasn't even there. Newlyweds Tonianne and Michael had offered me and Tricia to join them, had even gotten the tickets in advance, but neither of us went. There were four games left in the season and we were playing La Russa's playoff-bound White Sox. I still remember sitting in the public library with my friend Sherri. I remember looking at the clock and telling her that the game was about to start. I remember for the last inning or so rooting *against* Oakland's Mike Warren. Because that night of all nights—and not one of the 66 games that I attended that season— Warren was pulling a page right out of Vida Blue's 1971 yearbook. The kid had pitched a 10-inning gem in his previous start, beating the Blue Jays, 2–1. But against Chicago, he was even better. History-making better. Before 9,058 patrons that included my oldest sister and her husband but not me or my youngest sister, Michael Bruce Warren pitched a no-hitter against a team that won 99 games in 1983. As the White Sox swung and missed their way through a frustrating night, I had a tougher time explaining to my entire high school how I managed to miss the no-no. I can still see the faces, with their incredulous looks, followed by that haunting question: "You weren't there?!" Lucky for me, Hoback didn't go either.

John: "I remember the no-hitter but the only other thing I remember about Warren was that he looked nothing like a major league ball player. He looked more like some sick neighborhood kid who never got to come out and play. My memories of the '83 season are even fewer. Actually the losing seasons are a blur because I just can't picture the A's being lousy. My mind won't allow it. I can remember some of the players and a few select games but nothing else. Even when the A's stunk I never felt that they weren't going to win a particular game so I guess I didn't notice the losses piling up. With baseball there is always tomorrow so you just move on and get 'em the next day."

Seldom did the A's need to apply that philosophy more than after what took place on July 3 of that season. I still can't believe it happened. Or that I actually stayed for the whole thing. But there I was with Hoback, Tricia, our cousin Victoria, and six-year old Scott. The game played out innocently enough through six innings with the Texas Rangers taking a 4–2 lead into the bottom of the ninth. In dramatic fashion, the A's scored two runs to force extra innings. In the next five frames, neither team could muster much of a threat. Then in the top of the 15th, the Rangers scored. And scored again. And again. I have been to a ton of baseball games but what was taking place before my eyes was so off the radar, I am not even sure how to justifiably describe the insanity of it all. All told Texas scored 12 runs in that 15th inning, easily the most runs scored in an extra frame. And yet when the Oakland's took their turn at-bat, there we were chanting "Let's go A's!" Stupid kids.

Rickey (do I really need to include his last name?) gave us one last thrill for 1983: a third year in which he stole over 100 bases. No one else in the history of the game has done that, folks. He did it in typical Rickey fashion, first game back after a road trip, needing two for the century mark, and— naturally—stealing three. (By the way, I was there for that one.) Rickey turned a league-leading 103 walks into a league-leading 108 steals, which he turned into (a non-league leading) 105 runs scored. Just another solid, if not spectacular, campaign for our hometown hero.

When I first think of 1984, I can't help but look back on the evening of May 22. Abel and I went to watch the A's and the O's that night (a 6–4 win for the home team) and we returned home in good spirits; I remember that we were laughing as we stepped into Mom's house. It took two seconds to realize that something was terribly wrong. John was on the couch, hands over his face. When he heard us walk in, he looked up at us. He had been crying. "Uncle Don died," he said. I didn't know how to react; the words just didn't make sense to me. I don't even think Mom was there, she had probably gone to Grandma Toni's. I don't remember much else; at some point Aunt Minda came over, her face contorted. Just an awful, awful scene. Death is always so hard, but when it's sudden like this, it destroys you. One minute Uncle Don was listening to the ball game on his radio, the next paramedics were at his home, trying to revive him. He was fifty-one; gone way too soon. The wake was unforgettable. I remember Mom trying to be strong but failing, the pain forcing its way out for her brother. I remember it being the first time I ever saw my Dad cry. And he held nothing back. Uncle Don was a frequent visitor to our house, either alone or with his wife Rose. They'd sit for hours taking to Mom and Dad in the kitchen, two couples who were wed on the same day in 1956. Now one of them was gone. My namesake. Aunt Rose recognized that as she clutched my face the night of her husband's wake and looked at me with the saddest eyes. I remember Dad hugging Uncle Dan at the funeral, and telling him, "You still have me, brother." It was the perfect thing to say, the perfect way to honor the man who Mom wrote "did not have 'in-law' in his vocabulary." Strangely, if you look at the A's box score from the night he died, the same game that he listened to in his last living moments, the memory of Uncle Don springs to life: "D. Martinez" was one of the Baltimore pitchers used in that game.

The A's entered their 17th season in 1984, which happened to be the same amount of candles that I blew out on my cake that April. The home team competed quite nicely in the weak American League West thanks to a second straight .300 season by Carney Lansford, who was quickly making everyone (except Tricia) forget about Tony Armas. For the second year in a row, the A's finished ahead of the previous season's division champ and also improved from 74 wins to 77 victories, good enough for a fourth-place finish, seven games behind the first-place Royals. Jackie Moore took over for the fired Steve Boros in May and led us to a respectable 57–61 mark. It was an interesting collection of athletes. We had two former MVP's at the end of their playing days, Jeff Burroughs and Joe Morgan. Burroughs, who replaced Reggie as the AL MVP in 1974, was in his third and last season with the A's (as was ex-Dodger Davey Lopes). Both would finish their careers elsewhere. Morgan, the NL MVP in '75 and '76, would not. For the former Encinal High standout, his first season in Oakland turned out to be his last in a big league uniform.

But as three stars saw their lights go down in The (Other) City, one player found a rebirth of sorts. Dave Kingman came to town with 342 career homeruns, but he had only racked up thirteen the year before. In the eyes of many, acquiring this one-dimensional player was a gamble that was sure to bite Oakland in the A's. The eyes of many, it turned out, were near-sighted. Kingman made an immediate impact. In just his ninth game with the team, he lit up the Mariners for three homeruns (including a first-inning grand slam) and eight RBI's. He hit two in Boston ten days later, and two more in Toronto four days after that. On May 25, he passed his previous season total and it came in grand style against the Yankees. I was there that night with Abel and some friends. The game was tied at four going into the bottom of the 8th when the A's struck for two runs, the second on a bases-loaded walk. As the Yankees changed pitchers, we made our way up the steps (with the game running long, we decided that this would be our last inning). Meanwhile, PA announcer Roy Steelc reminded us of the Grand Slam inning, and that one lucky fan would drive away in a new car if an A's player were to hit a homerun with the bags full. Enter "Kong," with *Jaws* music blaring in the background and 22,000 fans cheering wildly. Kingman connected on the first-pitch and "drove" it out of the park, almost to the top of the bleachers where we were standing. I'd seen Reggie and Armas do some things to a baseball but this was ridiculous. Less than a month later, I was in the first deck with Grandma Toni, Tricia, Victoria, and Hoback for a matinee game against the Royals. In the bottom of the first, Rickey singled, Captain Murph walked, Lopes got a hit to load the bases, and Kong cleared them with his third granny of the season. With my granny in the stands no less. All told Kingman hit 35 homeruns in 1984 and walked away with the Comeback Player of the Year Award. "Come back" is what we A's fans were telling Rickey Henderson when management pulled a stunner and shipped our superstar to New York in December. For me it was 1976 all over again.

The A's lineup had a significantly new look in 1985, although the pitching staff remained pretty much intact. Tonianne always talked to me about how veteran players somehow seemed to end their careers in Oakland and this year was no different. The '85 version of Joe Morgan was Dusty Baker. Baker was one of many players to appear in uniform for both Bay Area teams, though the family didn't come to really dislike him until he became the Giants' manager. Another player dropping by for a cup of coffee was Tommy John, who joined us in mid-season, appeared in eleven games, and was off to another club. But while John started '85 with the Angels and ended it with the A's, Don Sutton took the opposite route when the club shipped the 13-game winner south in September. Strange times.

Steve McCatty, the second of Billy Martin's burnouts to leave the game prematurely (Mike Norris was the first although he made one last comeback in 1990), called it quits after the '85 season. I always enjoyed watching Cat pitch and he was more like Cat-*fish* in 1981: 14–7 with four shutouts in a shortened season. Finished second in the Cy Young Award voting that year, behind Milwaukee's Rollie Fingers. If only Billy's starters had Rollie in the pen, they might have hung around longer. It was sad to see it end so soon for the pitchers who had just four years before graced the cover of Sports Illustrated, the sky their only limit.

For Dave Kingman, well, not even the sky could hold on to some of his majestic clouts. Another 30 homeruns for the "washed-up" Kong were just about the only bright spots in a second straight 77–85 season. But as Kingman's career was winding down, a certain September call-up's was just beginning. "The real Roy Hobbs," they called him. Sparky Anderson said "he's built like a Greek goddess." (**John:** "Yes, he was built like the goddess, Steroidite.") Reggie gushed "he hits 'em where I hit 'em, except he's *right-handed!*" And like Reggie bursting onto the sports map the year I was born, Jose Canseco exploded into baseball's mindset the year I graduated from high school. He hit five homeruns in 29 games; Trish was there for his first on September 9.

All the hype surrounding Canseco entering the 1986 season was cemented in his monster rookie year in which he clubbed 33 homeruns and drove in 117 runs. Yeah, he suffered through an 0-for-40 slump but when he met the ball just right, there was something so Reggiesque about it. That was the case even when Jose struck out, which he did 175 times in 1986. Dave Kingman didn't just strike out (126 whiffs), he clocked out, ending his career on a bittersweet note: .210 batting average, 35 blasts, 94 RBI's. In his three seasons wearing an A's uniform, Kong hit exactly 100 homers. Not bad for a guy that was considered in the past tense as a player before coming to Oakland. Sadly, and perhaps justly, the power hitter will be remembered as much for his mood swings as his batting swing. The only player to have appeared with teams in all four divisions in a single season (back in 1977, when there were only four divisions), Kingman once sent a rat to a female Bay Area sportswriter. My brother remembers a sweeter side to Kong.

Abel: "I was with Sherri and her niece, Karen, who was dying for Kingman's autograph. He was not an easy guy to track down, often going out of his way to steer clear of fans after the games. But there was a guy who worked for the A's who told us where to find him (up by the arena entrance), and sure enough, he was right. I was amazed at how tall he was (6'6"), but even more surprised at his demeanor. Standing there in a T-shirt, blue jeans, and sandals, he signed for Karen and chatted with us for a few minutes. Not the bad guy that everyone made him out to be."

Another "A" to hang up his cleats in 1986 was pitcher Rick Langford, a true anatomy of a rags-to-riches-to-rags story. Yet another Billy Martin prodigy (or is it tragedy?), Langford lost nineteen games in 1977 and turned around to *win* nineteen just three years later. He completed 28 of his 35 starts, including 22 straight (you read that right); clearly, he was the last of his kind in a "finish what you start" world. After the '81 season in which he pitched the division clincher against the Royals, Langford's career started downward, culminating in 1986 with a 1–10 record. Matt Keough, who left the A's in 1983, also retired in '86, leaving Billy's Aces out of baseball just five years after taking the league by storm.

But as one era ends, so begins another. It is the rarest thing to know you are witnessing history in the making before anyone else is aware of it. But I had that feeling on July 7. The A's were stumbling along with a 29–44 record when Jackie Moore was relived of his duties as manager. Interim leader Jeff Newman fared even

worse in his short stint: 2–8. Enter Tony La Russa. And with his
first game coming against the Boston Red Sox (and their young
phenom Roger Clemens), who does La Russa anoint to start opposite The Rocket? Oakland's born-and-raised Dave Stewart. The Bay
Area was Stewart's fourth major-league stop and he arrived in May
of '86 with a spotty 30–35 record, not having won a game since
September 1984. In his first ten appearances here, only one was
as a starter. And Clemens? Well, in just his third season, he had
the baseball world in the palm of his hands. You could say he had
'68 numbers in '86 (24–4, 238 K'S, 2.48 ERA) and he got the honors to go with them (a Cy Young Award and a trip to the Series).
Clemens brought a 14–1 record to La Russa's debut and left it with
his second defeat. With the A's in front 3–1 after five, Rocket faced
three batters in the sixth, and not one of them treated him kindly.
Lansford's leadoff single was followed by the new (Canseco's two
run blast) and the old (Kingman's solo shot), which led to the Sox
standout's early departure. Stewart, for his part, was more than up
to the challenge against a dangerous lineup, and in doing just
enough of the little things, made a winner of himself and his intu-
itive manager. It wouldn't be the last time. With La Russa at the
helm, the A's went 45–31, and even though we finished with one
less win than the year before, good things were coming.

    And I felt it that night in July.

A whole lot of things took place in 1987 that I had no such premonitions of. I sure didn't expect to see Reggie Jackson on our
Opening Day roster. Or Dennis Eckersley, for that matter. I was
mildly surprised to see the A's trade rookie Rob Nelson to the
Padres a month into the season. I knew Stew was going to be good
but no way did I know he was going to be *special*. I didn't know
what to think when they inserted Mark McGwire at the first base
position where Nelson was to play (and excel) but if someone told
me he was going to hit 49 homeruns in 1987, I would have ordered
a double shot of what he was drinking. On a related note, it would
have been impossible to predict the phenomenon that swept the
Coliseum that season. I was at an April game with John when this
thing called Dot Racing appeared on the big screen. The guy behind

me summed up our thoughts when he told his friend, "I'm not *that* heated." Yes, all these things really did happen. And all it started when I opened the newspaper on Christmas Day '86 to see that my hero, Reggie, had come home. His smile was ultra-wide as he held up his uniform with the number 44 (not the 9 that we A's fans grew to adore). Honestly? He could have worn any number short of 666 and I wouldn't have cared. Reggie was home. *Our* Reggie. And of all the players that finished their baseball careers in Oakland, Reg was the most welcome and most fitting.

It was also a homecoming for one Dennis Eckersley, though no one was quite sure what to make of his arrival. Not even La Russa or pitching coach Dave Duncan. The fiery Eckersley, born in Oakland and raised in Fremont, had always been a starter in this league. But even though Jay Howell had led the A's in saves the previous two seasons, Tony and Dunc were of the opinion that Eckersely could resurrect his career coming out of the pen; a notion that the proud pitcher didn't exactly sign off on in blood. Howell hardly had the fans' endorsement, however, even though he was selected to the All-Star Game, which happened to be played in front of the home folks in 1987. I was at that game and I swear it was one of the most awkward sports moments I've ever experienced. There we were (me and John) celebrating the best that the league had to offer in our own back yard and then it reached ridiculous heights when McGwire (much more on him later) was announced. Easily one of the loudest ovations I ever heard. Then Howell's name was called and it was as if the Denver Broncos had taken the field. The dude was booed in his own stadium—at the All-Star Game! (Maybe it was the 4.86 ERA at the break that made his fifteen saves seemed watered down.) Howell made the night a complete success by giving up two runs—the game's *only* two runs—in the top of the 13th inning. Yeah, that'll endear him to the natives. If the fans had their choice, Howell would have been traded to the National League during player introductions. Howell saved only one more game in 1987 and with his season ending in August, there was a new sheriff—Eckersley—in town. He picked up eight saves after August 14 to finish with sixteen, tied with Howell for the team lead. Suddenly this whole bullpen thing didn't seem so bad.

Dave Stewart not only found his niche as a starter, he became the A's ace. In a year that Jim "Catfish" Hunter was elected to the Hall of Fame, Stewart started thirty-seven games and completed eight of them. For all the hoopla surrounding Reggie's return (including a homerun on Opening Night) and McGwire's out-of-nowhere fling with history, my favorite moment of 1987 was when I watched Number 34 beat the Indians on a chilly Wednesday night for his 20th win. That was the night he forever became "Stew" to us.

Forever ended for Reggie about a week later in Chicago. But to get to that day, we need to go back to McGwire to whom Reggie's torch was passed. Not that Canseco, the true heir to my hero's throne in every fashion, wasn't worthy of the baton. He enjoyed a fine sophomore season with 31 homers and 113 ribbies. But McGwire, who like Jose had given a glimpse of the future as a September call-up the year before, was off-the-planet better. Not that he started '87 with a bang—just four homeruns in April. Then he began hitting them in droves. Fifteen in May, including five in three games at Detroit, and two at Yankee Stadium to close out the month. Nine in June, including five over two days in Cleveland. Back-to-back with Canseco to beat Boston on The Fourth. Two more on July 11, right before the Break, the second one a two-run shot to give the A's the lead in the 8th. (I was there, screaming my lungs out.) Thirty-three homeruns heading into the All-Star Game— in his first season! Then the Reggie-like slide in the second half (shades of '69). Still, he set the rookie record with his 39th blast at Anaheim, surpassing the great Frank Robinson's record. Robinson, Mom's high school classmate, had held the mark since 1956, the year Mom married Dad. In 1987, Tonianne made Mom a grandma for the sixth time with her son Patrick. (See, it all connects, people.) And McGwire kept on connecting and sending baseballs into the stands. Number 40 came on August 29 and Number 48 on September 25, breaking Reggie's Oakland record (set in '69, the year Tricia was born). He hit one more four days later and had five games left for the magic 50. It never came. Meanwhile I listened at work on October 1st as Bill King called Reggie's last-at bat at the Coliseum, a single through the infield on a lazy Thursday afternoon. Less than 10,000 fans were on hand to say goodbye. Just three days later, at Comiskey Park, the A's fell to the White Sox, 5–2, and finished the season at 81–81, four games behind the Twins. The last time Minnesota had won the West (1970), the A's followed that up with five straight titles. Hmm....

But that Sunday in Chicago was about more than just mere coincidences. It was about one amazing player declining a chance at history as Mark McGwire chose the birth of his son over a shot at fifty homers. It was about a staple in center field giving us one last ride over a wall to a place where he so often kept baseballs from visiting; Dwayne Murphy, hero Number Two, hit a home run in his final at-bat as an A. (He retired after the '89 season.) And it was about the Greatest A of them all, Reggie Jackson, getting two hits, including one in his final at-bat, saying farewell to a Hall-of-Fame career.

You know something? This wasn't such a bad era after all.

But it doesn't beat the next one.

14 / Daddy's (Youngest) Little Girl

"God, I love baseball."

—Robert Redford, in *The Natural*

"Dave McKay."

That's the answer my youngest sister gave me when I asked what started her love affair with the A's. With Tonianne, it was Reggie. But at least he was a star! With Trish, it was Dave McKay. Before she spotted him, her interest in the game was casual at best.

Tricia: "Yep, I saw him warming up one day and I was like, 'ooh, baseball.' After that, the game sort of stuck on me."

Dave McKay. Dave McKay? Here's the rundown: After playing two seasons with the Twins (1975–76) for whom he homered in his first Major League at-bat, McKay was drafted by the expansion Toronto Blue Jays in 1977 where he spent the next three years before coming to Oakland for his last three seasons in the bigs. His final game on October 3, 1982 (he homered in this one, too) happened to coincide with the end of the Billy Ball era, though it didn't become official until seventeen days later. McKay served as the A's bullpen and first-base coach from 1984–95, mostly under Tony La Russa. They left for St. Louis in 1996 and have been there ever since, earning a World Series ring this past October.

OK, before this chapter begins to sound like The Life and Times of David Lawrence McKay, let me say again that he is the one that got my sister's *attention*. But while McKay's playing days were coming to an end, Tricia's time with the A's was only beginning. And she would go where no family member—not even me or Tonianne—had gone before. She and her friend Susan started out in the bleachers with the rest of us before upgrading to first-deck seats (somewhere around 1984).

113

"We would buy half-price, third-deck tickets and make our way down to the first deck. Because the crowds were so small at the time, we'd sit as close to the field as possible. We always went really early and we'd sit behind home plate during batting practice and then move to our seats afterwards. This allowed us to watch the players walk back to the clubhouse after practice. After awhile, they kind of got used to us being there and some of them started to acknowledge us. Clete Boyer (a holdover coach from the Billy Martin days) would throw souvenir balls to us. Wes Stock (who had coached the A's from '73–'75 and returned for another stint from '84–'86) always yelled out, 'hey girls.' I think he may have been deaf because he was so loud."

"I want to say we bought season tickets in '87, the year that the All-Star Game was played here. Susan's mom worked at the concession stands so she gave us rides to the games. We sat in 128, Row 1, right behind the A's bullpen, so between sitting there and behind the plate during batting practice, we got to know the players and coaches pretty well. One time Steve McCatty took Susan's math book and acted like he was doing her homework in the bullpen. Even some of the opposing players, like Paul Molitor and Billy Ripken (Cal's younger brother) would remember us from one visit to the next and would say hi to us."

"But it was the pitchers that really took to us, because of where we sat during the games. Steve Ontiveros, Gene Nelson, Todd Burns, Jeff Newman (who was the bullpen coach for a brief period) even Eck; all of them got to know us or at least knew who we were. We got to baking chocolate-chip cookies for them, mainly for Ontiveros or Nelson, but we'd give them to whoever might be passing by after practice. And they would share them with the others. We got to know Ontiveros and his girlfriend pretty well. I don't know how we got around to talking about it but we told him that Susan's mom did 'colors,' meaning she would bring fabric swaths and stuff like that to see what color clothes fit that person. He was interested in that but we never could click on setting it up, so finally one day he came over and said 'Let's just set something up now, why don't you come over for dinner one night?' So we did and he cooked us some hamburgers, and Susan's mom did the colors for him and his girlfriend."

"We had a good time out there in those seats. We started out with three seats, me, Susan, and her sister. We'd slip sunflower seeds and gummy bears through the cracks in the bullpen, stuff like that and they would give us water and gum. One time I was thirsty and Nelson gave me a Gatorade cup with water in it and I remember keeping it for awhile because one of the players had taken a drink out of it before Nelson handed it to me. I don't have it anymore though. Art Kusnyer (the bullpen coach from 1989–95) was really nice to us. During the winning years, it seemed like every player had some sort of fan club and they would hang their banners in the bleachers. So we decided to start the Art Kusnyer Fan Club and we made shirts that said that. He loved it and at the end of the year he gave me and Susan official team jackets. By that time, we had a total of five seats, me, Susan, her sister, her mom, and her mom's boyfriend. The year that we set the save record (1988), we made shirts that said 'The Best Bullpen in Baseball.' Each shirt had one of the pitcher's name and number on the back. I had Gene Nelson; he was my favorite."

Trish was the first in the family to attend Spring Training games (Arizona), and the first to see the A's play on the road (Anaheim). She and her friends always stayed at the same hotel as the team. It was in Southern California that they saw a side of Bill King they immediately wish they hadn't. "One day we walked down to the pool and there he was, wearing a Speedo! And we were like, 'Oh my God, he's wearing a bikini.' So every time we'd see him after that, we'd go, 'there's Bikini.' There was another time we were leaving the pool area and we saw Eck coming towards us, so we slowed down and waited for him. Not enough for him to notice but enough that he got on the same elevator as us. When he got to his floor he turned to us and said, 'see you later' and we were like, 'is that a promise?' In Arizona, we were hanging out in the hotel bar, although I guess it was a restaurant too. We were too young to be in a bar. Anyways, Dave Henderson saw us in there and ordered us drinks. 'Bacardi and Coke, hold the Bacardi.' There was another time when the A's were to play a Spring Training game at a different stadium than their home park, which was walking distance for us. We really wanted to go but Susan's dad wouldn't let us use his car. So we were talking to Hendu as he was boarding the team bus and told him that we had no way to get to the game. He pulled out his keys to his rental and said, 'take my car.' The best moment though was when Bill King got on the elevator with us and we whispered, 'it's Bikini.' Well, he must have thought we said his actual name because he turned around to talk to us. We lost it. Luckily, the elevator was made of glass so we could turn our backs to him while holding our laughs in. Susan's dad was left to talk to him. It was hilarious."

Tricia was a steady visitor to Oakland during those days and made memories to last a lifetime. But in 1994, it all came to an end. For a while at least. "I was mad," she said of the strike that prematurely ended the season. "I stopped paying attention after that." Little by little she came back, supporting her A's as they made the slow climb back to respectability and beyond. It was Trish who had me convinced that we were going to win the World Series in 2006. But I forgive her; we had one helluva season. Her faith in the team never wavers. The night the A's and the Angels duked it out for twelve innings last September, she kept telling me, "OK, this inning. We're going to win it *this* inning." And when Marco Scutaro drove in the winning run, my little sister jumped up and down and yelled with delight.

You'd have sworn that Dave McKay had just walked by.

15 / Feeling Bashful (1988–1992)

"This team has everything."

—San Francisco Giant scout, Hank Sauer,
offering his expert opinion on the A's to Dave Newhouse
of the *Oakland Tribune* in a May 1990 article.

I remember the press conference like it was yesterday. And for all the magic that Billy Beane has produced over the years, it's doubtful that he ever had a day like the one enjoyed by his mentor, Sandy Alderson. Fresh off a .500 season, and more importantly, back-to-back Rookie of the Year performances by Canseco and McGwire, the A's brass knew they had something special in which to build a winner. So in the words of the old man who dreamed of a dinosaur petting zoo in *Jurassic Park*, they "spared no expense." And they assembled, these stars, smiles broad, before the Bay Area media: catcher Ron Hassey, outfielder Dave Henderson, utility infielder Glenn Hubbard, outfielder-DH Dave Parker, southpaw starter Bob Welch, and pitcher Matt Young. Missing from the party were two more key additions: outfielder Don Baylor and lefty reliever Rick Honeycutt. All signed or traded for in the previous off-season, all with plenty of talent and experience, and yet all with something to prove. Manager Tony La Russa, careful to mask his excitement (and good fortune), offered these words: "My top goal is to make sure that the club is not carried away with the power potential of the team." Are you kidding me?

On Opening Night, the A's unveiled their new team with an old logo that was appropriate for their mammoth lineup—the elephant. First used by Connie Mack's Philadelphia club, the pachyderm's comeback coincided with a Murderer's Row of Canseco, McGwire, Parker, Henderson, and Baylor. Jose and Hendu showed off their

117

might in the opener with impressive homeruns but the real hero of this night was Dave Stewart. Stew gave up a hit (and his only run) in the first, and a hit in the ninth, but none in between before giving way to Honeycutt and eventually Eck to close out the 4–1 win. Talk about a formula built for success. And when the A's turned an 8–5 deficit on April 20 into a 9–8 win with four runs in the bottom of the eighth against the Angels (the last three courtesy of Hassey's dramatic two-out homerun), it gave them a half-game lead over Chicago, a lead they would hold for the remainder of the season. A 3–2 victory at Comiskey Park on April 23 left Stew with a 5–0 record; three starts later he was 8–0 and the A's were riding a thirteen-game winning streak that was extended by one the following night. Eck recorded five saves during the streak, bringing his early season total to twelve. The baseball world quickly took notice. In a nationally televised game at Cleveland on April 30, *Game of the Week* announcer Vin Scully gushed, "After seven innings, it's Oakland eleven…eleven!… Cleveland three."

The whole season was about numbers but there were two that stood out, side-by-side: 40–40. See, no one had hit forty homers and stolen forty bases in the same season, which was obviously unbeknownst to Canseco when he boasted to reporters in March about "joining the club." So Jose laughed and then set out to become its charter member. Along the way, he and McGwire invented a new way to celebrate round-trippers: with a forearm bash. The craze caught on at the Coliseum and a song (there's always a song) swept the stadium, to the tune of the Halloween anthem, *Monster Mash*: "And do the bash, do the monster bash." (Admit it, you're humming the song now.)

Tony La Russa's powerhouse was humming along, headed for the first division title since Billy Ball in '81. Oakland was a happening place and when I wasn't there with Abel (in the bleachers) or Rose (in the first deck) on weeknights, I was going alone on weekends. Sometimes, like Tone before me, I'd bring a little family member to keep me company. Such was the case the night Mark McGwire hit a grand slam in August to beat the Angels. I had five-year old Natalie with me in the wooden seats. A month later, I took my four nieces—Christina, Kimberly, Nat, and Stephanie—to a game against the Royals. (They were, at the time, just a little short of their 9th, 7th, 5th, and 3rd birthdays, respectively. In fact Steph was one day shy of turning three.) That afternoon, we saw a piece of history, when Canseco hit his 40th homerun of the season, leaving him just a handful of steals short of his 40–40 quest. (My cousins Scott and Nick still haven't forgiven me for taking the girls to the game, instead of them.) With the 3–2 win, the A's magic number was down to two. The World Champion Twins were in town the next night and a win against them would clinch the title. We had Stew going for us. I hung out with bleacher bums Kevin and Greg that night, even shared a couple of beers with them. Stew struggled early, as was his custom, but he bore down after giving up three runs through three. The A's also did all their scoring before the fourth frame; Dave Parker's two run shot in the third gave us the lead for good and another run was added to make it 5–3. And that's how it stayed as Eck got the final batter to fly out to left to start the celebration. AL West champs and it felt great! Great things kept happening to these A's as the regular season drew to a close. Jose stole his 40th base to go with his 40 homers. With that feat, he had gone where no player had gone before; not Mays, not Clemente, not Mantle. No one. Canseco, at 23 years young, was beyond spectacular. He batted .307, led the league in homeruns (42), RBI's (122), and slugging (.569), and even cut down on his strikeouts, while making great strides in the field. This stud of a player seemingly had no ceiling. The voters were convinced; they named him the first unanimous MVP since Reggie in '73. Want more A's? How about the bullpen setting the save record? Not as glamorous as what the right-fielder did, but arguably more significant. Yes, it was a season of numbers, and in one sensational Saturday afternoon, Stew won Number 20, Mac hit his 30th homerun, and the A's beat the Brewers for their 100th victory of 1988. When it was over, the A's towered over everyone else with a team record 104 wins. The "power potential of this team" that La Russa spoke of in April had been realized. Next up, Boston in the ALCS.

I was at work when the playoffs got under way at Fenway and I can still hear Lon Simmons' call of Canseco's fourth-inning blast that gave the A's a 1–0 lead. Now I understood what Tonianne meant when she talked about the pressure of the post-season. My heart was pounding the entire game. The Sox got one off Stew in the seventh, but we got it back in the eighth, thanks to a double by Carney and a single by Hendu, whose flair for the bright lights began in Boston in '86. Now he was doing it for us. Stew had worked out of a couple of jams early on, most notably in the second when he struck out four-time batting champion Wade Boggs with the bags juiced. Boggs had only gone down on strikes 34 times during the regular season. Eck came on in the 8th and retired the first five batters before Boston mounted a two-out rally in the 9th. Boggs stepped up to the plate with two men on and a chance to be the hero but for the second time in the game, he struck out. Game over. (Bill King, with as much mustard on the call as was on Eck's last pitch: "He *struck* him out!") I ran over to John's department and we embraced. One of those hard hugs. Later La Russa would describe this type of game as one that "makes your breath stink." Indeed. But the A's were feeling minty fresh in Game 2, even after Boston staked Clemens to a 2–0 lead after six. The lead lasted two batters as Hendu singled and Jose did the Monster Bash over the Green Monster (Lon Simmons, who was becoming quite masterful at making predictions late in the season, bragged on the air after Canseco's shot, "And I *told* you we'd be tied!") It wasn't tied for long as a clearly shaken-up Clemens gave up a single to Lansford, balked him to second, and wild-pitched him to third. McGwire brought him home with a single. 3–2, A's. The Sox squared it in the bottom half but we went ahead in the ninth thanks to three singles by the non-bashers: Ron Hassey, Tony Phillips, and the game-winner by Walt Weiss. Eck closed it out again and the A's were coming home with a chance to sweep. Me and Rose were there for Game 3 but Bob Welch's pitches appeared be to somewhere else. The first four Sox of the game reached base (three of them scored) and when Mike Greenwell homered in the second, Welch's night was done with the A's in a 5–0 hole. My third ALCS game in person was shaping up like the first two. I told Rose that I wanted to go home. She slapped me. Big Mac led off the second with a homerun to get us on the board; Carney's two-run dinger after Weiss' RBI double made it 5–4. With two outs in the bottom of the third, Hassey hit a rocket into the right-field seats, the A's led 6–5, and the place went bonkers. Just like that we were in front, and you knew it was over, even with six innings left. When Eck struck out Jim Rice to end it, we were 10–6 victors, and one win away from a Classic trip. The next day, Sunday, Stew took the mound again and he was staked to a 1–0 lead on a missile by Mr. 40–40. It was Canseco's third homerun of the series. Meanwhile our pitcher was Stew-pendous, and he left to a thunderous ovation after seven innings of four-hit ball. We tacked on two more in the 8th for a 4–1 lead and with me and Rose screaming our approval, Eck sealed the deal in the ninth. How Sweep it Was!

The Oakland A's were going to the World Series for the first time in fourteen years, or since I was a second grader at Woodrow Wilson Elementary. In another words, this would be a World Series that I could experience for myself, rather than depend on my older siblings for their tales of the "good old days." No, this World Series would be all mine to savor. And what was not to savor? The A's were clicking on all cylinders after sweeping the Red Sox, and their stars—Dave Stewart, Jose Canseco, and Dennis Eckersley—were shining bright. That their Series opponent, the Los Angeles Dodgers, appeared to have destiny on their side mattered little to me. We were going to make short work of LA, just like we did in 1974, but this time I was going to be there when it happened. The A's went into Game 1 fresh from a week-long layoff; the Dodgers were coming off an emotional seven-game NLCS win over the New York Mets. There was concern that Oakland would be a little rusty and the "experts" appeared to be right when the Dodgers jumped out to a 2–0 lead against Stew. Dad then went for one of his walks to Cherry Grove Park, which was to the right as you came out of our house. Dad *always* went to the right....

In the second inning, the A's loaded the bases for Canseco who picked a very good time for his first career Grand Slam, leaving a dent in the centerfield camera in the process. I rushed out to the front yard and screamed towards my Dad at the park: "Grand Slam, Jose! 4–2, A's!" (I always pictured him getting so excited that he swallowed his cigarette.) The Dodgers squeaked out a run in the sixth, while the A's kept wasting scoring chances (they left ten men on base). Not that I was worried; after all, it was almost Eck Time.

Stew's night was done after eight solid innings and in came Eckersley to nail the coffin shut. In typical Eck-onomic fashion, the closer quickly got two outs. Dad walked out again, this time going down the street to the left....

Everything else is a blur. Ex-A Mike Davis, signed by the Dodgers as a free agent exactly ten months before, inexplicably worked Eckersely for a walk. Suddenly a hobbling Kirk Gibson appeared from the dugout. My thought equaled the thoughts of every other being on this planet: no way does Gibson do anything but strike out. I remember Eck getting ahead in the count, I remember thinking how overmatched Gibson looked. Sometime during the at-bat Mike Davis stole second base. That made me a little nervous; now a cheap hit ties it up. I know the count went full, and I can remember hearing the roar of the crowd, a sound that reached epic levels when Gibson reached out and hit the most impossible homerun in my lifetime. The most *sickening* homerun in my lifetime. I don't remember who was around me (maybe Tricia?) but someone screamed, an awful, painful scream. The rest of the world was probably thinking "Holy Cow, did that really happen?" and calling their friends, excitedly. But not A's fans. A's fans were left all alone, we *wanted* to be alone, like Eck walking in a daze off that mound, lost, no one to cheer him up, this man who on a personal level had already known what Hell felt like.

I walked out of the house and walked a straight line over to Dad's truck and buried my face in my hands, not knowing whether I was going to cry or throw up. But then Dad interrupted me, his voice coming from the left. The *fricking left*! "Home run, huh?" I nodded meekly. "Shit." I then went into my room and fell asleep fully clothed, shoes and all. And when I woke up the next morning, I was convinced that the whole thing was a bad dream. That is, until I saw the sports page. Most A's fans will tell you they can't watch the highlight of the homerun, even now, nearly two decades later. But for some reason I can't help *not* to watch, as if somehow the ball will fall short of the warning track and Eck will walk off the mound pumping his fist.

Tonianne: "Michael and I were in Carmel with Patrick, who was 13 months at the time. We watched the game in our hotel room. That night Patrick cried (screaming in pain) the entire night. Coincidence? We didn't sleep and I don't think any of our "neighbors" did either. We snuck out at six am."

John: "There aren't many fans around the country that have experienced something like that. For Oakland fans though, this was the second of its kind. All you have to do is go back sixteen years to a game between the Pittsburgh Steelers and Oakland Raiders."

And so it was in Game 2 of the 1988 Series that Orel Hershiser was "immaculate" in shutting down the A's, 6–0. Oh by the way, he added three hits for good measure. Dave Parker had three hits, too; in fact, he was the only player in an Oakland uniform with a knock. And the teams headed up the coast, with the Dodgers knocking loudly on Destiny's Door. On the eve of my first World Series game in person, my stomach did somersaults. I woke up that morning still feeling nauseous but I was determined to make it to work. I didn't even last an hour. I spent most of the day, back home, throwing up. Why was this happening? Finally, I gave up the fight and gave my ticket to Ernie. Nothing that happened to me all day made me sicker than having to relinquish my World Series seat. The game itself turned out to be a pitcher's duel that ended on McGwire's homerun in the bottom of the ninth. I think I cheered and cried at the same time.

Rose: "We were tied 1–1 and Ernie just had to have a McGwire doll. He got back just in time to see McGwire hit his walk-off homerun and he held up that doll and claimed that the A's won because he bought it."

The next night I was back at the Coliseum for Game 4 but the Dodgers regained control of the Series with a 4–3 victory. In a way, this was more painful than the opener. Whereas Gibson got us with a swift kick to the groin, this contest was like three hours in the dentist chair. The Dodgers struck for two runs out of the gate, the first scoring on a passed ball by Stew, the second unearned, courtesy of an error by Hubbard. The A's got one back in their half of the first but LA went up 3–1 in the third with another unearned run, this time on a miscue by Weiss. Meanwhile, the shortstop's fellow Rookies of the Year continued to struggle at the plate (Jose and McGwire were a collective 0-for-6). The A's plated a run in the sixth to make it 3–2, but the Dodgers came right back with one in the seventh. It was that kind of night. The home nine rallied once more in their bottom half, with Dave Henderson scoring Weiss from first on a two-out double. One hit away from a tie game. Canseco walked and Parker reached on an error and suddenly last night's hero was up with the bags juiced. But Big Mac popped out weakly to first, killing our last real threat of the night. Damn ball took forever to come down, I think to torture us. And just for kicks, to make the evening complete, Jay Howell recorded the save.

The Dodgers' stunning upset was made complete the next night, a 5–2 win by Hershiser. As he did in Game 1, Mickey Hatcher hit a two-run homer in the first to get LA going. Hatcher had one (one!) round-tripper during the regular season before morphing into Gene Tenace in this Series. I hate Mickey Hatcher. But not as much as I despise Mike Davis, the former "A" who turned on a 3–0 offering from Storm Davis for a two-run shot in the fourth. I can still see it going. Come to think of it, it might still be going. That made it 4–1, and with Orel on the hill, the rest of the night was spent wondering what went wrong. Well, besides the Bash Brothers going a combined 2-for-36, which proved once and for all that good pitching beats good hitting. La Russa, in his address to the media, praised his ball club, saying "They didn't choke. They got beat because the Dodgers did more."

Man, 1989, was it really that long ago? Seventeen years have gone by, but it doesn't feel like it. I remember I felt the same way after losing to the Dodgers that Tone felt after the '71 playoffs: the best was yet to come. I mean, I *knew* we were going to win. Yeah, I was aware of the odds. The last team to repeat as American League champ was New York in 1977–78. Of the forty previous division winners, only one (yes, one) had come back to do it again the next season. Yawn. These A's were just too good, and furthermore, these A's had some unfinished business to attend to. Picture Goliath getting a second chance.

The A's wasted little time in showing that there were no ill effects from the previous October and they did it without their top gun. Jose Canseco, the reigning MVP, missed the first 88 games of the season with a wrist injury. But the A's, they just went about their business. Their first game of '89 played out like the '88 opener: Stew won it, Eck closed it, and McGwire picked up the slack for his sidelined Bash Brother with a long homerun in the third. A's 3, Seattle 2. Different year, same script. McGwire soon joined Canseco on the disabled list with a herniated disk. He missed fifteen games in April. Even without the Bashers, the A's started hot again, taking 18 of 26 in April. But the injury bug hit again in May, and once again, it was a former Rookie-of-the-Year that was victimized. Shortstop Walt Weiss sprained his right knee against New York and would be out of action for twenty-two games. Barely a week after Weiss went down, starter Storm Davis was sent to the DL with a trio of injuries. The very next day, Eckersley left a game against the Yankees with a strained rotator cuff. He would not pitch again until after the All-Star Break.

By now you'd figure that the A's were in third or fourth place, but with a patchwork roster, they hit the halfway mark with a 52–36 record, 1–1/2 games behind the first-place Angels. Starting pitching helped; Stew, Welch, and newcomer Mike Moore gave the team a chance every time out. Meanwhile there were still some decent bats in the lineup: Parker, Hendu, and the steady Lansford (he hit .336 in '89). Oh, and some dude named Rickey, who came back home via a trade from the Yankees in June. As **Carl Steward** of the *Daily Review* wrote, the re-acquisition of Oakland's favorite son was either "a killer shot in the arm or a fatal shot to the head." But not even Steward could deny the possibilities of Rickey leading things off once the Basher's wounds were fully healed: "On one hand, you have the prospect of an offensive lineup that is positively gaga—Rickey Henderson, Dave Henderson, Jose Canseco, Dave Parker, Mark McGwire, Terry Steinbach, Carney Lansford, Glenn Hubbard or Tony Phillips, and Walter Weiss. Juggle 'em however you want, but if you're the opposing pitcher, you're saying, 'Hey skip, I've got this awful pain in my gut today.'" Pain was surely in order for A's opponents now that the *M*A*S*H* unit that once made up our ball club was healthy.

The All-Star Game, and the first real game that followed, offered an October view. Our other local star, Dave Stewart, started the Midseason Classic opposite the (first-place) Giants' Rick

Reuschel. Local writers saw the pairing as a possible warm-up to a Bay Series. But there was still a lot of baseball to be played. The A's stars were aligned in Toronto after the Break and Canseco (finally) christened his season with a 2-for-3 night that included a double and an opposite-field homerun. And who was there to close out the 11–7 win? Eck, of course. Still, there was a roadblock to the playoffs that no one could expect: the Angels were presenting themselves as a genuine threat to the throne. The two teams were locked in a virtual tie for first and then matched each other win-for-win for five games heading into a late July showdown in Oakland. California left town a game up with a gutsy series win. And so it went for three weeks, the state rivals playing leapfrog in the standings, before the A's nestled in on August 21st and never looked back. The next night, some history was made in Texas, when the ageless Nolan Ryan struck out Rickey for his 5,000th K. No one else has approached that number and I don't believe anyone ever will. Meanwhile, Ryan and Rickey, taking the train to Cooperstown with records that may never be broken, would make history again in May of '91. But hey, that's for another chapter. This night, as was the case in many of Ryan's dominant games throughout his career, ultimately ended in defeat for the star pitcher. Welch and Eck shut out the Rangers on five hits to complete an amazing and rare stretch of three games in three cities for the A's. They played in Oakland on the 20th against the Twins, at Detroit on the 21st to make up a rain-out game, and in Texas on the 22nd, which happened to be Rose's birthday. And all the A's did was win all three games by a combined 13–1 score, take over first place for good, and conquer a legend on his night. From Rose's birthday to John's and another win over a one-of-a-kind hurler, this time Roger Clemens. When the A's beat him in May, they did it with Jose, Mac, Hendu, and Weiss sidelined with injures. And with Curt Young (1–4 at the time) on the mound. But it was Young who put the A's in first for good with his win at Detroit, and it was Young who beat Clemens again his next time out. This one was even harder to swallow for Rocket than the first, even though he was facing a much healthier lineup. He left after seven, down 5–1, having allowed only three hits (plus five walks). Only one of the five runs was earned. With their favorite punching bag out of the game, the A's went to work on Boston's beleaguered bullpen: the first nine batters in the bottom of the eighth reached base, against four relievers. Eight runs scored that inning; the final was 13–1, those thirteen runs coming on seven hits. Two weeks later, Clemens and the Red Sox gained some revenge; the A's dropped three straight at Fenway and saw their once-comfy lead slip to 2.5 games. Still, La Russa's club may have felt worse about the two *wins* that sandwiched the sweep at Boston. Both games featured Stew's bid for his 20th win, both victories were snatched away from him by ninth-inning, game tying homers—off Eck. Both times, the A's came back to win, with the stunned closer getting the "W" each time. Stew finally got his 20th at Minnesota on the 20th, and five days later, the A's clinched the Western crown for the second straight year. I was there with Scott. And on display that night, besides a Jose laser into the seats and a shutout by Mike Moore, was the underrated part of this juggernaut: its defense. All season long when player after player went down, two guys rose up: Tony Phillips and Mike Gallego. Yeah, you're saying "who" if you're not an A's fan, but we knew how important they were. And so did the rest of the team. That night, my second clincher in as many years, Tony and Gags flexed their muscle a bit. And the other two infielders, McGwire and Weiss, followed suit, making five or six "wow" plays on the night. Considering all the injuries and constant pressure from California and Kansas City, the whole season was worthy of a "wow." Say it backwards, even.

The playoffs started on a Tuesday evening in Oakland; with the Eastern champion Toronto Blue Jays standing in our way to Redemption City. Me and Rose were back in our customary seats in Section 127, Row 7. Great fricking seats. Stew was on the hill and, well, he was the Stew We All Knew. Struggled at the start, settled down, got himself a 7–3 win. Same as it ever was. His Oakland partner in crime, Rickey, was also a big hit. Without even getting a hit. After Mac led off the bottom of the sixth with game-tying shot, Phillips and Gallego stroked back-to-back, one-out singles. Rickey, who also walked twice, got hit by a pitch. Lansford then hit a shot to short for a sure inning-ender but Rickey slid hard into second and the throw to first sailed wide, scoring two runs. In the bottom of the eighth, with Gallego on third with two outs, Henderson walked, stole second (forcing a wild throw that plated Gags), and came home on a single by Carney. "Rickey Runs."

Rickey ran even more in Game 2, adding a little relish to the festivities. Once again, I was present with Rose. Canseco was not, out with a migraine. Rickey, with a little help from his friends, simply caused migraines. Felt in Canada. The top of the order made the most noise, with the first four batters collecting seven of the nine hits, including some valet work by Parker, who parked one into the seats in the sixth. The *very* top of the order—yes, that guy—was noisy, nagging, and not to be denied. Two hits in two at-bats, two walks, two runs scored, and a playoff-record four steals. Rickey also clapped his hands, pumped his fists, shimmied at third base, chatted with fans, and earned himself a *Sports Illustrated* cover. Oh, and he ruffled more than a few, blue feathers on the opposing team.

The Series shifted up north and the Jays got on the board with a 7–3 win. They didn't exactly stop Henderson, but they contained him enough. Meanwhile, Toronto's attention tuned to Parker, who went deep again, and took his usual slow trot around the bases, his fingers wagging like Yosemite Sam waving his pistols. Oh, those Swaggerin' A's! Game 4 was a thriller, a nail-biter, good to the last drop. Another quote from Max Mercy (*The Natural*) comes to mind as Rickey goes from base thief to slugger: "I've never seen anything like it. Anything he wants to do, he does." And what Rickey wanted to do this day was let his bat do his talking. He homered in the third to give the A's a 1–0 lead. Two batters later, Canseco, who had been curiously missing amid the A's Hot Dog Stand, hit one where even the hot dog vendors dare not go. Try the fifth deck. We don't even have five decks in our stadium. But they did in the Sky Dome and Jose sky-rocketed one into that section. Rickey couldn't keep quiet for this one, noting afterwards, "It was hit so hard, I fell of the bench." The Blue Jays wish he *had* fallen because in the fifth, the Oakland native went deep again, upping the lead to 5–1. But the Jays bounced back. Eck relieved Honeycutt with two on and one out in the eighth and promptly allowed both runners to score, making it 6–5. But Dennis closed it out in the ninth and we were one win away. Me, Trish, and Rose let out a collective breath at Mom's.

More drama ensued for what we hoped would be the clincher in Game 5. The locals were at it again, with Rickey walking in the first, stealing second, and scoring on Jose's single. Surely realizing that he didn't have a triple in the series, the left-fielder went out and got one in the third to drive in Weiss. The A's struck for two more without Rickey's aid and led 4–0 after seven. Now it was up to Oakland's Stewart and Fremont's Eckersley to seal the deal. Stew gave up a one-out homer to Lloyd Moseby (yet another Oakland prep star) in the eighth and a ringing blast by George Bell leading off the ninth. Eck gave up a single and a steal, the runner scoring on a sac fly for the second out. This was about the time that Toronto manager, Cito Gaston, decided he wanted to play some *Controversy* before the *Celebration*. The game was held up as the umpires checked Eck for possible substance abuse. On the baseball. Supposedly, the Jays felt that Dennis was scuffing the ball, an accusation that Eck took great exception to. When play mercifully resumed, the closer struck out Junior Felix to end it. As the A's rushed to the mound, Eckersley pumped his fist towards the Toronto dugout. Meanwhile, back at Mom's, our hearts were still pumping long after the game. Back to the Series!

The only problem that I had with playing the Giants in the World Series was knowing that we'd have to share the spotlight with them. I sure in the heck wasn't worried about losing to them. Any other year, I might have been nervous. But not *this* year. Had I known it was to be our last one, I would have reveled in it even more. Then again, nature kind of changed our perspective on things. The Bay Area media, meanwhile, was in its glory, and their only concern was what to dub this thing. The "BART Series" and "Bay Bridge Series" were the most popular, it seemed. At least, *before* the games got underway. We'd have other ways to name her afterwards.

The Series started on a Saturday night, with me and Rose stationed in 127, Tricia (as she was all season) in 126, Row 1 (behind the A's bullpen), and Abe was there directly above us in 227. As the starting lineups were announced, I couldn't help notice that things were somewhat backwards. First off, it was cold and gray, what you might expect if we were playing eight miles north. Secondly, we were playing the *Giants*, but surely as the Bashers were introduced, you had to kind of laugh at that. The Giants this night weren't giant at all. And it wasn't just the size of our players, it was their persona, too. Part swagger, part business-like approach, like "Hey, we're just here to pick up what we left behind last year and while we're doing it, we're going to bash and strut, and basically make life miserable for you." If SF had the Giants, we had the *Gigantics*.

Stew was on the mound and he was terrific. Just mowing them down like a teenager does to a lawn on a Saturday afternoon. Meanwhile it didn't take long for me to tap into my inner hatred for the Giants.

Rose: "As I recall, there was a family of Giants' fans behind us, a young couple and their two kids. Well, when Carney Lansford came up in the first inning, the little girl, who was maybe seven or eight, started singing, 'Carney, Warney. Carney, Warney.' You can see Don getting annoyed. I was too, but I wasn't going to say anything to the kid. Just then Carney got a hit, and Don turned to her and yelled, '*Yeah! Carney Warney!*' He was always embarrassing me. I think the family left after that. Would you want to sit near this maniac?"

Rose exaggerates but I guess I can relate because Tonianne would do the same thing to me. So we'll blame her. And Dad. The Giants were blaming Tony Phillips for their 1–0 deficit after his single brought home Hendu in the second. With Steinbach on third, Weiss hit a chopper towards first and Will Clark threw home. Steiny slid through the tag, jarring the ball loose and we had a 2–0 lead. Don't blink because now it's 3–0 as Rickey's single plates Phillips. I love beating the Giants. Leading off the bottom of the third, Scott Garrelts tried to sneak a low pitch by low-ball hitting Parker. That's like trying to sneak your girlfriend past your parents' bedroom. Parker deposited the offering into the right-field seats, before taking his wag-and-trot around the bases. Which gave the fans plenty of time to be bashful.

Abel: "I'll never forget being at Game One. I was in the second deck and Don was in the first deck. Parker led off the 3rd inning with a homer and me and Don did the best long distance bash ever."

In the fourth, Weiss followed Parker's lead with a lead-off homerun of his own to make it 5–0. Or four more than what Dave

Stewart needed this October evening. In the ninth, the first two batters singled and moved to second and third on a pass ball (as Matt Williams struck out). Stew got the next guy on strikes, too, and induced a ground ball to third from Candy Maldonado to secure a sweet shutout.

And something that Abel may or may not remember: walking out of the stadium, he was holding about twelve empty beer cups and screaming into the ear of some poor SF sap that we were going to sweep. Just a beautiful moment. The guy was actually shrinking by the minute. The Giants must have felt smaller after Stew's masterpiece and facing 19-game winner Mike Moore wasn't going to do much for them in that regard. Rickey (surprise!) led off the game with a walk, (gasp!) stole second, and (shocker!) scored on a double by Mr. Reliable, or if you prefer, Carney Warney. The Giants had the gall to tie the game in the third, which only served to anger the Elephants. In the fourth against Rick Reuschel, Jose walked, Parker doubled him home (missing a homer by *that* much), Hendu walked, Mac struck out, and Steinbach came up. The Giants tried that low-ball sneak thing again and Steiny crushed it. The place went berserk and I ran up and down the aisle bashing every fan in site. It was only the fourth inning, but this baby was over. The final, 5–1, and Moore was just as solid as Stew. Still hungry after last year's stunner, I was in the mood for Moore Giant Stew.

On Tuesday, October 17, at 5:04 pm, just as ABC was beginning its pre-game show for Game 3, the earth shook. Mother Nature, who moments before was at her sexiest, may have taken exception to her omission from the VIP list when her invitation arrived for the Bay Area Ball. This was her RSVP: a 7.1 quake that rocked this region and postponed the Series for ten days. Inside Candlestick Park, the fans cheered, not yet knowing the severity of the situation, but knowing that they were a part of history of a different breed.

ABC's **Al Michaels,** the believer of miracles, wasn't sure what to believe in at this point. "I don't know if we're on the air, and I don't even think I *care*! Well, folks, that is the greatest opening in the history of television, bar none!"

Soon reports came that the Bay Bridge, the very symbol of this World Series, had partially collapsed. Other stories told of a fallen freeway structure in Oakland and fires in San Francisco's Marina District. Like the people at the stadium that day, it took awhile for us to learn just how terrible this tremor was.

John: "I know you have the same memory as me, at least the first part. We were leaving BetLar to pick up Aaron and then go watch the game. I thought I had a flat tire and pulled over just after we went under the overpass at Whipple. As I got out I noticed about four other cars pulled over and the drivers getting out with the same puzzled look on their faces. It was then I realized that it was an earthquake. I didn't realize how bad it was until we got to Mom's and heard about the bridge and the Cypress structure. It was eerie especially when I went by our apartment and found a lot of stuff on the floor. After that it seemed like the remainder of the series, once they resumed it, was a strange blur."

I remember it took forever to get to Mom's house and there was this continuous blaring of sirens; that's when it started to hit me that maybe things were a lot worse than we had feared. Commissioner Fay Vincent sent the Candlestick crowd home with the announcement that there would be no baseball played here tonight. Celebration was replaced by chaos and confusion, and ultimately, mourning.

Tonianne: "I don't remember much. The Friday (the 13th) before the series began was my last chemo. I ran into Uncle Rick in Safeway on my way to the appointment. He was so excited; I don't ever remember Uncle Rick being excited about anything, but he was about this series. I was on tranquilizers for the first two games and I didn't see a single inning. I was finally able to go back to work on Tuesday the 17th but I left as soon as the bank closed because I was feeling sick. As I walked across the parking lot to my car I remember looking up at the sky and I actually said out loud, 'Yuck, it looks like earthquake weather.' After the quake, we went to Celeste's, where we were headed to watch the game, to check on her. At the time we didn't know that the game wouldn't be played. After a few more aftershocks and still not feeling good anyway, we went by Mom's, where it seemed everyone else in the family was. We sat around in the dark just talking. I was totally freaked by the quake and I don't even remember where I watched the final two games."

Baseball took a backseat to something greater, as a whole new perspective was placed on the game. Even the faces of our heroes had changed. So baseball waited. Waited as the Bay Area attempted to pull itself together. And when we needed her, baseball was there. There to put some normalcy back into our lives. There to give hope and diversion. Commissioner Vincent gave the go-ahead for the Series to resume on October 27. As I recall it, when we left work at the same time as we did ten days before, there was a general uneasiness going home. Like, can it really happen again?

Inside Candlestick Park, there was a festive mood, like "We made it." In a weird way, it brought this region, hardly antagonistic to begin with, even closer. Tony La Russa, for his part, had taken his team to Arizona, to stay sharp and focused. He found it impossible—and inappropriate—to focus on the task at hand in an area where the search for bodies continued. But now that baseball was again thrust to the forefront, La Russa had done what he thought was necessary to keep that edge. Stay the course. Eyes on the prize. If my own competitive fire had been reduced to a flicker during the layoff, it took just three batters for it to light up again. Scott Garrelts twice threw high-and-tight to Canseco, who was upset enough about being mired in an 0-for-23 Series skid. And so the Giant woke up the giant; the slumbering, slumping giant in the A's uniform, who promptly singled past the shortstop. Then it was Dave Henderson's turn, who hit what we all thought was a homerun (including Hendu, who did that little homerun hop) but instead it hit off the top of the fence for a two-run double (Carney had singled ahead of Canseco). Just like that, the A's were on top. In the top of the fourth, Hendu led off with a shot that *did* clear the fence and two batters later, Phillips joined the bashers with a blast of his own. Exit Garrelts. The Giants came back with two runs in the bottom half to close within 4–3, but the A's put it away with four in the fifth, the first three coming when Jose took Kelly Downs downtown and the last one coming on Hendu's second homerun of the night. Meanwhile, Stew was his usual stellar self. Already idolized within the community for his efforts on the field, the St. Elizabeth High grad had turned in his A's cap for a hard hat during the layoff, pitching in wherever he might be needed.

When La Russa looked to him in Game 3, Stew simply pitched: seven innings, five hits, eight strikeouts. Before all was said and done, he would earn himself the Series MVP. The A's, as a unit, earned straight A's this evening, tacking on four more runs in the eighth and steamrolling to a 13–7 win.

The next night, Game 2 star Mike Moore pitched opposite Don Robinson. Rickey got things started with a homerun to lead off the game. Relentless. With two men on and two outs in the second, Moore came to bat, with one career plate appearance to his name. So of course Moore doubled over the head of center-fielder Brett Butler to drive in both runners. While contemplating the American League's first hit by a pitcher in seventy Series at-bats, Moore again found himself in a unfamiliar role—base runner—as Rickey lined a single. Moore slid home safely to make it 4–0, as a shell-shocked Robinson headed for the showers. The A's doubled their advantage before the Giants rallied. With Eck on in the ninth to protect a 9–6 lead, Phillips put on one last defensive display. Interestingly enough, the versatile utility man had a hand in the last out of every game of the Series—at three different positions. Phillips fielded a bunt for the first out, and with two outs hustled to throw out Butler to end it. Eck, the face of despair just one season before, gloved the throw and pumped his fist at first base. World Champs at last! And yet the celebration was—justly—subdued.

John: I celebrated but it was nothing like the earlier championship celebrations. I also remember that I knew right from the start that the Giants had absolutely no chance of winning even one game. It turns out they never even had a lead. Knowing how their fans (and the SF media) were feeling was probably the biggest satisfaction I got out of the whole thing."

To me, these A's, men on a mission from day one, who found redemption under the most awkward—and awful—conditions, deserved a whole lot more than that. We all did. Especially my oldest sister.

Tonianne: "I don't remember celebrating. I do recall that all the kids got World Championship t-shirts for Christmas and that was the best! But the thing that sticks out about that Series is that when I needed it most, after the crappiest year of my life, I didn't get to enjoy it. I feel empty to this day."

The baseball world was void of one of its most colorful characters when Alfred Manuel (Billy) Martin, a Berkeley native and former A's manager, died in an auto accident on Christmas Day. On that day same day, Rickey Henderson, who thrived under Billy's style in the early 80's, "celebrated" his 31st birthday. Perhaps a fitting ending to the most bittersweet year in Oakland A's history.

By all accounts, the A's wouldn't have to wait too long to properly enjoy a World Series victory. With Rickey here from Day One and the team healthy to start the season, really, who was going to beat them? The champs won eight of their first ten and closed out April with impressive back-to-back shutouts. Stew beat Clemens (again) 1–0 and Welch blanked the Yanks. There was a lot of that going on in 1990: the A's swept the season series from New York, outscoring them 62–12 in their twelve games. Even when the A's lost, they entertained. On the eve of my 23rd birthday, they went up against a kid from Seattle, name of Brian Holman. The kid retired the first 26 batters he faced. One batter from immortality, he grooved one to pinch-hitter Ken Phelps, who drilled it into the right-field seats. One of the most confusing games I've ever attended. I mean, if you're going to lose, it might as well be a perfect game. History was made on June 11 as Nolan Ryan got what evaded Holman, except he walked two batters. Still, Ryan was carried off the field after his sixth career no-hitter. I won't lie; I cheered. It was amazing to watch. The Chicago White Sox were the only real challengers to the division title, but once the A's took back first place on July 8, it was theirs for good. The *Tribune*'s Dave Newhouse likened a day at the ball park to a trip to the candy store. Hmm, let's see, I'll take two of the Rickey Rolls, a Jose Smash N' Bash, and an Eck Saver. The numbers jump out at you like a 3-D movie. Canseco and McGwire combined for 76 homeruns and 209 RBI's. Mac's grand slam to beat Boston on August 15 made a 10-inning winner out of Stewart and gave the slugger thirty or more homeruns in his first four years. No one had done that before. Two nights later, Welch won his 20th game, making him the fastest to reach that mark in seventeen seasons. Stew got the best of Clemens once more for his 18th win (third against Rocket), and ten days later beat Minnesota for Number 20. It was his fourth straight 20-win season, and no pitcher since has come even close to approaching that feat. On June 29, he was part of a record-setting night when he threw a no-hitter at Toronto (a few hours later Fernando Valenzuela held St. Louis without a hit). Alas, Stew would find himself short on Cy Young Award votes as he did every other year, there was always one pitcher who did just enough to take it from him. This time it was his own teammate. Bob Welch, who had never posted seventeen wins in a single season, won a remarkable 27 games in 1990. That's an Oakland record. When you have a guy like the incomparable Eckersley closing out games, records are sure to fall. His own numbers bordered on the absurd: In 61 games (73-plus innings), Eck was 4–2, had more saves (48) than hits allowed (41), gave up just nine runs (five of them earned), and had a strikeout-to-walk ratio of 73-to-five (one was intentional). His ERA required a magnifying glass to read: 0.61. And then there was Rickey. He batted .325, led the league in on-base-percentage (.439), steals (65), and runs scored (119). Henderson also tied a career high with 28 homeruns. Ladies and gentlemen, your American League MVP. And for the third straight season, our Oakland A's led the Major League in wins (103) to run away with the team's ninth AL West title (Stew clinched it with a complete-game shutout for his 22nd win.) Next up: Boston.

The A's put on a pitching clinic to earn their second sweep of Boston in three years and their third consecutive trip to the World Series. They did it without hitting a single homerun in the series. Stew beat Clemens 9–1 in Game 1, followed by Welch's 4–1 victory the next night. Me and John skipped out on work for Game 3, won by Moore, 4–1. The Bash may have been absent but the A's were still plenty brash. Said **Canseco,** after the A's took a 3–0 series lead: "I'll say it's over. Use common sense." The next afternoon it was officially over, with Stewart besting Clemens, 3–1. One run allowed in each of the four games. Yikes. As for Stew-Clemens, it could hardly be called a rivalry. This was more like Roadrunner-Coyote. The Boston ace was ejected arguing balls and strikes during Oakland's three-run second while Stew pitched shutout ball into the ninth. Honeycutt came on to close and the A's were off to the Land of Milk and Honey.

And for the second time in three years, the unthinkable happened. It couldn't, could it? It didn't even take a miracle this time; this time we just got beat. What was this, "Revenge of the Seventies"? First the Dodgers, now the Reds. It wasn't even close. Stew started Game 1 against Jose Rijo. Rijo came to Oakland in the first Rickey trade and he was such a hit (17 wins, 22 losses) that we traded him after three seasons. Got Dave Parker in return, so it worked out for awhile. Rijo fit right in with the Reds and for the next six seasons, he was lights out. ERA under 3 every year. Meanwhile, Parker spent 1990 in total obscurity, well, in Milwaukee. Same thing. Not sure how much a difference he would have made in this Series anyway. But what the hell, we had Stew, our '70's Catfish, right? Riding a six-game post-season winning streak, he lasted four innings. Reds 7, A's 0. The next night, things start making sense again. (We watched this one at John's.) Jose hit a rocket to right and we jumped out to a 4–2 lead after three. Welch, our Cy Young, was dealing. But the Reds, they chipped away at it. They got one in the fourth and another in the eighth to tie it. Remember Mickey Hatcher from the '88 Dodgers? Well, the Reds had a Hatcher, too. Billy Hatcher. All he did was get seven hits in seven at-bats in Cincinnati. Which reminds me, if the A's had the best record for three straight seasons, why did they keep opening up playoff series' on the road? It took baseball forever to reward home-field advantage to the team with the best regular-season records. And they still don't have it right for the World Series. I know it sounds like an excuse, but it's not. The A's were head-and-shoulders above everyone, so they should have beaten the Reds no matter where they played. But I digress. Eck came on in the bottom of the tenth, and after getting the first out, gave up three straight singles. Ballgame.

The Series shifted to Oakland on Friday night and me and Rose got there late, just as Harold Baines' homerun reached the right-field seats. Baines, by the way, had come over in a trade with Texas in

August. That same day, we got Willie McGee from St. Louis. General Manager Sandy Alderson drew rave reviews for his shrewd moves. Three years later, Billy Beane would work as an assistant under Alderson, eventually taking over the reins. The A's rein as champs was about to come to an end as the Reds rocked Mike Moore for seven runs in the third inning, who left to a scattering of boos. Chris Sabo hit homeruns in the second and third innings and the Reds led 8–3. That's how it stayed as the A's were helpless—and hitless—against Cincinnati's vaunted bullpen. "The Nasty Boys" Norm Charlton, Randy Myers, and Rob Dibble kept the Bashers in check during nine innings of work in the Series. Outside the Coliseum, Rose fumed. Go to games all season long just to see it fall apart at the worst time. It just wasn't right. Game 4 pitted Stew against Rijo again. For the third straight game, we took an early lead. Stew was great. But in the eighth, they got to him. They didn't even hit the ball hard. But they got him for two runs. And that was that. Rijo gave up two hits. Two. We went 1–2–3 in the ninth. Carney popped up to first to end it. It was Carney who passed out shirts to his teammates in April that said, "Complacency Sucks. Stay Focused." Well, you don't win 103 games plus four in the playoffs by being complacent. But somewhere along the line, the fire burned out. La Russa had issues with his right-fielder who misplaced Hatcher's fly ball in Game Two. *Sports Illustrated,* in their World Series preview, had dissected ways for the Reds to pull off the upset, noting that "even if they do it, we'll be back next October trying to find ways to beat the A's." I wasn't so sure. Losing to the Dodgers was almost acceptable because it was our first time. The A's learned from that and you'd swear as long as they were healthy, 1988 would never happen again. But it did. For the first time since La Russa took over, I had no clue what to expect.

The 1991 season suggested that the rest of the baseball world had finally caught up to our A's. The division that they had dominated for three straight seasons was stronger than ever; not one of the seven teams in the American League West finished below the .500 mark. Three notable streaks came to an end. Stew went 11–11, far from the form that saw him win 20 games four years in a row.

McGwire slumped miserably (.201, 22 long balls, 75 RBI's), - easily missing the 30-homer mark that he had reached ever since he entered the league in 1987. And the only "A" in playoffs this year was the one stationed between the "L" and the "Y." Even Eck proved human. There were some bright spots. Rickey raced into the record books once more. Of his 58 league-leading steals, none was bigger than the one he swiped on May 1 against the Yankees. That afternoon, with Dad in attendance, he passed Lou Brock for all-time thievery with his 939th career stolen base.

In a trying season it was Jose Canseco—strangely enough—who was the most consistent. Strange because the former MVP had a history of off-field incidents that often overshadowed his play. They're all part of baseball lore (or is it, gore?); the speeding tickets, the loaded handgun, the 1–900 number, the late-night rendezvous with Madonna. Way too many things to mention here; this deserves its own book. (Oh wait, he already did that, didn't he?) For all his off-field hobbies—and we haven't even mentioned the "S" word yet—the A's made Jose the game's highest-paid player in June 1990. Which didn't sit all too well with La Russa and some of the players. Not when there were obvious "Jose Rules" for things like punctuality. But as long as Jose produced…and in 1991, he did that better than any player in an Oakland uniform. (A league-leading 44 homeruns to go with 122 RBI's.) Oddly, while the A's bit their lips, the paying customers voiced their displeasure. Perhaps they expected a 50–50 season with the fat contract he received the year before. In September, Canseco shot back at the fans with a "yea me or trade me" mantra, then one day later, hit a first-inning homerun *for* them. As he made his way back to the dugout he lifted his cap to the adoring crowd and for a split second, it felt like happy days were here again. But in the end it wasn't enough. Against the three teams that placed ahead of them—Minnesota, Chicago, and Texas—the A's were a combined 15–24. From three World Series appearances to fourth place, despite a respectable 84–78 record. And then to watch the Twins win their second title in five years; it was tough, man.

Any obituaries penned for the Tony La Russa era were slightly premature. No, the A's were going to give it one last push in 1992—their

25th season in Oakland—and they started off strong, winning their first five games. A rejuvenated Mark McGwire (no steroid jokes, please) was at the forefront of Oakland's resurgence, with five home-runs in the team's first six games. We lost a hard-fought one on my 25th birthday, in which Mom and Dad sent their wishes via the stadium message board. Pretty cool stuff. The A's flip-flopped with the Twins for the top spot the first two months of the season before having it all their own from June 2 through July 3. They spent three or so weeks chasing the Twins and were three out heading into Minnesota. In dramatic fashion, the A's swept the champs on their turf and left the Twin Cities tied for first. So who was the hero? Try Eric Fox. If you've never heard of him, you're not alone. Fox played 116 games in his career but he surely made his mark in that series. With the A's having won the first two games (in which Fox went 4-for-10), the young outfielder followed that up with a three-run 9th inning homerun to turn a 4–2 deficit into a stirring 5–4 win. I can still hear Bill King's voice on that one.

The year was an emotional ride on so many levels, and it all started with the strange surroundings of yet another right-field star traded away. It was after a 9–3 spanking of Boston that Carney Lansford had this to say: "First there are guys like Rickey Henderson and Jose Canseco. There there's everybody else." It's not far-fetched to say that even Rickey and Jose believed that. Rickey made a habit of showing up late to Spring Training and Jose's off-field antics are well-documented to a fault. Still Canseco continued to perform at a high level. Until this year. Which, in turn, gave the A's front office the out they had been seeking. Just one week after Lansford laid it on thick for the Cuban native, the brash Bash Brother was gone. I was at my brother-in-law's house and I had just turned the game on when I heard Bill King in a voice I did not recognize. He sounded in complete shock and utterly confused. Then the news: Jose Canseco had been traded. And not just during the game but while he was in the *on-deck circle*!

Tonianne: "I was never a huge Jose fan but I've never forgiven La Russa for the way he pulled him from the on-deck circle on the day he was traded. Jose didn't have any common sense, much less an ounce of class but La Russa stooped below the worst Jose-ism that day."

Rose: "Trish was there with Susan behind the bullpen and I was with Samantha in our seats. I knew something was going on by the action in the dugout and the buzz in the crowd. I actually said it was going to happen before it happened. Even though I grew not to like Jose, I still felt very sick that day. And seeing him on the news made me sicker. Samantha and I just sat there feeling sick. Trish and Susan were feeling the same way as us. I know the majority of the fans felt that way. They started leaving and so did we after one more inning. We ended up in Castro Valley and drowned our sorrows in ice cream."

The A's seemed lost that night and fell quietly to Baltimore, 4–0. One of their four hits was a single by Lance Blankenship, Jose's replacement that night. He also stole a base. That the A's would pull of such a stunner in the heat of a pennant race, seemed un-A's like, considering the sordid details. But often overlooked is the quality of players they received in return: starter Bobby Witt, reliever Jeff Russell, and outfielder Ruben Sierra. That was enough to get them over the hump. It seemed incredibly fitting that the A's clinched the American League West on a day they didn't even suit up. With Minnesota's loss to Chicago, La Russa's team won its fourth division title in five years. So much for the run being over. McGwire led the charges with 42 homeruns and 104 RBI's in just 139 games. While Stew was so-so (12–10), Mike Moore returned to '89 form (17–12) and ex-Met Ron Darling pitched in with 15 wins. Once again, the starters owed their success to Eck. In 69 games he earned a league-leading 51 saves and captured both the MVP and Cy Young Award. Only a handful of pitchers can make that claim and you might know two of them: Vida and Rollie (with Milwaukee). Fittingly, Rollie was enshrined at the Hall of Fame in 1992. Perhaps Eck had punched his own ticket to Cooperstown that season. One thing was for sure; it was because of him that the A's were back in the playoffs for the fourth time in five years. Toronto again.

I watched part of the first game at Mom's. We faced Jack Morris, the hero of the 1991 World Series (for Minnesota). In a game that would have made Jose Canseco proud, the A's bashed Morris for three homeruns. McGwire and Steinbach took him back-to-back in the second for a quick 3–0 lead. The Jays got one in the

fifth, one in the sixth, and one in the eighth to tie it. All three runs
came off Stew who was just outstanding in this one. As Dad
dropped me and Rocio off at my brother-in-law's house (where we
were staying at the time), I got him to come in to watch the ninth.
Good thing, too. Harold Baines led off the inning by crushing a
Morris offering into the seats and Eck came on to close out a hard-
fought 4–3 win as Dad and I exchanged hard high-fives. The next
night David Cone beat Moore 3–1 and the teams headed back to
Oakland knotted at a game apiece. The bats came alive for both
clubs in Game 3 with Toronto winning a 7–5 slugfest. We played
catch-up all afternoon, but couldn't break through with the big hit.
The next day, a Sunday, we watched the pivotal fourth game at
Ernie's house. This was one of those stinky-mouth games that La
Russa often talked about. Made worse by the heart-breaking manner in which we lost it. The A's rocked Morris again, to the tune
of five hits and five runs in a little over three innings. Through
seven, we had them, 6–1. With our bullpen? This thing was over.
But the Blue Jays showed how resilient they had become, a far cry
from the pushovers of '89. Roberto Alomar, on his way to the ALCS
MVP, led off the eighth with a double, his third hit of the day. Jeff
Parrett relieved Welch and promptly surrendered two singles, the
first of which plated Alomar. La Russa wasn't taking any chances
and brought in Eck, who gave up two more singles that scored two
more runs. 6–4. Then Eckersely got the next three to go down and
we breathed for a moment. The A's missed a chance in their bottom off with Blankenship getting thrown out at home, but we had
a two-run lead with three outs to go and surely the worst part was
behind us. Or so we prayed. After Devon White led off the ninth
with a single, the horror that we incurred in 1988 came back to
haunt us once more. As the shadows started to settle on the
Coliseum (supposedly to the pitcher's advantage), Roberto Alomar
took his place on the list of most despised opponents. He ripped
an Eckersley pitch into the right-field seats to tie the game and at
the same time he ripped out our hearts. Not again. Not to Eck.
Toronto won the game in the eleventh and we were one loss away
from elimination, and perhaps the end of an era in Oakland. But
Oakland was where Game 5 was played and Oakland-born Dave
Stewart was on the hill to give us one more day in the sun, with

pride in his heart and ice in his veins. I listened to the game at work as Stew closed out a gutsy 6–2 win, wondering if it was the last time. It was for 1992 as the Blue Jays won Game 6 by a 9–2 score to earn their first trip to the World Series, an event that had seemed exclusively ours for a while. The aftershocks came swiftly that October 14, as Carney Lansford called it quits. It took him forever to remove the uniform that last time. It was hard to say goodbye.

Goodbyes were in order just nine days later when Grandma Toni left us for a Better Place. She suffered so much in her last days but she greeted her visitors as best she could. Images of her in an A's cap ringing that bell, shaking her fists, and smiling after a win, well, those are what I take with me. She made an indelible mark on so many lives, mine included. Exactly one month after Grandma passed away, Don Jr., was born. I regretted that my only child would never meet his great-grandmother, but as my Mom cleverly reminded me, he'd still have a *great* grandmother. And of course, Mom was right.

I had trouble keeping up with everything. Two weeks after Don Jr. was born, Stew, our heart and soul, signed with Toronto. With the A's going in a new direction (the wrong one it seemed), Grandma Toni gone forever, and a bouncing baby boy to take care of, the times they were a-changin.'

In many ways for good.

16 / Awful Again (1993–1998)

*"Well, we committed twenty-four errors, and their
pitcher threw a no-hitter against us, but there is some
good news! Two of our runners almost managed to get
to first base, and we did hit seventeen foul balls!"*

—Alfred W. Lutter, portraying Ogilvie
in the 1976 hit, *The Bad News Bears*

Clearly our A's had seen better days. It started with Jose the
previous August, then Carney retired, and Stew signed with the
World Champion Jays. Walt Weiss was traded to Florida. Rickey
was shipped out again in July, joining Stewart in Toronto. McGwire
saw action in only twenty-seven games. Eck's ERA ballooned over
four. Oh yeah, this was the end of the era, alright. The A's finished
with a 68–94 record, and became the first team in league history
to go from first-to-worst in their division in successive seasons.
Even the good news was nothing more than a mirage: Reggie
Jackson entered the Hall-of-Fame in 1993…wearing a Yankee hat.
At year's end, we lost another star: Dave Henderson signed with
Kansas City. In six seasons with the A's he topped the twenty-homer
mark four times. But more than anything, we'd miss that wide gap-
toothed smile that made Hendu a fan favorite in Oakland. His
departure came two weeks after the "other" Henderson (yep,
Rickey) signed back on for his third go-around.

The 1994 season will go down as The Year Without a Series as yet
another work stoppage plagued baseball. It was also the year that
baseball divided itself into six divisions, rather than the four-group
format that had been in effect since 1969. In addition to the six

145

division winners making the playoffs, one wild-card from each league would earn a spot at the post-season table. But the strike changed all that in 1994 and there was no hurry to repeat the mess of '81, when there were first and second half "winners." Instead baseball kept from that embarrassment simply by canceling the playoffs altogether. There's a novel idea! Not since 1904 had there not been a World Series. The sport, it seemed, had hit rock bottom, and a quick glance at the American League West revealed even more ugliness: when play stopped on August 11, the A's were 51–62, just one game behind the first-place Rangers. In that regard, it was almost a good thing the strike hit when it did.

If 1993 was the end of the Tony La Russa regime, as we knew it, 1995 was the end, period. The season started late (April 26) thanks to the strike and the A's opened up against the defending champion Blue Jays. An old friend (Dave Stewart) was back on the hill with the A's but he looked plain old, as Toronto roughed up the 38-year old on its way to a 13–1 romp. On July 17 in Milwaukee, Stewart gave up seven hits and eight runs in two innings. Scott Baker, a San Jose native making his Major League debut, relieved Stewart and pitched 3–2/3 innings. We mention him here because his life in The Show lasted all of one game. Meanwhile, the man we came to call "Stew" called it quits that same day. There was some good news. Mark McGwire, healthy again (well, sort of) after a two-year hiatus, hit thirty-nine homers in 104 games. The A's, destined to a second straight last-place finish, actually had a chance at the .500 mark. They won their last six home games of the season to bring them to a 67–68 record. The finale, a 9–6 win over the Angels, had a "last-day-of-high-school feel to it," wrote Mark Purdy of the *San Jose Mercury News*. La Russa's contract was up and he would sign with St. Louis, taking pitching coach Dave Duncan with him. Rickey was on the move again, headed for San Diego. Eck was gone, too, soon to be reunited with his manager. Before long the Cardinals would be referred to as the "Oakland A's East." Perhaps caught up in the nostalgia of their final go-around in front of familiar faces, the A's lost their last nine games of 1995, all on the road. It wasn't exactly an exclamation point to an era, but as Purdy reported, they had already given their fans one last thrill at the Homecoming Dance. It was the kind of win we had grown accustomed to under the ownership of Walter A. Hass Jr., who restored Oakland's pride and power after buying the team in 1980. Sadly, and perhaps symbolically, Haas, 79, would not bear witness to La Russa's Last Stand; his long battle with cancer ended that very day, unbeknownst to anyone in the park until long after the game was completed. On that Wednesday afternoon, the 20th of September, Dennis Eckersely wasn't even supposed to pitch. Not with the A's winning 9–0 after eight. So the Fremont native reflected on an era gone by, an era of pumped fists, forearm bashes, and celebrations on the mound.…Then the phone rang as if to wake the closer from his dream and it was time to pitch. Pitch? The Angels had mounted an unlikely rally, closed it to 9–6 with a man on and one out. So Eck came on, like a hundred times before, to put the fire out. Double-play. Over. Afterwards he admitted pondering the finality of it all to Purdy. "Yeah, I was looking around and thinking about…" his words drifted off. Then the man who saved 320 games in an A's uniform made a sideways wave with his hand. The "goodbye" kind.

Baseball bid a permanent farewell to Charles Oscar Finley, who died on February 19, 1996, just three days short of his 68th birthday. Like Billy Martin before him, Finley was one of the game's most colorful and controversial men. The two came together briefly in 1980 as Finley made Martin his last managerial hire; shortly afterwards, he sold the team to the man who died just five months before him: Walter Haas Jr.

As the Beatles once sang, "You say goodbye, and I say hello," and it was a season of "hellos" for the Oakland A's in 1996. For the first time since July 1986, someone other than Tony La Russa was at the manager's post; Art Howe would lead the A's to a 78–84 record—good for third place—as baseball got in its first full season since 1993. Our closer was a 35-year old named William Howell Taylor. Better known as Billy, the second-year vet saved seventeen games. The roster was littered with never-were's; these players appeared in less than 150 games in their careers: Mark Acre (114), Willie Adams (25), Allen Battle (108), John Briscoe (102), Bobby Chouinard (111), Paul Fletcher (12), Webster Garrison (5), Doug Johns (116), Brian Lesher (108), Steve Montgomery (72), Kerwin Moore (22), Ariel Prieto (70), Dave Telgheder (81), and Steve Wojciechowski (34). There are at least five more players not mentioned here that I guarantee you never heard of. Shades of 1977–79. I could have inserted George LaHon in the middle of that mess, and you wouldn't have batted an eye. How did these guys even approach .500? It's shocking really. Their leader in wins was John Wasdin with eight, followed by Don Wengert and Carlos Reyes, with seven. Both of those fine pitchers lost more games than they won. Their team ERA was 5.20. Perhaps here's a clue how they managed to squeeze out 78 victories: them boys could hit. Leading the pack was a red-head named Mac. In 130 games, Mark McGwire, one of the last of La Russa's holdovers, led the league with 52 homeruns, a .467 on-base-percentage, and a .730 slugging average. Terry Steinbach, another old pal, made his last year in Oakland a memorable one with numbers he didn't come close to approaching in any other season: 35 bombs and 100 RBI's. Geronimo Berroa went for 36 and 106, making the middle of the lineup as formidable as anytime during the Bash days. Scott Brosius, who would gain more fame with the Yankees, joined the homerun derby with 22 (a career-high), while another future pin-striper (some guy named Giambi) hit 20 round-trippers.

If Art Howe had some pitching to go with his robust lineup, a return to the good old days might have been closer than we envisioned.

Make that a big "if." The A's took a huge step backward in 1997 (a year in which baseball introduced intra league play) and they reached into their past for some karma of the worst kind. Jose Canseco returned, but it wasn't the same warm and fuzzy feeling we had when Reggie came home. Yeah, the power was still there, 23 homers, but all other facets of his game were shadows of their former selves. Jose's season ended to injury in August and he was gone again, off to Toronto for one last Canseco-like season. Mac was gone, too, traded to St. Louis despite stroking 34 homeruns in 105 games. It was a desperate move by the A's, who needed pitching a lot more than an injury-prone slugger. Except for T.J. Matthews, who went 6–2 after the trade, the move proved disastrous, as the other two hurlers, Blake Stein and Eric Ludwick, appeared in a total of thirty-one games for the A's, while McGwire had 220 more homers left in his bat. A separate trade saw the team's other power hitter (Berroa) shipped out for more pitching but Jimmy Haynes (17–21 in Oakland) was not exactly the shot in the arm the A's had hoped for. Matt Stairs picked up some of the offensive slack (27 homeruns), but with their three big guns of 1996 playing for other teams by the following August, and with the team ERA actually worse than the year before, it was no wonder that Oakland stumbled to a 65–97 record, last in the American League West.

Behind the scenes lurked a man who would introduce a new way of thinking to the game of baseball, a man whose actions had little to do with what he felt in his gut. Billy Beane didn't do things on a hunch; no, his moves were *calculated*. For five seasons, he worked as an assistant to the mastermind that was Sandy Alderson. At the end of the 1997 season, Alderson stepped down and Beane assumed the role of general manager. Under his watch, the Oakland A's would be transformed into perennial contenders, despite playing with a slightly smaller bankroll than the league's upper echelon. He was a "can't miss" player who missed, but as the man in charge of the A's for the last decade, Beane has been right on target.

The A's improved by nine games in 1998, also known as Year One of the Billy Beane Project, but they still placed last in a division that had suddenly gone soft. The All-Star revolving door recycled another one, this time it was Rickey again, for the fourth and last (?) time. Can't blame a guy for wanting to play somewhere. For his part, Rickey played nearly a full season (152 games) and led the league in walks while capturing his twelfth stolen base title, *eighteen* years after his first. Amazing. Ben Grieve, with the sweetest swing in Oakland since, well, Rickey, earned Rookie-of-the-Year honors. While Matt Stairs hit one less homerun than the year before, his RBI total, um, "climbed" from 73 to 106. Jason Giambi came into his own with a solid season (27, 110, .295), and aptly filled the leadership void left by his friend McGwire. Oh, and a young-un named Tejada played in 105 games. But most importantly the A's had...ta-dah...pitching! Kenny Rogers (forgot he pitched for us, didn't you?) went 16–8 and was an absolute terror at home: 11–0, 1.96 ERA. Filthy. Jimmy Haynes and Walnut Creek native Tom Candiotti won eleven games each and Billy Taylor saved thirty-three. Meanwhile, the new general manager wasted little time showing off his Midas touch; with the second pick of the free-agent draft, the A's selected Mark Mulder. Little-by-little, the pieces were setting in place for a championship revival.

As A's fans, our family takes the cake. And we bake them, too.

My Uncle Dan (middle) hangs out in the bleachers with his buddies. Note the "Bucket O' Beer at their feet. (1973)

Two legends: My oldest cousin Jimmy, and Catfish Hunter (roped off area) in Anaheim. (1974)

My oldest brother Ernie Jr. enjoys a "suite" seat, while paying homage to Catfish Hunter. (2004)

My brother John (left) and my cousin Paul (right) pose with Reggie Jackson. (1970)

Tonianne and then A's manager, John McNamara. (1970)

My Dad raises his arm to meet Joe Rudi's glove at the National Baseball Hall of Fame. (1988)

That's me, admiring my new A's sweatshirt, with my name on the back. (1972)

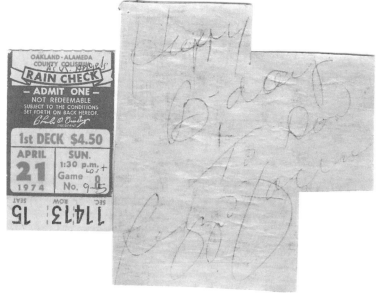

The game ticket stub and the birthday greeting of my baseball hero. (1974)

The Marquez 8 (minus Ernie Jr.) pose for Tonianne's high school graduation.

I'm the smiling brother, while Abel watches on. Must mean I got the sports page that day. (1977)

My cousins Nick (left) and Scott in the old bleachers. (1979)

A's star Rickey Henderson and my cousin Scott. (1980)

My six oldest nephews and nieces in their new World Champion A's shirts. Back l-r: Kimberly, Ernie III, Christina, Natalie. Front l-r: Stephanie, Patrick (Christmas 1989)

A's star Dave Stewart points my nephew Patrick towards the camera. (1989)

Tonianne and Patrick show off their Green and Gold at Disneyland. (1990)

Another game over, Tonianne takes Scott (foreground) and Nick up the bleacher steps. (1979)

My cousin Scott in the A's uniform that would get him on TV. (1980)

My cousin Scott agonizes over another defeat. Note the Red Sox fan smiling behind him. (1980)

My cousin, Nick.
(1980)

My niece Kimberly held by my
sister-in-law, Yong. (1981)

My cousin Rebecca shows off her
"AmaA'sing" shirt. (1982)

My nephew Patrick in his new A's
hat. (1987)

My nephews Patrick (left) and Aaron. (1989)

My niece Stephanie celebrates an A's win with my nephew Patrick. (1988)

Even as a baby, Don Jr. knew exactly who was Number 1. (1992)

Ernie Jr. holds Carrin on her Baptism. Not sure if the priest blessed the A's hat. (1992)

Dad holds my niece Jillian, while my god-daughter Brittany looks on in her A's shirt. (1994)

Tonianne and my youngest niece, Vanessa. (2002)

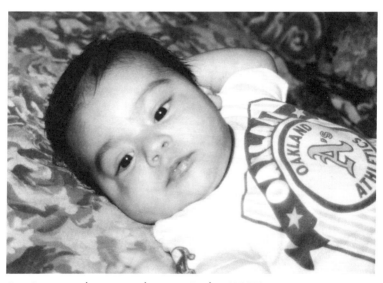

Scott's son, and my second cousin, Emilio. (1997)

My cousin Geoffrey sits on the Coliseum grass at A's FanFest. (2006)

The whole gang gathers for Breast Cancer Awareness Day. Tonianne is on far right. (2001)

Breast Cancer Awareness Day. (2005)

Aunt Marie with her youngest daughter, and my god-daughter, Liz at Breast Cancer Awareness Day. (2005)

Me with my god-daughter Christina, and my youngest sister Tricia, at Spring Training. (2004)

Don Jr. with my brother John after the Hall-of-Fame induction of Dennis Eckersely. (2004)

*My dad with my great-nephew
Nathaniel. (2006)*

*Christina's husband Greg holds
Ethan at my great-nephew's first
A's game. (2005)*

*My god-daughter Christina with her son, and my
great-nephew, Ethan.*

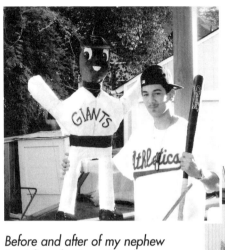

Before and after of my nephew
Patrick and a Barry Bonds
piñata. Yeah, we're sick. (2005)

Christina's husband Greg cleverly
shows his disdain for a certain East
Coast team. (2006)

Ethan prefers popcorn to peanuts and Crackers Jacks, but there's no denying who he is rooting for. (2006)

With the A's future looking bright, my great-nephew Nathaniel just had to wear shades. (2006)

l-r: My great-nephews Ethan and Nathaniel, and my nephew Xavier. (2006)

17 / Passing the Torch

"There are three things in my life which I really love: God, my family, and baseball. The only problem: once the season starts, I change the order around a bit."
—former ballplayer, Al Gallagher

Grandpa Abe's babes had long since finished having babes of their own. In fact his babe's babes were having babes…and so on. Good thing, too, because we needed someone to take the baton for the next great era of A's baseball. My four oldest siblings had the 70's, while the bottom half of the Marquez 8 took over for the Bash Years. All of us can say that we have seen our team win at least one World Series in our peak years as fans. Although most of the extended family's allegiances still reside with the A's, few members (for various reasons) have followed as closely us. It helps that they've been in our backyard all these years. But there are some; first one that comes to mind is Uncle Dan. He and Aunt Marie get out to a few games each year. Aunt Genie did the same with Uncle Paul before she passed away in '02, and their son Paul Jr., a mainstay in the 70's with John, Lenny, and David (the latter two Aunt Sue's oldest boys), still frequents the Coliseum today. Aunt Mac and Aunt Minda cast more than a casual eye on the goings-on of our beloved ball team. Aunt Minda's son Wayne, six months my senior, recently told me that he and his daughter Erin went to a handful of games this past season. Same for Aunt Joanne's son, John. Further proof that a great tradition has been passed on. Within our immediately family and Uncle Dan's, there are specific details that illustrate this even more.

Scott was born in May 1977 and his brother Nicholas followed some nineteen months later in December 1978. Uncle Dan's only sons got an early introduction to A's baseball, thanks to Tonianne, who began taking the boys to games when they were toddlers. She would pack peanut butter and jelly sandwiches for them and they would take their afternoon naps right there on those wooden benches. Sometimes she'd buy them hot dogs, even put in a special request for them: hold the bun. To me, even as we've drifted apart somewhat (time does that), they are—and always will be—my little brothers. (But don't get all teary-eyed, they're still punks.) After Tone stopped attending games on a regular basis, the boys would hang out with me at the Coliseum. And even though they're stuck on that one game when Canseco hit his 40th homerun, and I took my nieces instead of them, we had plenty of great times out at the ball park. On one occasion, Scott, who was maybe twelve at the time, was talking to a girl on one of the pay phones. (Wow, times have changed, haven't they?) As Nick and I waited (and probably teased him), a fight broke out on the field between the A's and the Indians. Me and Nick rushed toward the seats to get a better look and Scott soon followed, leaving the phone dangling. The poor girl had no clue what was going on. When the A's clinched the AL West in 2000, Nick gave us one of our greatest "increasers" with a called homerun. To quickly explain, "increaser" is the opposite of "buzz kill" (or as we call those, "*de*creasers"). So if you have a nice buzz going, and somebody says something to heighten that feeling, it's an "increaser." OK, yeah, so anyway, the A's had just gone ahead 2–0 on a Randy Velarde homerun in the eighth when Olmedo Saenz stepped into the on-deck circle behind Giambi, who would fly out to left. Nick, who was fourteen the last time the A's made the playoffs, was feeling it. We've all been *there* before. So he leaned over and told us that Saenz was going to hit one out. Sure enough, he crushed one. A no-doubter. And just like that, Saenz had "increased" the A's lead. I swear we have our own language. Although this next one came totally by accident. (Scott's going to get me for this.) Mom held a belated baby shower for Rocio in '92, so Dad and I paid Uncle Dan and the boys a surprise visit. Somehow we got around to talking about the 70's A's, and the three elders took turns shouting out player's names. "Reggie!" "Catfish!" "Vida!" Just then, Scott chimed in, and really it wasn't a bad call at all. "Bando!" Complete silence. Well, except for the crickets. And Nick's laughter. He was dying. And ever since that day, if you say something that you think is going to get a great response, or maybe a laugh, and it doesn't, it's a "Bando," folks. Poor Captain Sal. He deserves so much better. So does Scott. The boys are grown up now with boys of their own (Scott has Emilio, Nick has Nick Jr. to go with his step-sons Thomas and Tito, step-daughter Trevina, and daughters, Destiny and Mariah, my youngest god-child). Scott still gets out to games with me, though it's harder for Nick, living in Modesto. Nick claims to be more Raider fan than A's fan but it's all for show if you ask me. The Martinez brothers say that they got their competitive spirit and superstitious behavior from me, but I have no idea what they are talking about.

Uncle Dan's girls don't blame me for such things; then again they are little calmer when it comes to their teams. OK, except Liz and the Raiders; but she reminds me so much of Nick in that regard, we'll just blame him. Aunt Marie's eldest daughter Jessica is no stranger to the Coliseum confines. Neither is Rebecca (August '80) or Danielle (April '83) who attend a few games each year. To Scott and Nick's disappointment (at the time anyway), another girl was born to the Martinez household; Elizabeth, who came to us on October 7, 1986. And for me, a god-daughter. Little Liz, as I sometimes still call her even though she's twenty years-old, *definitely* has more Raider in her than A's, but I am working on that. She and Rebecca were at my house the night we clinched the West this past season and I am pretty sure a smile crossed her face. But bless her heart, she knows what the A's mean to me. After we lost Game 1 of the ALCS to Detroit, Liz sent an e-mail to console her Nino, and wish my team better fortunes in Game 2. I'll never forget that.

By the time Uncle Dan and Aunt Marie's youngest child was born, I had been an uncle myself, five times over. First is Christina, Ernie and Yong's oldest, born in Korea on September 22, 1979. The A's were mired in a 1–12 stretch at the time but picked Chris' birth date for their one win. And Matt Keough, who went 2–17 in '79, was the winning pitcher that day. Seriously, what are the odds? My oldest god-daughter has aptly handled the torch that was passed from Tone to Trish to her. She and her husband Greg have been my game partners for the last four seasons. (Their son, Ethan has joined us for the last two.) Christina is aching for a World Series to call her own; after all, it's her turn.

Christina's sister, Kimberly, came next for us, the second oldest niece, in October '81 (Matt Keough won on her birthday, too), then Carol gave us Natalie in September '83 (just one day before Mike Warren no-hit the White Sox). Ernie III was born in December 1984, the first grandson to Mom and Dad. Natalie's little sister followed in September 1985, as Stephanie graced us with her presence. On her 21st birthday, we celebrated with an A's game, and Bobby (or Bob-ay as Steph called him) Kielty delivered a present in grand style. When the redhead stepped to the plate, I pleaded with him to come through. "Come on, Bobby. I'll go to war for you." Steph, our little soldier girl, followed that up with, "Come on, Bob-ay! I *am* going to war for you!" That apparently was enough for Kielty, who crushed the next pitch into the right field seats for a grand slam. Just for the record, no A's player has *ever* hit a bases-loaded homerun on *my* birthday. Tonianne delivered Patrick to us in September 1987 (what's with all the Fall babies?), her and Michael's only child. Dave Stewart missed out on his 20th win that day; a year or so later, Stew and Patch would pose for a photo together. I've gone to only a few games with Patrick, mostly Breast Cancer Awareness Days, but I get a kick out of his reaction to my tales of the good old days. Gives him chills. Abel had his first child on October 14, 1990. Brittany Marie was born that day, my third oldest god-daughter. Just four days before the A's beat Boston to win their third straight American League pennant. Brit tells of a story when she was barley two and was at a game with her Mom. "I was yelling to Rickey Henderson at the top of my lungs (trust me folks, these are healthy lungs), 'Uncle Rickey! Uncle Rickey!' And I guess all the people around us gave me this look, like 'as if,' but I kept yelling anyway. And then Rickey turned around and waved, and Mom said that I couldn't stop smiling." Next in line was Carrin, born to John not in the Fall, but in February 1992. But me and Rocio went right back to autumn form with the birth of Don Jr. that November. When the babes of Abe (and Teresa) and John (and Jodie) are born in 2007, it will mark the first time since '92 that two grandchildren were born in the same year, (discounting the births of Xavier and *great*-grandchild Nathaniel in

'05.) Carrin may have not been able to provide a baseball story for me, but check out her picture on the day of her Baptism; yep, she's wearing an A's hat. As for my not-so-little son, well, baseball has yet to appeal to him the way it has his old man. But there is still time. Abel's second oldest, Jillian, came in—no kidding— September (1994), giving us four consecutive dates in which one of the grandchildren has a birthday: Stephanie (19th), Jill (20th), Patrick (21st), and Christina (22nd). Nikkole followed Jillian in October '98, and keeping in line with World Cup tradition, Abel's fourth (and Teresa's second) came four years after that, when Vanessa joined the family in May 2002. The four-year-between-kids streak ended in '06, as Abel and Teresa decided to go with an odd year in hopes of bringing in that elusive boy. Another streak came to an end on New Year's Day 2005, when John and Jodie gave us Xavier, the first grandson born to Mom and Dad since Don Jr. more than twelve years before. Xavier is sandwiched between two great-grandchildren, Christina's Ethan in December '04, and Natalie's Nathaniel in January '05. So after the girls ruled the Marquez roost (nine of the first twelve grandkids), we've had three boys in a row, with two to be decided in 2007.

Carol: "Nathaniel's first game was last year (2006) when Tone and Mike got the sky box for Patrick's graduation. I love it when we can enjoy an A's game as a family. Like when Tonianne participates in the Breast Cancer Awareness Days; thirteen years and counting for our survivor sister! We were all there together when she first participated. Remember when she directed traffic in the parking lot after one of the playoff games?

Nathaniel is like Xavier when he sees a ball game on TV, he always claps his hands and screams, "Yeah A's!" He also holds up his 'one' finger because I always tell him the A's are number 1."

John: "Xavier is a nut when it comes to watching baseball (doesn't have to be the A's) and playing it as he's watching. If he can't get his A's hat just perfect (he likes to wear it like Dwayne Murphy wore his), he'll wear it backwards, which is most of the time. He runs after every swing whether he hits it or not and will announce what's going on. He will then slide either feet first or head first. I have it on video because when he gets in front of people he won't do it unless he has a couple of hours to get comfortable.

He copies player's stances, bunts (he says, 'I bump it'), looks up and says, 'I got it!,' and says, 'You're out-a-dere!' One of the days that Nathaniel was over, Jodie had walked out of the room and heard Xavier screaming. She ran in thinking Nathaniel had bit him but all he was doing was trying to touch Xavier's A's cap."

(He sounds like a kid I used to know.)

As we move deeper into this decade, the next generation of A's fans looks healthy indeed.

18 / Economics 101 (1999-2003)

"Oakland has now increased its payroll to the point that it now ranks third in the Bay Area among all McDonald's franchises."
— Sandy Alderson, former A's general manager.

As has always been the case in Oakland A's history, there is that one "not-quite-there" year that sets the tone for greatness to follow. It's a unique pattern. When the A's captured the AL West crown with 101 victories in 1971, it followed a season in which they won 89. Before the '81 title, they went 83–79 in 1980. Preceding the first title under La Russa's watch in 1988, the A's posted an 81–81 mark the year prior. In all three instances, if you go back just four seasons before the championship flag was raised, you'll find a losing record: 1967 (62–99), '77 (63–98), and '84 (77–85). Tradition would hold true once more as Art Howe's team put it all together for one shiny, glimpse-of-the-future season. In going 87–75, the A's posted a winning record for the first time since 1992. Offensive starts were aplenty as three players hit more than 30 homers and drove in over 100 runs: Giambi (33, 123), Stairs (38, 102), and newcomer John Jaha (35, 111). The latter, a la Dave Kingman in 1984, won Comeback Player of the Year for his efforts. Giambi also hit .315 and walked 106 times; no A's player before him had provided such all-around skills at the plate. The pitching staff kept up with the offense for a change; although Gil Heredia led the team with just thirteen wins, he had plenty of support: TJ Matthews (9–5), Omar Olivares (7–2), and Kevin Appier (7–5, after arriving in July from Kansas City via a trade). But the guy that everyone was talking about, our Catfish in-waiting, was a 6'0", 160-pound righty from Columbus, Georgia named Tim Hudson. In his very first start,

157

on June 8 in San Diego, he pitched five innings and struck out eleven batters. Five days later, he earned his first big-league win, with seven solid frames against the Dodgers. In his nineteen other starts of 1999, Hudson pitched into the sixth inning in all but two of them. On September 10, he ran his record to 10–1 with 7–2/3 innings at Tampa Bay. The victory was symbolic, as it came one day after Jim "Catfish" Hunter lost his bout with Lou Gehrig Disease. He was 53. Hudson finished the year with eleven wins against just two defeats.

With Jason Giambi leading the offensive charge, and Tim Hudson heading a young and talented pitching staff, A's fans had reason to expect great things entering the new decade.

The A's got off to a slow start in the year 2000, something that would become as much their trademark in this decade as their scorching summers and their autumn heartbreaks. They began the season 8–12, and as late as May 29, owned a losing record (at 25–26) with their next two games at Yankee Stadium. New York had rediscovered the magic that was missing since the late 70's, having won the two previous World Series, thereby putting a stamp on 212 regular season victories. But the A's stuck it to the champs, winning two straight at the Babe's Crib, and avoided the wrong side of the .500 mark for the remainder of the season. Take note, boys and girls; this is what we call a "turning point." Like they say in the Big Apple, "Start spreading the news." The A's returned home and beat up the National League West seven out of nine times, then went on a 5–1 trek through Minnesota and Kansas City (losing only the first game). Winning their first four back in Oakland brought their season-high streak to nine and when the dust had finally cleared, the A's had used their two victories against the Yankees as a nifty 20–4 springboard. During that span, they scored ten runs or more six times, including a 21–3 football romp at Kansas City. There was no shortage of swingers on these Swingin' A's. Only these guys didn't swing at each other. Hardly. Theirs was more a frat house than a clubhouse, with blaring music and remote-control car races. Still, some of them surely looked the part of their 70's namesakes. Jason Giambi adorned the cover of *Sports*

Illustrated as "The New Face of Baseball"; his scraggly hair, bulging muscles, and full-length tattoos for all the world to see. So maybe Jason wasn't the kind of guy you brought home to meet the folks, but he was plenty adored by the home folks. His 43 home-runs led this new band of bashers, and his cohorts followed suit; Miguel Tejada (30), Ben Grieve (27), Eric Chavez (26), and Matt Stairs (21) all hit twenty or more round-trippers.

Art Howe's underpaid overachievers cooled off as summer heated up, but they did manage to avoid a sweep at Pac Bell Park with a 6–2 win in the series finale on July 15. The Giants' new home drew rave reviews in its first year of existence, but as A's ads cleverly pointed out on billboards throughout the Bay Area, "While they were building a stadium, we were building a team." One of the key pieces of Oakland's architectural plans was Barry Zito, who won big in his big-league debut (10–3 over the Angels) on July 22. Another was Mark Mulder, who threw seven shutout innings at the Halos the very next night. Not to be outdone, Tim Hudson beat Seattle three nights later to run his record to 11–3. The trio quickly formed a friendship off the diamond; on the field, they fed off each other's success. All the while they drew the attention of adolescent girls everywhere. Chicks may have dug the long ball, but apparently they dug guys who kept the ball in the park, too.

The A's went through one more tough stretch: a six-game losing streak in August, in which they were outscored 56–17. But from there, they went on a tear, winning thirty of their last forty-seven games. It was all so unexpected, which is what made it so exciting. Nowadays, you just wait for the A's to get hot; you know it's coming, you just don't know when. But that year, it came out of nowhere. On August 12, they were looking up at the Seattle Mariners, owners of a seven-game lead in the AL West. But the M's swooned as the summer came to a close, and the A's, despite going 8–10 to finish August, entered the stretch run just 2–1/2 games out of first. Then Jason Giambi did what crunch-time players do: he took over. On September 2, the slugger embarked on a thirteen-game hitting streak. He homered seven times during that stretch, with a pair of two-homer games. Against Tampa Bay on September 15, he went 3-for-4 and collected seven RBI's. In the last eight games of the season, JG hit five homeruns and had eleven ribbies. He raised his average fourteen points in September from .319 to .333. Simply put, the dude strapped the A's on his back for a month and had a certain fan/writer showing his appreciation with a three-letter salute. I was at a late-season game with Scott and Nick, and after another Giambi homerun, I started chanting "M-V-P." My cousins, well, they sort of laughed at that, but I kept up with it. Before long, it caught on with the crowd, and soon everyone was singing the same tune. It was beautiful.

Tim Hudson proved to be Giambi's equal as the A's found themselves involved in two pennant races, the division and the wild-card. Huddy was lights out starting on August 28 when he tossed a stirring one-hitter at the White Sox. I remember watching this one on TV, and as Huddy masterfully set down the Sox, announcer Greg Papa was going nuts in the booth. He loved calling Hudson by his nickname and that night Papa put a little extra on it. "The Stinger has got it going on tonight!" That night began a season-ending, seven-game winning streak for the new ace of the A's.

To say our boys were clicking on all cylinders would toe the line of all-time understatements. Pitching and hitting came together like a scrumptious combo meal. Super sized, of course. In that last month, the A's won games by scores of 8–0, 10–0 (twice), 11–0, 10–3, 12–3, and 17–3. In their last road series of the season, they went into Seattle for a crucial four-game set, and left town having won three of four. Quite possibly the division was won right there. Back home for seven games to close out, the A's won six; their only loss a 14-inning defeat. On that last Friday of the season, I was there to see Giambi hit his 42nd homer ("M-V-P!") as we inched closer to the playoffs with a 7–5 win. The next day I took Don Jr. to the Halloween store instead of the game, but Abel beeped me on his Nextel with some news that was positively frightening. In a good way. The first four batters had reached base in our half of the first, and from there, Abe kept on calling me as the A's played ring-around-the-Rangers. Terrence Long hit a bases-loaded double to make it 7–0 and Randy Velarde followed with a two-run homer. Nine runs in the first! Abel called again after the last out. "I'll let you hear the fans." I actually had people stop and look at me in the store as the roar of the crowd filtered through my Nextel. Chillsville. The A's weren't even close to finished; they struck for five in the fifth and eight in the seventh en route to an astounding 23–2 shellacking. A loss by Seattle that night would clinch the division for the A's but I secretly hoped the Mariners would win (they did) to set up Huddy on Sunday. A game I wasn't about to miss. Oh and there we all were in one place, three generations hooked on A's. That day at the Coliseum were all three of my brothers, my youngest sister Tricia, Uncle Dan, my cousins Scott and Nick, my nephews Ernie III and Patrick, my nieces Christina and Stephanie, Scott's son Emilio, and Don Jr. The Stinger was on the hill going for a rare double: his 20th win and an A's title. I don't know if Scott or Nick or Christina realized it at the time, but they were about to discover what it was like to have Catfish or Stew in a big game. Hudson was brilliant, just brilliant. In eight innings of work, he gave up four hits, walked two, and struck out ten. The A's got one in the seventh thanks to the lesser known Giambi. Jeremy doubled and scored on Ramon Hernandez' single. When Velarde and Saenz did some eighth inning yard work to make it 3–0, it was only a matter of time. Jason (Izzy) Isringhausen came on to close, and the next thing I knew, John had his arms wrapped around me. It was one of my biggest thrills as an A's fan, watching this little-known, low-budget team win the West, and to be surrounded by so much family made it even sweeter.

The last time I had been to a playoff game was Game 3 of the 1990 Series. But the A's were back (after an eight-year layoff) and so was I. And wouldn't you know it but we drew the World Champion Yankees in the first-round. The A's actually posted a better record than New York during the season and were awarded home-field advantage. The first game was on a Tuesday, barely 48 hours after the division was won. Me, Scott, Nick, and a few of their friends got third-deck seats. The Yankees scored first and had an old friend—Roger Clemens—on the mound against us. Different decade, same results. The A's chased the ageless All-Star with three runs in the fifth and one in the sixth on their way to a 5–3 win. We were back the next night for Game 2, the little brothers and I, and some co-workers. But Andy Pettitte made sure we went home with just a split after putting the handcuffs on our lineup for most of the night. Mariano Rivera closed out the 4–0 victory and it was on to the Big Apple. On one hand, I felt pretty good about things. We were going to New York at one game apiece, but we had gotten there with Gil Heredia and Kevin Appier pitching in Oakland. Now it was Huddy's turn, and after that, Zito, who went 7–2 in his rookie year and easily had the team's best ERA among starters (2.72). Hudson pitched well enough to win Game 3 but when your team makes almost as many errors (two) as they have hits (four), it makes it tough to get the "W." The Yankees won it 4–2 and sent Clemens out against Zito to wrap up the series. But a funny thing happened on the way to Elimination Day; the bats came alive for Barry, and the A's rocked the Rocket for a stunning 11–1 triumph that tied it up at two and sent the teams back to Oakland for all the marbles. I didn't have tickets to Game 5; in fact I went to the Raider-49er game that afternoon in San Francisco. By the time I reached my friend's car after Tim Brown hauled in the winning touchdown in overtime, the Yankees had lit up Heredia for six first-inning runs. All things being equal, I would have preferred Hudson in that situation. But because we needed him just to get into the playoffs, he was only available for one game in this series. The A's, for their part, didn't go quietly. Not right away anyway. They sent Pettitte to the showers in the third by laying ten hits and five earned runs on him. When I reached my house, it was 7–5 after four. And that's how it stayed. Against the vaunted Yankee bullpen, the A's managed three hits.

The 2000 season itself was a huge success. They had gone the distance with the champ, and with a young nucleus of players coming back in 2001, this was only the beginning of another great era in Oakland A's history.

Baseball purists (at least those partial to a certain green-and-gold colored team) who had frowned upon the current playoff format since its inception in 1994, finally found a reason to accept it. Because this would be the year that their A's only shot at a post-season berth would be as a (cough it out, old-timer), *wild-card*. In Seattle, once home to Alex Rodriguez, Ken Griffey Jr., and Randy Johnson, the Mariners showed that they were still a pretty good ball club without three future Hall members. In 2001, they were historically good. But while the M's burst out of the gate in April, the defending champion A's had trouble just getting the latch open. They started the season 2–10. You know things are going bad for the good guys when Roger Clemens beats them. Which he did to close out the first month, dropping the A's to 8–17, and a whopping twelve games behind Seattle. That Art Howe's Fun Bunch finished the season fourteen games out isn't the story; it's that the A's kept up with the Mariners' incredible pace the rest of the year. To put that in perspective, here are two teams that didn't: Anaheim and Texas, who finished 41 and 43 games out, respectively. After a heart-breaking, extra-inning loss in Toronto dropped the A's to a season-high ten games under .500, the champs turned it around in record style, posting the most wins and largest margin of victory by a wild-card team. Once again, Jason Giambi led the resurgence. The reigning MVP may have been even better (and was surely more valuable) in 2001. "G" batted .342, with 38 bombs, and 120 ribbies. He also led the league in doubles (47), walks (129), on-base percentage (.477), and slugging (.660). On a team that meticulously studied a player's worth and saw value in previously unexplored numbers (like pitches per at-bat), Giambi was a statistician's dream. But his monster season wasn't enough to beat out Ichiro for the MVP crown. (You could hardly blame the voters on that one; his Seattle team *did* win a record-tying 116 games.) On the other side of the A's infield were two young, Latin players coming into their own. Third basemen Eric Chavez (32 home runs, 114 RBI's) and Miguel Tejada (31, 113) gave the A's a solid triple threat. The trio was particularly robust in a thrilling 4–2 win over the Yankees on August 12. Having won ten straight games (including five on the homestand, against Boston and New York), the A's shocked the three-time defending champions with a little bit of Yankee magic. Miggy and Chavy hit back-to-back homers in the fifth to make it 2–0, and after the Yankees tied it in the eighth, Giambi faced Mike Stanton with two outs and a man on in the ninth. I watched this one at home as Jason worked the count full, fouling off a few pitches until he got one to his liking. And when he did, he crushed it high and deep into the right-field stands. Bedlam.

If the A's could boast of their fearsome threesome in the middle of the lineup, they could be equally proud of their Big Three on the mound: Tim Hudson, Mark Mulder, and Barry Zito. Having chased the .500 mark for the first half of the season, Oakland finally reached—and surpassed—that point heading into the All-Star Break. In a sparkling three-game sweep of the Arizona Diamond-backs, the A's, you could say, were up in arms. Mulder set the tone on Friday night by retiring the first twenty-one batters. (To illustrate my sometimes-superstitious behavior, I did not move from my bed until the 'Backs got their first hit. It didn't matter that I had to go to the bathroom during the last four innings.) Mulder "settled" for a stirring one-hit shutout. In the A's aces' little game of "anything you can do, I can do…just as well," Hudson matched his teammate's complete-game performance the next night, allowing a meaningless ninth-inning score in a 5–1 win. Then it was Zito's turn. The second-year southpaw faced off against Curt Schilling, who four months later would help bring Arizona its first World Series title. Zito was up to the task but plenty, as he left after six innings with a 2–1 lead and ten strikeouts on his time sheet. Three A's relievers—no doubt starving for action—closed it out. Three games, two runs allowed by the amazing trio. When play resumed after the break, Mulder pitched his second consecutive complete-game shutout with a 6–0 blanking of the Dodgers. Fifteen days later, he did it again, handcuffing the Royals on four hits. During the eleven-game winning streak in early August, the Big Three combined for almost as many wins (6) as they did runs allowed (7). Mulder was kind enough to share his can of Run Remover with fellow lefty Zito; in four starts from August 9th through the 30th, Barry blanked Boston (6–0) and Cleveland (9–0), and pitched six shutout innings at Baltimore. After an 8–6 loss at Tampa Bay to open the season's final month, the A's went on another winning streak. Zito's complete-game 4–2 victory, in which he struck out ten Rangers, made it eight in a row. It came on the evening of September 10, 2001.

The next day, Tuesday, September 11, our world as we knew it, changed forever. Although it is appropriate to mention that fateful day, to attempt to do so in detail is not. I can tell you where I was and what I was doing, as can everyone else, but to write how the physical tragedy affected me some three thousand miles away, doesn't seem right. Sports, as it had done through other tragic moments, took its proper place, first as an afterthought, then as a diversion and a return to normalcy.

Baseball made an emotional return on September 17, with the A's taking the field one day later. They immediately picked up where they left off, winning their ninth game in a row. After splitting their next two at Texas, they swept a six-game homestand to run their September record to 16–2 (they'd finish the month 17–4, a year after posting a 22–7 record). It was on Sunday, September 23 that Mark Mulder won his 20th game and sent the A's back to the play-offs (as a wild-card) at the same time. It also completed a three-game sweep of Seattle; overall the A's took nine out of nineteen against the Mariners. Afterwards, Art Howe led his team on a lap around the Coliseum to shake hands with their faithful. I was at home wishing I was in Oakland. The A's won their last six games and closed the books on the regular season with a 23–3 flurry. So they didn't catch Seattle but there was no catching them either; their 102 wins outdistanced every other team in the league by at least seven games. The downside to their wild-card standing? Starting on the road against the World Champion Yankees, despite owning a better record.

I remember those first two games very well, me and Scott watching them in the back room of my old house in Hayward. Johnny Damon, long before his cult hero days, got it going in the very first inning with a single, a stolen base, and a run scored on a sac fly by Giambi. These A's weren't supposed to play "Billy Ball." But there was Damon, doing like Rickey used to. And against our favorite whipping boy, Clemens. Damon was a pain in the ass all night, with four singles and a walk in five trips to the plate. In the fourth, Terrence Long hit a rocket off the Rocket and the A's had a 2–0 lead. Clemens' night ended after a lead-off walk to Giambi in the fifth when his hamstring tightened up on him (yeah, right). When Jason led off again in the seventh, he faced off against reliever Sterling Hitchcock. Sadly for New York, this at-bat carried little suspense, as the slugger sent Sterling's Mr. Spalding high into the upper deck. Then in the eighth, T-Long went long again to make it 5–1. After a shaky outing by Jim Mecir brought the champs to within 5–3, Izzy slammed the door with a 1–2–3 ninth to preserve the win for the A's and Mulder. A huge win reminiscent of 1988 in Boston. Game 2 was delayed by President Bush's emotional speech but the A's kept their focus. Huddy paired off against Andy Pettitte, and The Stinger was masterful. With just one run to work with, the lanky right-hander pitched eight shutout innings, allowing just six singles and a walk. The A's struck for one more in the ninth and Izzy nailed down the 2–0 win, as me and Scott hugged and our phones rang into the night. The whole family was there for Game 3, the night that we were going to put an end to the Yankee Dynasty. Before they announced the starting lineups, a video tribute to our amazing A's was shown as The Who's *Baba O'Reilly* blared over the PA system. I got chills just watching it, and I couldn't help but think that maybe the kids were more than alright; maybe they were all grown up and ready to move on. But a lesson was learned that night, of Yankee aura, and perhaps of destiny. I went to the bathroom after the A's went down in the fourth so I didn't even see Jorge Posada take Barry Zito deep for the game's only run. The next batter doubled, but Barry gave up no other hits in his eight innings on the mound; in the biggest game of his life, he had done more than we had hoped for. Meanwhile the A's posed little threat to Yankee starter Mike Mussina. Aside from the fourth inning when they had back-to-back singles, the A's were hitless through six. Then came the fateful seventh. Everything happened so damn quick. A pop-up to the shortstop, a fly ball to center, and then a two-out single by Jeremy Giambi. The crowd stirred, hoping for anything. Terrence Long ripped a ball down the right-field line and when Shane Spencer threw wildly towards home, it looked as if we were going to have a tie game. Do I really have to tell you the rest? Derek Jeter came out of nowhere to cut the ball off, flipped behind him to home plate and Posada tagged out Giambi, who tried to score standing up. It was a bang-bang play that ultimately took the bang out of the A's. With two outs and a man on second in the ninth, Jason's younger brother had a shot at redemption, but he grounded out to second to end it. As my family filed past me, I stared in disbelief at the playing field, shaking my head at the missed opportunity. Finally, **Mom** came up behind me. "Come on Don; it's over." And two days later, it really was. Oh, we went back (me, John, and Scott) the next day but the air had been let out of our A's. Corey Lidle was roughed up for six runs in a little over three innings and the Yanks tied up the series with a 9–2 win. The telling blow came in the third inning when right-fielder Jermaine Dye hit a foul ball off his leg. Dye, who had driven in 61 runs in 59 games after Beane traded for him in July, broke a bone and was lost for the season; a season which, incidentally, ended one day later. The A's put up a fight, jumping on Clemens yet again. Damon doubled in the first and scored on the elder Giambi's single. In the second, Long doubled and scored on the *younger* Giambi's single. But the champs scored two to tie it, and added a single run each in the third and fourth innings. Jason Giambi singled home a run to make it 4–3 in the fifth but he showed frustration towards Miguel Tejada for not taking third base on the play. Once again the inexperience of the A's proved costly as Eric Chavez hit a long fly ball that would have easily scored Tejada and tied the game at four. Afterwards, the former MVP scolded the future MVP in the dugout. In his last game as an "A," Giambi showed off his leadership skills at the plate, too: 4-for-4, with two RBI's. His single leading off the eighth against Yankee Savior Mariano Rivera was the A's last hit of 2001. Afterwards, New York celebrated the 5–3 win with hugs, tears, and one huge sigh of relief. Up until Arizona shocked the Yankees in that year's World Series, no team in four years had posed a bigger threat to their supremacy than the young squad from Oakland. It was a tiny consolation considering how close the A's were to dethroning the world champs, but once the hurt wore off, we looked excitedly towards another season.

And then just two months later came the kick to the groin. Our MVP, our leader, our star power, our *Reggie*, went to the dark side. Jason Giambi, who was so much a symbol of the A's-Yankee rivalry, a Hair to their Squares, decided to shed his Samson look for Steinbrenner's hard, cold cash. We had seen our heroes leave before. Reggie, Rickey, Jose. But all of them had been traded away. This was Catfish-like, but at least Catfish had just cause. No this was a betrayal of the highest order, and rather than seal his newfound earnings with a kiss, Giambi kicked dirt on the team that had admired him, and the town that had supported him. In training camp, he told his new Boss, "Here we don't rebuild, we reload." And in an appearance on David Letterman, he gave his top ten reasons for skipping town, one of them being, "Have you ever been to Oakland?" Yeah, he was officially one of *them* now. But according to my youngest sister, there would be a steep price to pay for the millions of dollars that he'd earn.

Tricia: "Rickey, Armas, McGwire, Stew, Eck; for those guys I was definitely heart broken. As for Giambi, I was just *pissed*. Hence the curse that I put on him and the Yankees. He will not get a ring before we do."

The A's would soon discover that life without Jason Giambi would not be that much different than life *with* the tattooed slugger. They would learn that 30-homer, 100-RBI men were a dime a dozen in the land of inflated long ball totals. Clearly they realized that the key to their success remained, as it always has, in their pitching. Namely that three-headed monster called HudsMuldZito. While the trio of Catfish Hunter, Ken Holtzman, and Vida Blue are the last teammates to win twenty games in the same season, this version of the Big Three put a new twist on the number that every starting pitcher strives to reach. Huddy got there on the last day of the 2000 season and Mulder accomplished the feat in 2001. In '02, it was Zito's turn, giving the A's three different 20-game winners in consecutive seasons. Barry was better than good in this, his third year; he was "barry" good. With a 23–5 record and a 2.75 ERA, Zito won the award that had evaded his playmates the previous two seasons: the Cy Young.

At the plate, everything began and ended with Miguel Tejada. Like Barry Zito, who led the league with thirty-five starts, Miggy was as durable (he played in all 162 games) as he was dominant. Although he didn't work the count nearly as well as his former teammate, the free-swinging Dominican was positively Giambiesqe, with a .308 average on 204 hits (including 30 doubles and 34 homeruns) and 131 RBI's. And he had every bit of Jason's flair for the dramatic. Like Giambi two years before, Tejada earned his Most

Valuable Player honors with plenty of late-season magic. Miggy had some help, most notably from Eric Chavez, who tied Tejada for the club lead in homers, while driving in 109 runs. Chavy also earned his second straight Gold Glove following another stellar season at the Hot Corner.

Any concerns about life A.G. (After Giambi) were squelched with an unusually fast start, as the A's went 15–11 in the season's first month. That was quickly negated by a poor showing in May, and the team fell nine games behind Seattle as summer approached. But for a team under the weather (not to mention a game under .500), better days were on the way in the form of one hearty spoonful of National League medicine. A 6–2 loss to the Giants on June 15 was the only blemish during a fifteen-game stretch as the A's sandwiched two seven-game winning streaks around that one defeat. After feasting on the Senior Circuit, Art Howe's club found itself twelve games to the plus side on June 23, and upon winning the first two of a three-game set at Yankee Stadium in mid-August (including a 16-inning marathon), the A's reached their peak (for the moment) at nineteen games over the .500 mark.

On August 13, the Oakland A's snapped a modest two-game losing streak with a 5–4 win over Toronto before 17,466 fans at the Coliseum.

The next afternoon, more than 40,000 sun-soaked spectators watched Eric Chavez spark a 4–2 victory with a three-run bomb in the first. After a day off, the Chicago White Sox came to town. Corey Lidle, fresh off back-to-back starts in which he didn't give up a run in fifteen innings of work, made Jermaine Dye's second-inning homerun stand up with seven more goose eggs in a 1–0 thriller. For a while it seemed as if Art Howe was pulling a hero out of a hat each night. Mark Ellis' three-run jack made a 9–2 winner out of Mulder (eight innings, five hits, one earned run), and Terrence Long helped finish off the Sox sweep with two homeruns in a 7–4 win. Chicago played six games at the Coliseum in 2002 and lost them all, while being outscored, 49–17. As the Green and Gold took to the road, another pending work stoppage loomed. But for the time being, there was just no stopping these amazing A's. Huddy stifled Cleveland, 8–1, and Chavy collected five RBI's with a homerun in the first and ninth innings. The third baseman was at it again the next day with another two-run shot in the first to spearhead a 6–3 win. Meanwhile David Justice, acquired from New York during the off-season, sprinkled a little Yankee aura on for good measure. As legend has it, the right-fielder kept telling his teammates before each game something to the effect of, "We can't sweep the road trip if we don't win today." Not wishing to disappoint the veteran leader, the A's, well, they just kept on winning. And Justice did his part, too, with a sixth-inning, bases-loaded triple that put the finishing touches on a 6–0 masterpiece by Lidle. The Hollywood-born starter gave an Oscar-like performance, allowing only a single and a walk (both with two outs in the first inning) to run his scoreless streak to 31 innings. Mulder finished off the four-game dusting of Cleveland with a 9–3 win. On to the Motor City. For the second time during the streak, Zito was the beneficiary of a two-homer game by an A's player not necessarily known for his pop. This time it was John Mabry turning the trick in a 9–1 romp at Detroit. Ten in a row and showing no signs of slowing down. Homeruns by Chavez, Justice, and Long provided ample support for Hudson the next day as the A's scored four in the first, four in the second, and three in the third. The juggernaut rolled on, 12–3.

When the Detroit Tigers jumped out to a 7–2 lead after four innings on Sunday, August 25, it looked like Defeat had finally come knocking on Oakland's door. But the A's left her standing on the porch, as they struck for nine runs over the final three innings and escaped town with a 10–7 win and their streak intact. In Kansas City, Lidle saw his scoreless stretch snapped but he was still plenty strong (seven innings, one run, three hits) in a 6–3 taming of the Tigers. With Mulder on the hill, Justice hit another homerun and rapped out three hits for the second straight game as the A's won 6–4 for their fourteenth straight win, tying the '88 club for the longest run in Oakland history. The streak officially became "The Streak" on getaway day when Zito took advantage of a six-spot in the first and carved out a 7–1 gem. Miguel Tejada (yeah, you were waiting for his name to pop up again, weren't you?) gave a glimpse of what was to come when he hit his only home run of the road trip. Up to this point, Miggy had somehow avoided the spotlight; while his teammates came up big in crucial spots, he "quietly" hit

.413 with fourteen runs and nine RBI's during the three-city tour. As for the A's, they made good on the challenge set before them by David Justice: an absurd ten-game sweep away from home and a team record fifteenth consecutive win. Coming back home, one had to wonder if they had anything left for an encore.

When the first-place Minnesota Twins arrived at the Coliseum on Friday, August 30, they must have thought it was October, with the amount of media that had set up camp there. It wasn't just the opposition that wanted a piece of the streaking A's. Both teams scored a run each in the first and second innings but Chavez came through with a two-out single in the fifth to plate Ramon Hernandez, and back-to-back doubles by Ray Durham and Scott Hatteberg sealed the 4–2 win for Hudson. The next game, a rare Saturday night affair, showcased some of the drama that had been curiously missing during this incredible ride. Me and Scott watched this one at home as the A's scored two in the first, went up 3–1 on Chavy's seventh-inning blast, then fell back into a tie when Minnesota rallied for a pair in the eighth. The A's mounted a threat in their bottom half and when Tejada was intentionally walked to load the bases, Chavez came through once more. His sizzling single up the middle scored two, and while 42,000 fans went nuts at the Coliseum, me and Scott delighted in Art Howe's reaction on TV: whistling and excitedly pointing out to Chavez at first base. What a scene. The 6–3 win concluded an eye-popping 24–4 August. As the calendar turned to September, The Streak stood at seventeen games. And on that first day of the ninth month of 2002, the family gathered in Tracy at Abel's house for Vanessa's baptism. Miggy got things going with a two-run jack in the third. Torii Hunter touched Mulder for a two-run job in the sixth to tie it. Undeterred, the A's got the lead right back when Mabry led off the bottom half with a homerun. An insurance run was added that inning and the 4–2 lead held into the ninth. Then disaster struck. Not once, not twice, but three times. Matt LeCroy and Corey Koskie hit back-to-back homers and in the blink of an eye, the game was tied. Billy Koch replaced the beleaguered Mulder and quickly got two outs. We breathed a little. Then Michael Cuddyer sucker-punched us with a rocket into the bleachers to make it 5–4. The only thing heard amid the utter silence at the Coliseum was the Twins celebrating their unfathomable comeback. Back at Abel's house, some talked of finding a way to get Tejada up again. Me and Scott agonized in the kitchen. Facing closer Eddie Guardado to start the ninth, Ramon worked a walk, and Durham followed through with a single. The pacing in the kitchen increased, with quick, nervous glances at the TV. Olmedo Saenz struck out, and up to the plate stepped Miguel Odalis (Martinez) Tejada. Yeah, like Reggie before him, Miggy had some Martinez in him. On this day he had some Reggie in him, too. With a 17-game winning streak on the line, Tejada homered deep into the left-field bleachers, turning the baseball world on its ear and transforming Vanessa's baptism into a family hug-fest. It would have been crazy to think that the A's could continue their winning ways in such improbable fashion, but that's pretty much what happened the next two nights. The lowly Royals were next and they jumped out to a 5–0 Labor Day lead off of Zito. Meanwhile, the A's appeared to be going through the motions after riding the tidal wave for nearly three weeks. But that all changed in the bottom of the fifth when Dye took exception to a high-and-tight pitch, promptly singled, and came home on a Justice homerun. The sleeping giant had awakened. Justice again delivered the big hit in the sixth, a two-run single to give the A's a 6–5 lead. After KC had tied it in the eighth, Long tripled to lead off the ninth, win number nineteen just ninety feet away. Two intentional walks and a force-out at home brought us back to Tejada, and he singled home Greg Myers for the game-winner. Strangely, the schedule makers planned a day off for the two teams between Monday and Wednesday, which gave the A's extra time to ponder their place in history. As it was, they had tied the American League record, held previously by the 1906 White Sox and 1947 Yankees. The one-day delay also allowed them to step out of the circus tent and catch their breath. Wednesday, September 4 was the culmination of a dream run. Every year, baseball crowns a World Series champion. But twenty-game winning streaks? Those come once in a blue moon, folks. My cousins Scott (Martinez) and John (Sanchez) were our family reps that night, and part of a regular-season record crowd of 55,528. Batteries recharged, the A's made it known from the start that Number 20 would be theirs, and that no last minute heroics would be necessary. A six-run first led to an 11–0 lead after three innings. If this was a boxing match, they would have stopped it right there. But somehow the Royals got up off the canvas and delivered some heavy blows of their own. They scored five in the fourth and—shockingly—five more in the eighth to close within a run. Then in the top of the ninth, the comeback was made complete as Luis Alicea stroked a two-out, RBI single off of Koch. To illustrate the A's penchant for late-inning magic, the goateed closer won *eleven* games in 2002. And he would be a winner this night, too, compliments of a one-out, walk-off, history making blast by Scott Hatteberg. After blowing an 11–0 lead, the A's reached back for one more bit of magic and sent the partisan crowd home with memories to last a lifetime. Unbelievable.

John Sanchez, cousin, "It was a game unlike any other and it all happened on "Dollar Wednesday." We arrived almost an hour early, rare for a family bringing seven restless kids along. On the way to the game I sold five $1 tickets for forty dollars. The first three for $30 and the last two for $5 each. I felt like a millionaire; I had beer money!

We bought fifteen one-dollar hotdogs and made our way to our seats on the third deck, my Hornito's tequila tucked nicely in the baby's bag. Great seats supposedly, right in the first row! We would later find that sitting in the first row isn't so cool with people walking back and forth through the aisle all night! The Coliseum filled up quickly and before long, a record crowd of over 55,000 screaming A's fans began to spill over into Mt. Davis. A rarity for a regular season A's game.

The game began and the A's came out swinging. The Royals seeming to succumb under the pressure of the moment, committed several errors in the first three innings and the A's opened up a huge lead. The crowd was raucous and the chants filled the air with 'Let's go A's,' 'MVP' chants for Tejada, and the wave rolled around the Coliseum a full three times—all 55,000 plus fans seeming to participate.

The A's lead didn't last too long as the A's bullpen soon began to struggle giving up multiple run innings. The lead continued to dwindle until the ninth when Kansas City completed the unbelievable comeback tying the game at eleven runs apiece. That meant at least one more half inning and another trip to the men's pissing trough. The fans didn't seem to mind though, everyone somehow knew that the game was in hand and after Scott Hatteberg rounded the bases for his game winning home run, the crowd celebrated as if the A's had just won game seven of the World Series.

The celebration continued all the way through the BART ramp with chants like 'Streak! Streak! Twenty!', and the all too familiar 'Yankees Suck!' Of course the BART tunnel was jammed beyond belief, not a single fan had left early and we all squeezed inside the bridge and enjoyed the spoils of victory.

A night to remember, the streak reached its apex that evening as the A's lost in Minnesota two days later. But they accomplished a feat breaking records and defying the odds, catapulting the team from third to first place. Another amazing feat for the night included my eight-month old son Daniel eating an entire hot dog with only one tooth! The next day after the smoke had cleared and the victory was ours, we turned in our collector-item ticket stubs for personal pizzas at Round Table."

Indeed the A's impossible streak ended on Friday night at Minnesota by a 6–0 score. The run had left them thirty-seven games over .500 and with a three-game advantage in the American League West. To put in further perspective the magnitude of such a stretch, the Anaheim Angels went 18–2 and *lost ground*! As for the A's, they followed up their first defeat since August 12 with impressive back-to-back shutouts at the Metrodome. In the series finale Zito won his 20th game with seven innings of three-hit ball.

Shortly after the streak ended, I visited Hawaii for the first time. It was there in my hotel room that I was told by Carol that Aunt Genie had passed away. So we came home to a funeral. Like Uncle Donald before her, she loved her family dearly; she always knew what everyone was up to, and would proudly tell those who didn't know. I regret that her passing has distanced her son Paul Jr. from some of us, though not intentionally. But we never got the chance to sit down and capture some of his A's memories. I have no doubt that he has many to share.

For the third straight season, the A's had a healthy final month (18–8) and they secured a playoff spot with a 4–2 win over Texas on September 20th. Six days later they beat Seattle 5–3 in ten innings for their 100th victory and their second division title in three years. It marked the first time in Oakland history that the A's reached the century mark in consecutive seasons. Only Giambi's Yankees won as many games (103) in 2002. And yet for all their achievements, the A's could not rest on their lofty laurels. It was playoff time again, this time the Twins.

I went with Scott to Game 1, and for awhile it looked like Minnesota's farm club had suited up for the series opener. A pair of Twin mistakes led to three first inning runs, a "single" by Scott Hatteberg in the second (that actually fell out of the reach of four infielders) brought home another, and a third error resulted in a fifth run, as the A's took a 5–1 lead on the generous visitors. One of the Minnesota miscues was committed by third-baseman Corey Koskie but he made up for it with a third-inning, two-run shot off Hudson to get the Twins back in it. Doug Mientkiewicz chased Huddy with a lead-off shot in the sixth, and before the inning was over, the A's were staring at a one-run deficit. In the seventh, A.J. Pierzynski put the finishing touches on a 4-for-4 day with an RBI triple and the Twins went on to a stunning 7–5 win. I went home and tried to sleep off an afternoon hangover that consisted of too many beers and too many Twins crossing home plate. Neither was an issue in Game 2. I listened to this one at work as Chavez got it started with a three-run homer in the first. The A's put it away with a five-spot in the fourth and two relievers mopped up for Mulder in a 9–1 series-squaring victory. In Minnesota, Ray Durham led off Game 3 with an inside-the-park homer and Hatteberg followed with a more conventional homerun to get the A's off and running. After the Twins tied it with a pair in the fifth, Dye homered in the sixth, and the Green and Gold got two more in the seventh for a 6–3 win. With a chance to advance and Hudson on the mound in Game 4, the A's barely made it out of the gate as the Twins rolled to an 11–2 laugher. Back home for our third Game 5 in as many seasons. Abe and John joined me and Scott at my house. Mulder pitched in and out of trouble all afternoon but he left in the seventh trailing only 2–1. Billy Koch entered the ninth inning, having pitched in a league-leading 84 contests. He saved forty-four games to go with his eleven wins. But like Izzy before him, there was never a sense that things were kosher when he was on the mound. His 3.27 ERA in 2002 suggested as much. And so it was when we needed him to be like Eck for one inning, Koch was more like *wreck*. Pierzynski touched him for a two-run homer and the Twins added one more to pad their lead to 5–1. Those hoping for a Miggy Reprise must know that he struck out to end the eighth. But good old Chavy led off with a single and after Dye forced him at second, Justice hit a ringing double. Then Mark Ellis turned on a Guardado fatty for a three-run, no-doubt-about it blast into the left-field seats. 5–4, one out, and the Coliseum in an uproar. After Long flew out, Randy Velarde singled to right. Then Durham, who was 3-for-5 with a homerun, popped up meekly to second base and just like that, it was over. How horribly ironic that the biggest thrill of The Streak happened on *that* field against *those* Twins, and now *they* were doing the celebrating. Cruel indeed.

Accessories. My thesaurus describes them as "trimmings," "garnishes," "frills," and my person favorite, "side dishes." The 2003 baseball season, at least in our little part of the world, offered no such samplers, no fries with that shake. There were no MVP's or Cy Young award winners on this squad. In fact, no one in an A's uniform hit .300, won twenty games, or socked thirty homers. And there was certainly no outrageous winning streak to lose our heads about. Yeah, there was the usual mad dash to the finish line (22–11) but even that appeared mild compared to years past. The only thing that resembled anything close to normal was Eric Chavez striking gold at third base for the third consecutive year. Even the manager had changed, and well, how could that be? Art Howe's teams won almost three-hundred games over his final three seasons, good enough to earn an invite to the Autumn Ball in each of those years. So maybe the A's didn't leave the dance with the best-looking girl, but let's face it, playfulness and charm only get you so far. Money talks a good game at these events; it's just not the sort of place for guys who search the sofa for loose change. (Billy Beane had a different view of these so-called playoffs, referring to them as nothing more than a crapshoot.) But in the end, for all of his success, none of these things were enough to save Art Howe from losing his job. The man to replace him was practically a Howe clone. Ken Macha, like his predecessor, was born in Pennsylvania. Both began their playing careers with the Pittsburgh Pirates; in fact, Howe and Macha made their big-league debuts in the very same year. The latter was only up long enough for five games that season, but he made pinch-hit appearances in all five contests, and was successful in three of them. In his last game of 1974, Macha and Howe both had pinch-hit singles. While Howe went on to play in 891 games, seeing action in every season except one (1983) from his rookie year to his retirement in 1985, Macha's career actually spanned a longer period of time (1974–81), though only about a quarter of the games played (180). His last Major League appearance, ironically, came against the A's in Oakland. Howe had previous managerial experience before taking over for the departing Tony La Russa in 1996; for Macha this was his first go at it, after serving as his former teammate's bench coach for four seasons. Both were students of the game and generally liked throughout the sport. Just two Pennsylvania gentlemen trying to earn a living in a game they loved.

As for the A's, they didn't miss a beat. In one of their most consistent seasons to date, the Green and Gold never dipped under .500, or below second place the entire season. Which would set them up nicely for another exciting pennant race (or in their case, *chase*). The Seattle Mariners held the AL West top spot from May 16 to August 25, including an eight-game lead as late as June 13. But the A's went 60–37 from that point on to capture their second straight division title, and third in four years. In season that tiptoed away from the norm, even their method of clinching was unorthodox....

After the A's disposed of Seattle on Sunday, September 21 (12–0), I was feeling a whole lot better about our chances to win this thing and a little bit better about myself. (We had lost the previous three games that I had purchased a ticket for, including a 9–2 shelling on Saturday which dropped our lead to three games with seven left.) The next night, the family gathered at The Englander for Christina's 24th birthday and a Monday Night

Football clash between two old friends—the Raiders and Broncos. With the football game turning ugly early and the A's cruising against the Texas Rangers (thereby cutting their magic number to two games), Christina and I decided that we'd head out to the 'Net Tuesday night for what we hoped would be the clincher. There was only a twenty-five percent chance that the champagne would be popped open that evening, but we were willing to take those odds.

As I reached the office on Tuesday morning, I spotted a penny on the ground, picked it up and thought to myself, "This is our night." It reminded me of former Raider cornerback Willie Brown, who would often find loose change on the field before games and then go out and have a pick or two. Hey, if it worked for Willie, it could work for me, and I took a good, long look at that Lincoln. Shoot, that baby had "clinch" written all over it. Actually, it said, "In God we Trust," but I digress. All day long, I had this nervous energy about me. I wasn't the only one. A little before noon, I called Christina to make sure we were still a go; she thought I was replying, rather punctually, to an e-mail she had just sent me—making sure we were still a go. (Cue the Twilight Zone music.) My oldest godchild had good reason to doubt me—I had a 6:00 appointment at my son's school and work was its usual charmingly hectic self. But I should have known better than to question her. Christina wasn't going to miss this for the world. After all, there was family history to uphold. First there is Tonianne, who supported the club upon its move to Oakland through its glory years and its darkest of days, followed by Tricia, who took the baton from Billy Ball through Bash Ball. Fans like them come along once in a decade. No really, Tone was born in '59, Trish in '69, and Christina in '79. But her aunts have something that she does not; playoff and World Series memories to last a lifetime (or at least until I've finished this book). Perhaps the passing of the torch would come tonight.

I met Christina and her friend (now husband) Greg in the parking lot at about 6:45. Over semi-cold Budweiser I told them I had been to three clinching games but all of them had begun with the magic number at one. This would be different, I said. Little did I know how much so. The A's struck for a first-inning run while we were will still out in the lot, and as we made our way in, we learned the Angels had done the same against Seattle. Things were definitely looking up. The out-of-town scoreboard was littered with important games being played across the nation, but to us, California was where it was at. And an interesting game of tennis ensued, as we turned left to watch the live action and right to see the scoreboard. Left, pitch, right, scoreboard, left, pitch, right, scoreboard. There were moments where our game was ahead of theirs, at others, the roles were reversed. If given the choice, we preferred that the Mariners lose first and the A's would win shortly thereafter. But surely we'd settle for any scenario so long as the next day's papers had an "X" next to "Oakland" in the standings.

In the bottom of the fourth inning, banged-up All-Star catcher Ramon Hernandez drove in Miguel Tejada with a single and the A's were ahead 2–0. Turn right, still Angels 1–0. Texas got a run back in their half of the fifth, but me and 23,210 of my closest friends were like, "what, me worry"? As the seventh inning got underway, the A's were still 2–1 to the good and the Angels' lone run was still standing, however precariously. At about that time, Scott began to give us updates of the Seattle game (which we were getting by watching the scoreboard, but Scott's Nextel was just a bit quicker). Hey, I'm a nostalgic kind of guy, but there are certain luxuries that make you say "screw the old days." Former "A" Ryan Christenson, he of the lofty .172 average, worked his way on for the third time in the game. Scott beeped in to tell us that A's TV man Greg Papa had announced Oakland's playoff schedule. Greg "talk too soon" Papa had done it again. As Scott relayed the message, Jermaine Clark, he of the even loftier .125 average, stroked a double that tied the score and ended rookie pitcher Rich Harden's night. The large screen in the sky showed that the Mariners were still drawing blanks through seven frames, so half of the news was good. Well for two innings, anyway. Both games moved on, the A's into the bottom of the eighth knotted at two; Seattle into the ninth, three outs from defeat. While we waited for what seemed like an eternity for the "9" to turn into an "F" down in Anaheim, Scott confirmed our biggest fears—the Mariners were mounting a threat. Meanwhile, Tejada turned a two-on, one-out situation into a wasted opportunity, as he hit into a tailor-made 6–4–3 double play.

And then, as if that cruelty wasn't enough for A's fans to endure, the baseball gods injected us with a double dose of heartbreak. Once again, it was the bottom of the lineup that struck gold for Texas: Todd Greene, batting .225, ripped closer Keith Foulke's first pitch of the ninth inning for a tie-breaking homerun. Milliseconds later, Scott called in with the sickening news that Seattle had tied Anaheim. For a minute there it looked as if there would be no magic number shrinkage this night. Christina and Greg fidgeted in their seats. They're not quite accustomed to this thing called playoff pressure and it certainly didn't help that the last beer sold was two innings ago. Me, I'm a seasoned vet, not quite in John or Tonianne's league, but close enough. So why was my stomach churning with Jermaine Dye at the dish, one strike away from lights out at the 'Net? Because we practically had the sweet taste of champagne on our lips, only to have the bottle snatched away, to be sealed tightly for another night. But Dye, much maligned, still not quite right from that injury that knocked him out of 2001 playoffs, he came through. Double to the wall, Chris Singleton scampered home to tie it, and this "seasoned vet" was slapping five with people he never saw in his life!

Neither the Angels nor the Mariners scored in the first extra inning of their game, while ours headed into the bottom of the tenth, still knotted at three. Erubiel Durazo rapped a one-out single, and then in a rare display of small-ball, the designated hitter stole second base, while Chavy swung at strike three. Two outs. They intentionally walked Miggy, and unintentionally walked Hatteberg, to bring up Adam Melhuse to pinch-hit with the bags full. Melhuse delivered a base-hit and Durazo scored to win it. Now all we had to do was wait out the game down in Anaheim, which was being shown on the big screen. Tim Salmon endeared himself to A's fans everywhere on this night when he hit a homerun with one out in the bottom of the eleventh to beat Seattle and clinch another Oakland title. What a night!

The A's may have taken a road less traveled to the playoffs, but once they got there, it was like déjà vu all over again. Different team, same heartbreak. This time against the Red Sox. Boston. Why was I so threatened by *Boston*? Why did I harbor such ill feelings towards its baseball team, which hadn't won a World Series since 1918? It wasn't always this way. Even after they swept the A's in

1975 and ended their three-year reign as champs, I sided with them against the Reds in that year's Fall Classic. I always liked George Scott, the original "Boomer." I was a huge fan of Jim Rice; still say he deserves a plaque at Cooperstown. I revered Carl Yastrzemski. When he homered in his final Coliseum at-bat in 1983, I saluted him with a standing ovation. It was in the late 70's that New York and Boston renewed its once-heated rivalry, and their fans began to appear in large numbers at opposing stadiums. Like Oakland. I loathed the Yankee fans, but the Sox followers didn't seem to bother me much. And yet in that famed '78 playoff game, I cheered for the Bombers. Call that Reggie Influence. I did not become fully aware of Boston's title-less plight until 1986 when the Red Sox self-destructed against the Mets in the World Series. Up three games-to-two, a two-run lead, no men on, and one out to go. One out to end 68 years of frustration. One out that never came. In the matter of four batters, the Mets pulled off one of the most stunning comebacks in post-season history. The collapse was made complete the next night in Game 7. Boston's shot at Series redemption was thwarted at the hands of La Russa's A's; in both 1988 and 1990, the Sox were swept out of the American League playoffs. The resentment between New York and Boston heated up once more in 1995 and has not let up since. It's not just the fight for supremacy in the American League East where the teams have finished 1–2 the last nine seasons; it's also the extracurricular activities that have served to spice up this already fiery relationship. And while the Yankees methodically added to their World Series total with four titles in five seasons (which they delightfully flaunted in the direction of you-know-where), the weight of the Evil Empire squashed Boston even deeper into its state of despair. Each disappointment played out like a Shakespeare tragedy, as the Red Sox Nation wondered if their turn would ever come. The sport networks capitalized on Beantown's annual lament, known to most as "The Curse of the Bambino." On one hand I couldn't stand the East Coast bias displayed on ESPN and other channels. On the other hand, I couldn't keep from watching baseball's most compelling drama. And as much as I detested New York, I always chose them over Boston in their head-to-head wars. Always. And there were three reasons why. The first one made the most sense: their fans. Where did they all come from? Yeah, they came out to support the team in the 70's but this was something else. The more they lost, the more they came out; like it was somehow chic to be a Sox fan. They were like roaches and just as pesky. And surely just as indestructible. What did they care if an A's fan shouted "Nineteen, eighteen" in their faces? It didn't matter because they had already been through the most damning defeats and heard the worst of every insult from every Yankee fan they had ever encountered. But don't think it kept me from trying to get under their skin, even though the real truth was they got under mine.

Another reason why I didn't want to see the Sox end their Series drought was that there was something almost poetic to their suffering. Surely no full-fledged member of the Nation would buy into the idea that the Red Sox would be "just another team" if they were to win it all. But for me personally, a Boston championship would change how I viewed their rivalry with the Yankees, if only because the Sox seemed to be running their operation in much the same way as their "evil" nemesis. The whole Wall-Street-executive versus blue-collar-worker was already in danger of losing its appeal; in fact it was becoming increasingly difficult deciphering between David and Goliath. In truth, both had become giants.

And then there's Bill Simmons. I imagine for most, he needs no introduction, but I will do it for those who do other things with their lives besides eat, drink, and sleep sports. Simmons is a columnist for *ESPN: The Magazine* and ESPN.com. He has the greatest job in the whole world and not just because it's ESPN. It's the greatest job in the whole world because he actually gets to write about his favorite teams, completely biased, and yet unabashedly, for ESPN. Like what I am doing here, in this book, with the A's, he does for…ESPN! And in case you haven't figured it out, Simmons is a Sox fan. It was around 2003 that I started reading his work, so any animosity I already had towards the so-called Nation was intensified. The thing that really burned me up about Simmons was his public denouncement of any "Curse" (and let's face it, there wasn't one), but whenever his team lost in heartbreaking fashion, he quickly resorted to the standard "why us" mantra.

By the time Game 1 of the 2003 ALDS rolled around, the dynamics of baseball's most intense rivalry had reached epic proportions. In fact most people outside the Bay Area viewed our series with the BoSox as a mere undercard to the main event that lay ahead. Boston, for all its alleged curses and demons, seemed primed to stick it to the Yankee bully once and for all. The A's, battling the first-round blues for three seasons, had other ideas. Me and Ernie had seats for Game 1; Scott and Nick were there, too. On the mound: Huddy vs. Pedro. The crowd was as electric as any that I could remember, with more than a fair share of Red Sox fans in attendance. Todd Walker, the game's third hitter, stroked a solo homerun off Hudson, but the A's touched The Untouchable for three runs in the third. The Stinger gave way to Ricardo Rincon with a man on and two out in the seventh, and the A's clinging to 3–2 lead. But Walker took Rincon deep for his second homerun of the night, and suddenly we were down, 4–3. Down to our last out in the ninth—as we were in our division clincher—Durazo singled home Eric Byrnes to tie it, and sent the game to extra innings. As we reached the twelfth inning, we didn't care who won, just that the game would end soon (well, not really, but it sounded good at the time). In our bottom half, the team that dared not to play small ball, did just that. After Durazo walked, Chavez forced him at second. With two outs, Chavy stole third base as Hatteberg worked a base-on-balls. Hatty took second on a no-throw, and the Sox intentionally gave Long a free pass to load the bases for Hernandez…who bunted (yes, bunted) home Chavez with the game-winner. Unreal.

Simmons: "I mean, what can you say? How often can this happen? Do other baseball teams lose games like this?"

Obviously he hadn't been watching the A's very closely the previous three seasons, but as we were soon to find out (again), there was at least one other team to "lose like this." Being that Game 2 was an afternoon affair, I gave my tickets to Mom and Uncle Dan, who were treated to a Zito masterpiece. Barry tossed seven innings of five-hit ball, struck out nine, and came away a 5–1 winner. One more to advance. Well, we certainly had been *here* before. Saturday night in Fenway for Game 3 and I was on a date. A concert. We'll just leave it at that. But outside the theater, they had the game on, big screen and all. So while waiting for the concert to start, I kept close tabs on the action. I wasn't close enough to hear the announcers so I had to trust my eyes for this one. But even had I been *at* the game, it would have been hard to believe what I witnessed in the sixth inning. With Boston in front 1–0, the A's had Durazo on first, Byrnes on third, and Tejada at the dish with just one out. Miggy hit it back to the pitcher Derek Lowe, who threw wildly to home plate. Byrnes never touched home plate as he was blocked expertly by catcher Jason Varitek, who then retrieved the ball, and tagged out the hobbling baserunner. Chavez walked to load the bases, and then things got ultra weird. Hernandez hit a ground ball to shortstop Nomar Garciaparra, whose error allowed Durazo to score the tying run. Meanwhile third baseman Bill Mueller was called for obstruction which, by rule, allowed Tejada (who was at second) to take the next base. Any other base would be taken at the runner's peril. Clearly confused, Miggy stopped running between third and home, and was out by thirty feet, the second A's player of the inning to be "thrown out" at home. Yeah, imagine trying to watch *that* with no sound. The game trudged on into the tenth, tied at one. With a man on and one out, Trot Nixon hit a two-run shot off of reliever Rich Harden, and the Nation celebrated a win that normally went against them. Game 4, a Sunday, and we went to Ernie's to watch it. Tim Hudson against John Burkett (if you're looking for Mark Mulder, his season ended in August). Hudson's season ended on this day, after one inning. Strained left oblique muscle. Whatever the hell that is. Soon rumors began to swirl around that Huddy injured himself the night before, while fending off obnoxious Sox fans in a Boston pub. I'm not making this up. In the sixth, the A's turned a 2–1 deficit into a 4–2 lead, on the strength of Jermaine Dye's two-run jack over The Monster. High-fives all around at Ernie's. Twelve tantalizing outs away. The Sox got one back in their bottom half but after no runs were scored in the seventh, we were six outs from advancing. Keith Foulke, who was as close to "lights out" of any A's closer since Eckersley, the one guy that didn't make Tricia nervous the way Izzy and Koch used to, came on in the eighth to finish it off. Foulke, who was born on October 19, 1972, a day in which the A's scored two runs in the bottom of the ninth to win Game 4 of the World Series, gave up two runs in the eight inning of this Game 4, and we never recovered. It was neither quick nor painless. Foulke got Damon to ground out, and after a Garciaparra double, induced a fly ball from Walker. Manny Ramirez, ever dangerous, singled to make it first and third, with David Ortiz coming up. Big Papi (Simmons called him "Poppy") was a still a year away from icon status in Boston but he gave a view of things to come with a ringing double off Foulke. Nomar and Manny scored, sending the Fenway Faithful into a frenzied state. After a lifeless 1–2–3 ninth by the A's, we were all tied up again. Game 5, back at Oakland, and if Simmons thought he was tired of endless highlights of The Babe, Buckner, and Bucky, well, how many times was FOX going to bring up our inability to close out a playoff series? In eight previous chances to eliminate an opponent—once in 2000, three times in '01, twice in '02, and now twice in this series—we were 0-for-8. Simmons wasn't there when Ruth was traded to New York. He had no recollection of '46 or '67, or even '75. But I had seen the first-round collapses of my A's first-hand. I had seen them lose a Game 1 ('02), a Game 2 ('00), a Game 3 ('01), and a Game 4 ('01) in person. Losing this one would make it complete. Me and Ernie again, and it was either going to be joy and relief, or the worst kind of pain. Barry against Pedro, and through five, Barry held a 1–0 edge. But Varitek led off the sixth with a homerun, and you could see that Zito lacked the zip that he had displayed earlier. Damon walked, Garciaparra popped up, and Walker was hit by a pitch. At that point, I thought to myself, "Come on Macha. Bring in a fresh arm." It came one batter too late. Manny Ramirez crushed a three-run homer and just like that, it was 4–1. Ramirez took an extra moment to admire his work, and how could he not? It's a swing that still haunts me to this day. The A's scratched for two more runs off Martinez, one in the sixth, another in the eighth. He was far from dominating, but he was good enough. 49,000 fans came to their feet in the ninth as the Green and Gold gave it one last go. The first two batters walked and you could sense something special was brewing. After our favorite bunter (Hernandez) sacrificed the runners to second and third, Macha inexplicably pinch hit Adam Melhuse for Dye. One lousy fly ball from a tie game, and he brings in a back-up catcher for Dye? On one hand it was hard to argue; Melhuse was 3-for-4 in the series at the time. On the other hand, Melhuse went down on strikes for the second out. A third walk loaded the bases and brought up Terrence Long, whose strikeout sent the A's into a long and lonely winter.

Simmons: "I just want to win. I don't feel sorry for myself, and I don't care about the past, and I don't think I deserve these things any more than (other) fans or anyone else. I just want to win. And I think every Sox fan feels that way."

That night, me and Ernie ended up doing shots of Jack Daniels at the Whiskey River Saloon in Hayward. Had we known it would be our last playoff game until 2006, we might have closed the place down.

Yes, Bill Simmons, this kind of thing happens to other fans, too.

19 / Grandpa's Little Girl

"You ever got your heart broken?"
"Yeah. When we lost the pennant in '87."
—dialogue between Kelly Preston and Kevin Costner
(who portrays a Major League pitcher as well as
Preston's love interest) in *For the Love of the Game*

Reggie and Tonianne…Tricia and Dave McKay…Christina and…?
Hint: he's not a player.…

Here's *her* story:

I started going to some games when I was at Sonoma State. Of course, fraternity guys love sports. And being that I grew up in a family where baseball was a religion we practiced regularly, I knew a lot about baseball. So that helped me score some serious points with the frat boys. We would watch it on TV somewhere like Paradise Pizza, or we would go to the games. And since I already knew the game, and still watched from time to time, it was easy to follow in the footsteps of my aunts and uncles and become a big-time fan.

That was also the era of the Big Three. I loved Tim Hudson. Just LOVED him. I think it was partly the Texas Southern background, or maybe because he was the smallest of the three, making him kind of an underdog. Or maybe it was because he looked so fierce when he pitched. At the time, I was living with two sorority sisters who I turned into baseball fans. Katie liked Mulder, and Lori, well we told her to like Zito.

(Quick side note: At first, Katie laughed at my fanatic behavior toward the A's. But soon after living with me, she was so schooled in the game of baseball, she could tell when an ump made a bad call, or even recognize the sound of a homer right off the bat

187

when listening to a game on the radio. She now lives in New York with Lori, and still supports the A's to this day. And she still has her Mulder Bobblehead on her desk and shows it off proudly.)

As for me, it was "the boys" who got me back into being a "fan." It gave me a common interest with them. And when I moved from Sonoma State to Corte Madera, it was easier to get back in it since I was closer to Oakland. Plus I was making a whole lot more money, and even my roommate was a huge fan. His dad was a season ticket holder, but he didn't go to every game, so we would go a lot in his place.

But what really got me into it that year, 2002, was…again…a guy. My dad was going with friends from work a lot. This is when $2 Wednesdays were really popular. So they would buy tickets, leave work early, and tailgate. I would join them. Dad knew I was a big fan so he would invite me a lot. That's when I really started to notice Greg. Him and Dad had hung out a lot before, but I was getting to see him so often that I really started to notice him, and really started to like him.

2003 came around and things got a lot hotter for the A's, and for me and Greg, too. We were doing the $2 Wednesday thing again. Then, Greg's season ticket partner upped and moved to Reno, leaving Greg with the remainder of the tickets. When my dad told me this, I casually mentioned, 'Well, let Greg know that I'm always available if he needs someone to go to the game with.' And he did! So Greg and I were going to games just by ourselves. Plus, this was the second year the A's were giving out Bobbleheads, but it was the first year that people really took notice of them. So me, Greg, Mom, and Dad were going to all of those games too. I had moved back to San Leandro in August of 2003, and I remember that the four of us were going to another Bobblehead game, and my dad had told Greg the day before, 'Why don't you pick Christina up and you guys can meet us at the game.' I was like, 'WHAT?!?!' I guess my dad had NO idea I had a crush on this guy.

October was approaching, and like I said earlier, the A's were hot in 2003. Me and Greg, and even my Nino were there the night the A's clinched the division title. The A's had won, and now we just needed the Mariners to lose. But most of the fans didn't leave the stadium; we were watching the game on the big screen. And then, the Mariners lost, and the place went crazy; people were screaming, celebrating, hi-fiving. I turned to my Nino and gave him a hug. Then I said, 'what the heck,' and I turned to Greg and gave him a hug. It was the first time I had showed him any affection.

We had already made plans to go to the playoffs together, and had our tickets. We went to Game 1, on October 1st, which happened to be the same night I came back from a trip to New York to visit Katie. That game went twelve innings, and the A's won. It was beautiful. Then they won Game 2, and I believe we were at that game too. There was no game on October 3rd, but that was the day Greg and I finally admitted to liking each other. That's the day we consider our "dating" anniversary. Unfortunately, we weren't at a game that day, because it would have been all too fitting, but I was just glad it finally happened. We didn't end up going to Game 5, which was brought back home. Greg was actually in Massachusetts for work during that time, and I remember him calling me and telling me how much he hated being there. Of course, everywhere he went, there were Boston fans cheering like crazy.

So that started our relationship. Unfortunately, the A's season ended too quickly for us, though we did have our Raider season tickets to enjoy. Plans had already been made to get season tickets for 2004, long before the season ended. I had asked my Nino if he wanted to join us in our plan. I mean, at the time, Greg and I weren't dating, so I wasn't sure a two-ticket plan between the two of us would be the right thing to do. So, I ended up getting four tickets, one for me, one for Greg, and two for Nino. Little did I know what 2004 what bring for us. Opening Night was April 3, 2004, our six-month anniversary. Yes, only a girl would recognize and honor that date. But I felt it had a lot of significance since it was Opening Night. And we had planned on going, and having a huge tailgate, and just having a great time. Well, two days before that I ended up finding out I was pregnant and Greg and I were going to have a baby. Wow, huh?

That threw our life into fast-forward. We moved in together, bought a house, got engaged, and had a baby on December 3, 2004. Ethan Gregory. He was a fan from the start. We went to a lot of games while I was pregnant, though we missed a lot during the first half due to morning sickness. But as soon as the 2005 season started, Ethan was right there with us for the games. We took him to as many games as we could, so long as the weather was warm enough. His first word was "A's," no joke. He knew how to make a little #1 with his finger and say "A's." And he had a great instinct for the game. He always knew when to clap, even at seven months old. It was unbelievable.

Greg and I got married in April 2006. The A's weren't home that weekend, or we would have had our rehearsal dinner at a game (again, no joke). We did have the A's present all throughout our wedding. The colors were—you got it, green and gold. (Though it wasn't the Kelly green and it was more of a soft yellow.) My garter was made of A's logo material. Our favors were beer koozies because we figured they would be great for tailgates. And our table numbers were A's jerseys with the players names and numbers on them, and the seating cards were made to look like game tickets. What can I say, we are A's fans.

So yeah, my "re-introduction" to the A's started because of guys. I admit that. But its always been genuine and real. I am a HUGE A's fan. And I just feel very lucky to have found someone who loves them as much as I do. And I know my family appreciates it too.

20 / More Heartache (2004–2005)

"Losing feels worse than winning feels good."
—legendary broadcaster, Vin Scully

The A's had barely broke for Spring Training in 2004 when the news came from the East Coast that Uncle Rick had died. We rushed first to Uncle Dan's (Grandma's last surviving son), then to Mom's, where we mourned another Martinez taken away from us way too soon. For me, there was a little extra sorrow involved; I had made plans to visit Uncle Rick and his family in the summer.

As for the ball club that my uncle rooted for, even from his home in upstate New York, well, it was another year, another home-grown star gone elsewhere. This time, it was Miggy. Told by the A's before the 2003 season that they had no intentions of offering him the kind of money he deserved, Tejada signed on with Baltimore. We'd miss his bat and his energy, but we'd get by. After awhile you sort of get used to these things. If anything, the A's were more balanced in '04, with Eric Chavez leading the charge with another solid season at third. Aside from picking up another Gold Glove, Chavy hit 29 homeruns and drew a league-leading 95 walks. He was joined in the 20-homer club by Jermaine Dye (23), Bobby Crosby (22), Erubiel Durazo (22), and Eric Byrnes (20). Crosby, the heir to Tejada's throne, won the Rookie of the Year award, the fifth "A" to be so honored.

For me personally, the biggest thrills of 2004 didn't involve actual ball games (well, not ones that counted in the standings anyway). The first one came in March when Tricia and I went to Spring Training in Arizona courtesy of our god-daughter Christina, who joined us there with Greg and his parents. It was a special treat to

191

watch Eric Chavez homer in his first at-bat after signing a six-year contract as the A's took three straight from the Angels. Then in July, I went to Cooperstown, New York for Dennis Eckersley's induction into baseball's Hall-of-Fame. Don Jr. and John made the trip with me. Earlier in the day, we visited the place where Eck's plaque would soon hang among the greatest players this game has known. As an extra treat, long-time A's announcer Lon Simmons was awarded the Ford C. Frick award, presented annually to baseball broadcasters. But it was Eck who stole the show, as he "closed" the ceremonies with an emotional speech.

The first five months of the season pretty much followed the same script of previous years. Once again the A's were at pedestrian speed out of the gate, only to turn it up come the summer. Mark Mulder, fresh off an injury that ended his 2003 season prematurely, was back in form; he started and won the All-Star Game, and was 17–4 through the end of August. In large part to the lefty's resurgence, the A's held a three-game lead over Anaheim heading into the final stretch. But September, which had been so kind to Oakland over the years, turned its back on the defending American League West champs. You could say they were due for a tough final month, and at 12–15, it wasn't even that bad. Mark Mulder, however, was very bad. In his last seven starts he reached the seventh inning just once, and saw his ERA balloon seventy-one points. His fallout may have been a mystery to most but there was no secret as to why the A's found themselves in a dead heat with Anaheim heading into a season-ending series against the Angels in Oakland. Best two-out-of-three for all the marbles. But as the calendar turned to October, the horror of playoffs past reared its ugly head once more. I was with Abel and his family for Friday night fireworks, but the Angels supplied their own sparks, chasing Mulder after two innings en route to a 10–0 rout. Facing the possibility of missing the post-season for the first time since 1999, the A's took a 4–2 lead into the eighth, as Zito gave way to the bullpen. I left my seat where I was hanging with Mom, Tone, and Rose. With our season resting on the arm of Jim Mecir, I needed one more beer to get me through. He faced three batters and promptly gave up two singles. Exit Mecir, enter Rincon. Darin Erstad doubled off Rincon to bring both runners home. Tie game. After an intentional walk, a pitching change, another beer, and a fly ball to left for the second out, Garrett Anderson singled home Erstad to make it 5–4. Un-fricking-believable. The A's went quietly in the eighth and ninth, and the Angels became the third team in three years to celebrate on the Coliseum turf.

Billy Beane had seen his stars leave before but this time he wanted something in return. But who to trade? In a matter of three days, right before Christmas, we received a most staggering response. Beane dealt not one, but two, of his pitching aces, and in the process, turned the baseball world on its ear. First, he shipped Tim Hudson to Atlanta, and before the buzz had died down from that shocker, he sent Mulder to St. Louis. First reactions were that Beane had lost his mind. Others hinted that his pride may have gotten the best of him; for all his achievements, there were far too many people that pointed to Hudson-Mulder-Zito as the real key to the A's success. Perhaps he was eager to show that he could split up the Big Three and still win. In retrospect, these may have been Beane's best moves yet. They were no doubt his gutsiest. While the jury is still out on the three players the A's got in return for Hudson, there has been plenty to like about starter Dan Haren and reliever Kiko Calero, who came over in the Mulder trade. And with prospect Daric Barton waiting for his shot in 2007, this has the potential of pure larceny. Not that everyone was happy with it at first.

Tricia: "I have put up with a lot of trades but Hudson and Mulder *really* upset me."

What Beane saw was two brilliant, but injury-prone pitchers, on the decline. To wit, Hudson has gone just 27–21 with Atlanta, after winning seventy percent of his decisions here. And this past season, he set career highs (lows?) in losses, runs, earned runs, homeruns, ERA, and batting average against. In the National League, no less. Mulder enjoyed moderate success in his first season with St. Louis (16–8), but his second campaign was cut short by injury and he finished 6–7 with an ugly 7.14 ERA. Worse yet, the Cardinals won the World Series with him on the sidelines. Fellow GM's shook their heads at the seemingly Midas touch that

Beane possessed. Even if they didn't provide the immediate desired results.

The A's still had Barry Zito and Rich Harden, who was primed to step into an ace's role. Joe Blanton, a first-round draft pick from Kentucky won twelve games. Haren won fourteen to tie Zito for the team lead. Offensively, the A's were a different team in 2005. Only Eric Chavez and Nick Swisher hit more than twenty home-runs. But the lineup was littered with "gamers," guys who played with passion and fire. Newcomer Jason Kendall, who manager Ken Macha almost had to beg to take a day off, caught 150 games. Mark Ellis recovered from a career-threatening injury and hit .316. Mark Kotsay batted .280 and drove in 82 runs, good for second on the team. He also played a stellar center field. Yes, just when you thought you had Billy Beane figured out, he'd switch gears on you. On-base percentage was sooo last year, now he was looking for guys who could take away a hit as well as they could provide one with their bat. And his bullpen was its strongest since he took over the GM post, with Calero and All-Star Justin Duchscherer setting up Rookie-of-the-Year closer Huston Street. Beane showed he still had some magic left at the trade deadline when he brought over Jay Payton in one deal and relievers Joe Kennedy and Jay Witasick in another.

A 6–2 loss to Cleveland on May 29 left the A's at 5–20 for the month and 17–32 on the year, twelve games out of first. They recovered to win their last two games of May, and then went on one of their patented runs: 19–8 in June, 20–6 in July, and 17–11 in August. It was on August 11 that they climbed into first-place with as wacky a win as you could ever dream up. The A's had split the first two games of a three-game set with the Angels, which left the division rivals tied for the top spot heading into a Thursday after-noon affair. Anaheim led 4–0 heading into the bottom of the seventh, as Abel kept tabs on-line. A Payton homer preceded sin-gles by Kendall and Ellis, but Kotsay and Crosby made outs. As I shouted a work question at Abel, he suddenly thrust his arms in the air and shouted "Home run, Chavez! We're tied!" Normally, I'd have to wait to make sure he was telling the truth, but there was no way he was faking this one. I ran over for a string of extra-hard high-fives. There we were in the middle of another stressful work day and we were celebrating as if we had seats near the dugout. What a moment. We turned on the radio for the bottom of the ninth and I'll do my best to describe the ending. Ellis singled, and was forced by Kendall, who went to second on Kotsay's base hit. Crosby forced Kotsay, while Kendall took third. Crosby took second without a throw from the catcher Jose Molina, but as Molina tossed the ball back to pitcher Francisco Rodriguez, Rodriguez took his eye off the ball for a moment, and the ball got away from him long enough for Kendall to score! Bill King was so excited by the strange turn of events that we didn't fully comprehend what took place until after the commercials. All we knew was that we had won. Baffling.

In the end, Anaheim got the best of us, as the A's once again ran out of gas in September (11–17), thanks in large part to season-ending injuries to Bobby Crosby and Rich Harden. For the second straight season, the Angels celebrated a division title at the Coliseum.

Greg: "Rough year. Down at the start, hope in the middle, disappointed in the end. I am not a bandwagon kind of guy (how can I be when I support a team with a $60M payroll going up against teams with twice the money or when I continue to root for our Oakland Raiders, 0–3, oh and by the way, see you on Sunday). I'm a home town fan, love being one, and will continue to support our teams. I'd even support the Warriors if they'd change their name to Oakland. But, I have decided to reflect on this season differently. For me, it was a wonderful year. Christina and I continued to support our young Oakland A's as one of the few season ticket holders. We passed on our tradition to Ethan, our first child, and we believe his first phrase will be "Go A's." That or "Yankees Suck"; either is fine with me. Ethan started the season at four months old asleep in our arms in the middle of a cheering crowd and wearing the cutest little knitted A's hat made by his Aunt Toni. He ended it at ten months old and *standing* on my lap cheering on the A's along side his mother and father. After many late nights in the concrete bowl, we call McAfee Coliseum, with Ethan on my lap and wide awake three hours past his bed time it is clear he is an A's fan. All you have to do is watch this kid's eyes light up when the fans roar for a Chavez HR or a Kotsay double (32 for the year through last night). In passing on our tradition, we've been successful. We've turned our individual interests in the A's into a common interest that brings Christina and I closer, and now we've made it a family event. We look forward to cultivating the next generation A's fan and future bleacher bum. Between innings I find myself wondering…will Ethan be a Street, Blanton, or Johnson fan, or will he favor the "more experienced" Crosby? Regardless, I look forward to watching my boy grow up in the Green and Yellow of the Oakland A's while those big hearted rookies establish themselves as big league players. It's about tradition. Passed on from one generation to the next. Ethan's lucky enough to have that tradition passed down from both his Fisher and Marquez sides. Eventually we'll add Spring Training to Ethan's experiences and hopefully a fifth world title. And in a couple years, we'll make the move from two season tickets to three so Ethan can stand on his own seat and watch Chavez go yard over the right field wall."

John: "I see many similarities between this club and the '71 A's (although *that* team made the playoffs), minus the "R" factor. Obviously Reggie was a huge factor but you're not going to find someone like him very often. What I did see were some guys that aren't intimidated by the 'Big Boys' like the teams of the past few years. Kotsay, Payton, Swisher, Ellis, Crosby, Scutaro, Johnson, Kendall, Blanton and Street remind me of Reggie, North, Rudi, Bando, Campy, Green, Epstein, Catfish and Rollie. I think Kendall was the leader. Problem is, he has the heart but not the tools. You'd like to get 10–15 homers from your catcher. Also teams ran on us like crazy. Maybe Barry can slip him a little juice. What I saw at the end was players trying too hard to make something happen on offense. They were swinging at pitches they normally wouldn't swing at—a sign of pressing and being overanxious. And the guys that should have carried us still proved to be gutless when it came to big games. You talk about missing a guy like 'Mr. October'; right now I'd settle for 'Mr. September.' Chavez needs to put his bat where his mouth is and step up to the plate. I'd compare Blanton to Catfish, Street to Rollie and Harden has Blue-like stuff. I'd like to include Zito and compare him with Holtzman but he seemed to be at his worst in big games this year which is very un-Holtzman like. What was surprising was we tanked it at home in August and September. We had one of the best home records again going into those months but after taking two of three from the Angels, we got swept by Baltimore and lost two of three to the Royals. Then we came back and lost two of three to the Yankees and got swept by the Mariners—all at home. That was pretty much the beginning of the end. I remember the A's of the '70s getting off to slow starts so that isn't always a huge factor if another team isn't running away with it from the get-go but you can't always put yourself in a huge hole and not expect to run out of gas especially with five rookies being such a big part of your makeup. Looking to 2006, we won't need help with starting pitching, our defense is solid, and the rookies will have a year under their belt. I like Macha but it may be time for a Dick Williams clone. Someone who will close the doors to the clubhouse once in awhile and air things out when the team is slumping. We've run out of gas the last two Septembers and you can't let that happen. I think the experience is going to be a great help for next year but the A's are going to need a big gun to get over the top. They need at least one hitter in the lineup that makes the opposing team rethink the way they pitch and right now we don't have that guy."

Tonianne: "First, the good: Jason Kendall diving head first to tag the runner out at home. Kendall scoring from third on the throw back to the pitcher! A portrait of a player who wanted to be on a winning team! I was thinking about the '70/'71 seasons on my way to work this morning. Same kind of teams, same kind of manager. Macha's a lot like McNamara, no killer instinct, no "finish 'em off" attitude. The real difference is that we don't really have a leader who stands out. Kotsay comes close but he's not Reggie. We have the same youth, the same potential. We have a lot of fun but in the end that's not enough to take it all the way to a championship. We're missing a couple of vets who have done it and know what it's like to play down the stretch. The A's had some good runs in the middle but overall they lacked consistency. How many times did we score twelve runs one game and nothing the next two nights? How many more games would we have won had we scored just *one* more run? What was it that Dick Williams used to say? Fundamentals? It's time for the A's to go back to fundamentals, basically winning games with good pitching and timely hitting. We don't need a manger who says, 'If we can just split with them, we'll be okay.'

We need someone who intends to take each series, no matter who we're playing."

The A's must have heeded my sister's advice because at the end of the season, they parted ways with manager Ken Macha. A few days later, he returned to sign a new deal. In the short period between Macha's departure and bizarre homecoming, speculation arose as to who was next in line to lead our team.

John made his pitch with this "phone conversation" between Billy Beane and Lou Pinella:

(Ring, ring)
LOU: "Hello this is Lou."
BILLY: "Lou? It's Billy. No not Martin. Beane"
LOU: "Beane? Yeah I've been beaned plenty of times"
BILLY: "No, it's Billy Beane, you know, GM of the Year.
LOU: "Oh, *that* Billy. The one with no money right?"
BILLY: "Actually we've got a new owner and he's willing to spend a little. I was wondering how you'd feel about sporting the green & gold."
LOU: "Green & Gold? Are you kidding? I'd look like a freaking 300 pound parrot with hemorrhoids."
(Ring, ring)
LOU: "Hold on Billy, I have another call coming in."
BILLY: "No that was me. Get it? Maybe you wouldn't look good in green and gold but a few rings would take the attention off of your beer belly."
LOU: "Oakland fans hate me."
BILLY: "Ah, they'll get over it, especially if you bring a championship. Besides, you won't know if they're booing you or Lou-ing you."
LOU: "That's true."
BILLY: "That *is* true."
LOU: "Can you guys change to pinstripes?"
BILLY: "Tell you what; I hear that you're looking for an owner who is committed to winning. That's us. You bring us a title and you can come dressed as Ethel Merman for all we care."
LOU: "Hey, I just may take you up on that."

BILLY: "Ok but don't take too long. My next call is to Joe Morgan."

A'S FANS: "Ahhhhhh!!!!!!!!!!!!!"

Sadly, this chapter ends as it began. Bill King, the voice of the A's for twenty-five years, passed away on October 18. I can go all day about what he meant to us, but more than anything, Bill King exemplified a sense of security. As players came and went, he was always there. And in recent years, there was nothing sweeter than coming home from work on a Saturday afternoon, and falling asleep to his soothing voice, only to awake in time to hear him call the last outs of another A's win

21 / No Respect

"My psychiatrist told me I'm going crazy.
I told him, 'If you don't mind, I'd like a second opinion.'
He said, 'All right. You're ugly too!"'
                    —the late comedian, Rodney Dangerfield

As an A's fan, I admit to having a chip on my shoulder the size of Mt. Davis. Maybe it's because the A's, for all their success, are still perceived as second-class. Need proof? How much time do you have? The A's had two strikes against them the moment they arrived from Kansas City in 1968. First off, they reside in a city that has been, still is, and probably always will be, a football town. Secondly, the A's were ten years too late in moving westward. The San Francisco Giants made the trip in '58 and have smugly disregarded their East Bay neighbors as nothing more than an annoying tag-along; the red-headed stepchild in green and gold.

By the time the A's set foot here, the Raiders were a powerhouse in the American Football League, having won an astounding 37 of 42 regular-season contests, and had thus created a cult following among the citizens of Oakland. The A's were the unknown entity, and it would take a while for them to escape the shadow cast by the Silver & Black. For every magic moment manifested by the boys of summer, it seemed the giants of the gridiron would outdo them come the fall. So while Catfish was perfect in May of '68, the Raiders shocked the Jets in November, as a girl named Heidi pranced across TV screens nationwide. When Reggie made the families of Ruth and Maris sweat out the 1969 season, novice Raider coach John Madden did likewise to opposing coaches and officials

201

en route to a shiny 12–1–1 record. The following year, a man named Blanda worked miracles and somehow upstaged the efforts of a boy named Blue. (Vida would gain his revenge in '71.) It took the A's their fifth season in Oakland to understand the sure way to one-up their football counterparts: bring home a title. Every year the Raiders would add to their gaudy regular-season totals, only to get knocked off in the playoffs by the eventual Super Bowl champion. As if to say, "You had your chance, now it's our turn," the A's brought Oakland its first major championship. And second. And third. Aside from that little disparity, the good times rolled for *both* teams in the early 70's. On the field, they combined for nine first-place finishes over a five-year span; off the field, fans took to their colorful and often controversial style. And they rooted for each other. When the A's were defeated in the 1975 playoffs, thus ending their bid for four consecutive World Series titles, their biggest star urged the Raiders to put an exclamation point on a half-decade of dominance.

"Maybe Al Davis and John Madden can pick up where we left off," Reggie Jackson said, his melancholy mood turning hopeful. "Come on Raiders, bring Oakland a championship!"

One area the A's could never match their football brethren was at the turnstiles. It's not that their fans didn't appreciate their winning ways; they just didn't particularly care for the man that signed the checks. A curious way of thinking considering that the man who ran the football operations in Oakland had a fault or two of his own. And so it was Al Davis who moved his Raiders out of Northern California in 1981, and it was Charlie Finley who sold his A's to the Haas family who not only kept the club in the Bay Area, they transformed the faltering franchise into a model organization and the envy of Major League Baseball. But Al Davis is anything but dumb and he scheduled the Silver & Black for a visit to their old stomping grounds in the summer of '89 (which happened to be a World Series year for the A's), just to see if the hearts in Oakland still pounded for his Pride and Poise Boys. That August night, in which Raider fans welcomed their Prodigal Sons home with wide-open arms, paved the way for the team's permanent return in 1995. Which so happened to follow a baseball season that for the first time since 1904 did not have a World Series. Which so happened to come at a time when the A's were lousy on the field and their future in Oakland, as it almost always is, was in question. No, Al Davis is anything but dumb. So the A's once again found themselves in the shadow of the Raiders. Even though it was the Raiders who abandoned Oakland for thirteen seasons. But timing is everything. And the A's were hardly a hot item. Consequently, it made them vulnerable to the power of Al. Soon renovations were being made to the Coliseum, renovations that would benefit the football team. The bleachers that became my second home during my adolescence and early adulthood were "remodeled." Luxury boxes were added, as was a section of seating atop the new bleachers, dubbed simply, "Mt. Davis." In honor of you-know-who.

And while the love affair between the football team and its rabid fans rages on (despite four consecutive losing seasons), the disdain that the Raiders have reserved for their roommates—especially since returning in 1995—is disturbing. It's a shame, too, when you consider that the A's and Raiders enjoyed equal success at the turn of the century. For the first time since the glory days of the early 70's, both clubs earned playoff invitations three years in a row. Sadly, they will never attain the camaraderie that those teams of yesteryear shared—and shared willingly.

When it comes to the A's and the San Francisco Giants, "shared" and "willingly" go together like "jumbo" and "shrimp." Needless to say, the big brothers across the Bay never wanted the A's here in the first place. Worse yet, the A's more than invaded their safe haven, they conquered it. Six World Series appearances, four of which they won, fourteen trips to the post-season overall. Funny, but you'd swear that the Giants were the Yankees of the National League, the way their fans carry on about them. Fact is they have yet to win one World Series since they left New York at the end of the 1957 campaign. Almost a half-century in San Francisco, zero league titles. Not even one that the old-timers can hang their hats on. Even Cub fans have that. OK so none of them are still alive, but that's beside the point. When they moved on to that great big diamond in the sky, they were at peace knowing their teams had given them at least one moment of bliss. Tell me, have the San

Francisco Giants so rewarded their fans for nearly fifty years of unwavering support, most of which were spent braving the wicked winds at chilly Candlestick Park? No, sir. But hey, the Frisco Faithful scored one hell of a consolation prize—a state-of-the-art stadium to freeze their yuppie asses in, and drown their sorrows at. Yeah, they brag about Barry and their recent run of success but still no titles. You want to have some fun? Attend one Giant's game and ask the first usher you see where the "World Series trophy room" is. Ask more than one. Sure it's cruel, but well worth the admission price.

And it doesn't compare to the countless times we've had to hear about how sinfully wonderful San Francisco is and how woefully downtrodden Oakland is and "don't you just love the tradition, the restaurants, the Golden Gate Bridge, and Fisherman's Wharf, and, oh yeah, isn't Pac Bell Park the loveliest creation since Eve herself? I mean, when Barry is muscling one high and deep into McCovey Cove, you just feel like you're in Heaven. But it's better than Shoeless Joe in the "Field of Dreams" because it's not a dream, it's real, and it's not Iowa, it's San Francisco!" To which I reply, "Gag me with a Tofu Burger."

But seriously, that's just the half of it. They really do believe they have some sort of right to cast a condescending eye across the Bay just because they were here first. And they have the audacity to revel in their "rich history," when they have hardly prospered at all. The numbers speak for themselves. The A's have played in twice as many Fall Classics, and own a 4–0 edge in Series triumphs, including a sweep of their cross-town rivals in 1989. So dominant was Oakland in those four games that the Giants did not hold a lead in any *single inning* of the series. Alas, that World Series will be most remembered for these numbers: 5:04 and 7.1, as a major earthquake rippled through the Bay Area mere moments before Game 3 was to take place. Baseball, indeed, took its proper place behind life itself and to the many real-life heroes that came forward during that horrible, horrible time. Strangely enough, many Giant fans believed that the tremor was some sort of sign, perhaps even a wake-up call to their slumbering team. It seemed awfully pompous to assume that they were more deserving of a Series win after all their precious city had been through, obviously forgetting that Oakland was equally affected by the quake. While both cities showed their true grit under unprecedented circumstances, the on-field drama never got a chance to unfold. The A's, on a mission since their shocking Series defeat just one year prior, pummeled the Giants by the scores of 13–7 and 9–6 to win their fourth league title. Our little-town team had beaten the big-city Giants in the most convincing fashion possible and we never got the chance to fully celebrate. To this day, when I trade insults back and forth with Giant fans, I almost feel guilty for using "1989" as my ultimate comeback.

The media doesn't help matters. A man can fall asleep waiting for A's highlights on *SportsCenter*, but hey, the Yankees and Red Sox come first. We get it. But the local press isn't any better. When the A's were winning all those titles in the 70's, it was a "Bay Area" accomplishment. Suddenly, we were "their" A's. But when the Giants (or 49ers) excelled, it was exclusively San Francisco's to revel in. And the notion that the A's have worn out their welcome will never go away completely. Like when Dave Del Grande suggested in his column for *The Daily Review* in 2004 that the Bay Area wasn't big enough for two baseball teams (hardly an original thought). Not surprisingly, he chose to send the A's packing, figuring that San Francisco (think dollar signs) would be better equipped to copy the newly crowned Red Sox' recipe for success.

My reply: "Let's ignore for a second that Dave Del Grande is a "reaction" journalist who preys on easy targets like the A's because he's smart enough to know that their fans will speak out on their behalf, and let's face it, hate mail is *still* mail. But now to the truth of the matter. The Boston Red Sox did not win solely on the strength of their vibrant front office. They won because they were willing (and able) to open their checkbooks to the Schilling's and the Foulke's, who would increase their chances come playoff time. In fact, Boston *should* have won this year, and the only reason not to bet the mortgage on them was because history forbade us to do so. OK, so why punish Beane whose system has netted him 90+ wins the last five seasons, even though he's had to do most of his shopping at the second-hand store? The A's have a long history of grooming talent that dates back to their days in Philadelphia and Kansas City. The downside is that their budding stars often come to full bloom in other teams' uniforms, and it's no great mystery why. A's fans are an insecure lot. Most of them prefer security to winning. Security in knowing that 1) the team is going to stay in Oakland and 2) that the players they become enamored with are going to hang around for awhile. Compare the Finley era to the Haas era. More fans attended games during the Haas regime because they felt like they were getting something special for their dollar, even though Finley's 70's teams were ultimately more successful. Today's fans aren't frustrated with Beane's system; they're frustrated with not having the means to fully reap the rewards of that system. But it's still a system that should be rewarded, not punished. So if one Bay Area team is to hit the road, let it be the team with no trophies on the mantel. Just be sure to leave the checkbook behind, boys. And take Del Grande with you."

When baseball experts dive into a discussion about the dominant teams of the 1970's, they mention Cincinnati's Big Red Machine first, followed closely by the pitching-wealthy Baltimore Orioles, and the slugging New York Yankees. The A's—the team that won five straight division titles and three consecutive World Series'— fall in somewhere after that. What makes this especially unnerving is that the Reds, who ran roughshod over the league in 1975–76, fielded pretty much the same squad then as they did in '72, when they fell to the A's in seven gut-wrenching games. And that was with Oakland's star right fielder, Reggie Jackson, on crutches. How about the 1973 A's, perhaps the best of Finley's championship teams? They had the league MVP in a healthy and rejuvenated Jackson, plus a trio of 20-game winners in Hunter, Holtzman, and Blue. That team, like the 1969 Orioles, met up with the Miracle Mets in the Fall Classic. But unlike the Birds, Oakland averted a monumental upset to capture a second straight crown. And before Reggie's Yankees shook up LA in 1977 and 1978, he and the A's made short work of those same, though less-seasoned, Dodgers in a '74 Series that could have very easily ended in a sweep. Strangely the late 80's A's get the most ink of any Oakland ball clubs, despite suffering two of the biggest upsets in World Series history. But boy did they steamroll the competition during the regular season. And maybe that was the whole deal with those 70's teams; they didn't impress the way the Big Red Machine or the Bronx Zoo did. Instead, they won like the 2005 White Sox, in the same manner that Tonianne mentioned when talking about Dick Williams: with fundamentals. Pitching, timely hitting, and defense. Winning only the games they had to win. Knowing that they weren't going to beat themselves. They were a throwback to the throwbacks. But they played before sparse crowds, wore strange uniforms, fought among themselves, and were owned by a man who himself downplayed their performances (at arbitration time, naturally). Unfortunately, that is what history remembers most about the Mustache Gang.

It has become the stuff of legends, minus the happy ending (yet). Billy Beane, like Charles Finley before him, part genius, part madman, tinkers with his A's every year looking for that perfect match. He's working with a lot less coin than some of his more popular *compadres*, but Beane sees that as an opportunity, not a handicap. He's the little boy who sells the cow for mere beans only to find that there's magic in those beans (as there surely is magic in Beane) and he and his A's climb the beanstalk to do battle with baseball's giants. For seven years Oakland has stood toe-to-toe with the New Yorks and Bostons and Anaheims only to have the giant awake in late September or early October to send little Billy spiraling down the beanstalk. No goose with golden eggs. Just plain old goose eggs in the World Series department. But Billy, he's a stubborn boy and he'll keep trading those cows like he did Giambi and Tejada and Hudson and Mulder. And he'll keep coming home with packages of Kendall and Kotsay beans. But he won't be satisfied until that beanstalk grows and grows, way up high, past all those giants. Where he can stand at the top and defiantly say, "Look at me now." Because until he is able to do that, the baseball world will continue to see his A's as nothing more than a fun, exciting, yet harmless little ball club; the Little Engine that Almost Does. And until Beane reaches the highest floor of the Beanstalk Hotel, he is just a kid with a few bucks trying to buy in at the Big Boy's table; a nerd with a computer who somehow managed to alienate his fellow GM's. In many cases, he's gotten the better of them, but without the ring, he may never gain their full respect.

Respect.

Damn, there's that word again. Sing it, Aretha.

22 / Starting Over (2006, 1st Half)

"This year's love had better last
Heaven knows it high time
And I've been waiting on my own
Too Long"

—David Gray, *This Year's Love*

Sunday, March 19: Hope Springs Eternal

I have often pondered this question when it comes to my sports teams: Is it better that they perform well during the season, only to falter in the end, when it counts the most? Or do I prefer them to be awful all the time, so that I am not trapped into thinking that this might be the year? I don't know. I look at the late 70's through the mid-80's and even though the A's swam in mediocrity for a decade, those were great times for me. But maybe that's because I was in my teens and I was going to enjoy the games whether the A's won or not. When the team went through seven years of famine from 1993–99, I had more or less lost interest. But maybe it's because I was married with a son and my priorities had shifted a little. I just don't know. But I know this: the A's have broken my heart for the last six seasons and every season I come back thinking *this* is the year that we break through. So in a strange way, I have answered my own question. I'd rather have the opportunity to win and take the chance that it'll end bloody. It's almost like falling in love and you go through that honeymoon stage where everything is perfect and just as you start to think that she is the one, something goes wrong. And this happens year after year. So you start to become a little guarded, a little jaded. You spend the cold months of November through February getting over the last

209

one but then comes spring. You feel like a new man, ready to conquer the world. And you meet *her*. And she's beautiful and funny and you have all these things in common and boy, can she…*cook*. After some bumps in April, the relationship starts to really take off around June and you're skating; this is bliss. Crazy things pop into your head. An October wedding perhaps? But you don't want to jinx it, so you keep those thoughts to yourself. As summer turns to autumn, you start to feel the relationship turning, too. And you start to think, "Was this too good to be true?" Now you wait for that moment, it's coming. The girl and the circumstances may be different than the year before but the result is always the same. And she takes your heart with her and you swear you will never put yourself in that position again. But of course, you do.

Man, I sound like a freaking Red Sox fan. Always expecting the worst. Well, how can I not sometimes? How many teams have experienced a six-year string of misfortune such as this?

2000: Terrence Long loses a ball in the twilight; Yankees score six in the first inning of the fifth and deciding game.

2001: Jeremy Giambi doesn't slide in Game 3; A's miss chance to sweep, and ultimately lose three straight.

2002: The Twins parlay four hits, two errors, two wild pitches, and one hit batsman into a seven-run inning to win Game 4, go on to take the series back in Oakland.

2003: Two A's are thrown out at home in the same inning of Game 3; Hudson comes out in the first inning of Game 4 due to an injury he suffered the night before in a Boston pub. A's lose Game 5 at home, blowing their second 2–0 series lead in three seasons.

2004: The body of Mark Mulder is abducted in August (well, not really); the A's stumble in September, miss playoffs for first time since '99.

2005: The injuries to Bobby Crosby and Rich Harden are too much to overcome; for the second straight year, A's fall short of the post-season.

In five of the last six seasons, an opposing team has celebrated on our field: the Yankees, Twins, Red Sox, and the Angels twice. And yet the optimist in me says we must have played some pretty fantastic baseball just to get to that point.

So here it is March 19, and Oakland is geared—and according to some experts, *favored*—to make some serious noise come October. The team is hungry and healthy and perhaps even deeper than in recent years. The addition of Frank Thomas and Milton Bradley should only strengthen an already solid lineup. And even though the A's have put my heart through the meat grinder the last half-decade or so, I am ready for the challenges of a new relationship.

Monday, April 3: Let's Get it On

I love Opening Night. Everything is brand new; it's a clean slate for all. It's a night of firsts. And it's a night to become acquainted (or reacquainted) with the players that you hope will take you deep into October. As I drank my first MGD of the season in the parking lot before the game, I told Greg that in six or so months I'd be pouring one of these cold ones over his head. That's right; Opening Night is *the* night for World Series optimism.

We sat in the Field Level Outfield seats tonight; right field area, section 103, row 25. "We" being Christina, Greg, Ernie III and myself. Tonight was my first look at the "new" stadium and its tarp-covered upper deck. It was weird not seeing people up there but not a bad look overall.

The Yankees are here, which only added to tonight's festivities, especially with former Cy Young Award winners Barry Zito and Randy Johnson taking the hill. The Yankees in town translates to Yankee *fans* in town and we were surrounded by a bunch of them. Not exactly a fun night for that. As the New York starting lineup was introduced amid both cheers and boos, The Third (as I call Ernie III) yelled into my ear, "This team is fricking *stacked*!" Well, duh. Still, there was no way to see *this* coming.

It started well enough. Jason Giambi struck out to end the top of the first, leaving a couple of men on base as we shouted our approval. The second inning was not so fun. By the time I got back from a trip to the ATM, the bad guys had broken through for three runs. Then with the bags juiced, A-Rod sent a rocket into the cheap seats to make it 7-zip, and the Yankee fans were giving us the "it's over" sign. Well, it *was* over, even Yogi would tell you so. But it was early and the tickets were paid for so we sat around to see if the A's could make it interesting. Frank Thomas crushed a home run in his first at-bat in Green-and-Gold but there was little to cheer for after that.

Thankfully, the atmosphere, the cold beer, and knowing that there were still 161 games to go, made losing 15–2 on Opening Night an easier pill to swallow than you might expect.

Tuesday, April 4: The First Win

I brought my co-worker and friend, Vince Contreras, tonight. We were in section 127 under the overhang, which was perfect, considering the Bay Area's month-long impersonation of Seattle. Christina and Greg took the evening off, leaving me to win this one on my own.

We arrived a little late, with Rich Harden already in a jam; a clean-shaven Johnny Damon on third and Derek Jeter on second. But the young gun got out of it in style, striking out A-Rod, Gary Sheffield, and Giambi in succession.

The mood wasn't nearly as festive as last night, which could be expected if we were playing the Devil Rays, but come on, these are still the Yankees. Their fans were ever-present, but much more subdued, perhaps fatigued from cheering their team to two touchdowns the night before. I watched from the beer line as Nick Swisher homered to tie things up at one, and got back to my seat in time to see Mark Kotsay drive in Marco Scutaro with a sharp single to right. The 2–1 lead was short-lived as the Yankees broke through with a run in the fourth and forged ahead in the sixth on a Jorge Posada base hit.

In the bottom half, Eric Chavez stepped up. "Come on, Eric, pretend it's June and get a hold of one," I thought to myself, as I reached for my beer. The roar of the crowd caught my attention and I looked up to see the ball heading towards the right-field bleachers. Tied again. And it stayed that way until the bottom of the ninth, thanks to some stellar pitching from the pen: Justin Duchscherer, Joe Kennedy, and Huston Street. Vince turned to me and said the A's "are going to win it in this inning." Great. He's been to one baseball game in his life prior to tonight and already he's throwing out predictions. Well, he was right. Milton Bradley led off with a walk and Jason Kendall laid down a beauty of a bunt to get him to second. After an intentional walk to Swisher, Scutaro took his turn at bat. A career .255 hitter, the Venezuelan often turns it up a notch in the clutch, and he delivered again with a shot over the head of leftfielder Hideki Matsui to bring home Bradley with the season's first win.

Thursday, April 6: Early Season Giddiness

After the A's came back from their Opening Night shellacking to take two out of three from the Yankees, I thought today was a perfect day for a family e-mail (those written by me will be preceded by "DM"):

DM: I know that professionals are supposed to act the part. You know the clichés, "take one game at a time," "stay on an even keel," blah, blah, blah. But for the A's to get hit in the head with a frying pan on Monday night, and come back to win the next two games against that monstrous lineup speaks volumes about their resiliency. (As resilient as a team can be after three games anyway.) They refused to blink after seeing stars in the opener and let the Yankees make costly errors and leave runners on base. (New York netted a grand total of one run after the fifth inning the last two nights; can you say "shut down"?) And after falling behind 4-love last night, they took advantage of Yankee mistakes, collected clutch hits, and, (gads!) ran the bases with a purpose not seen since Rickey was here. Too early to get all giddy here (the A's wouldn't allow it anyway), but a nice about-face heading into Seattle.

Abel: The A's are about "one series at a time." The fact that our first series came against the best offensive lineup in baseball will only help as the early part of the season progresses. Every lineup our staff faces now will look like a minor league team.

Rose (speaking in the third person): Rose, what are you going to do now that the A's have taken two from the Yankees? I'm going to Disneyland! (She really is, next week.) Yippee!

DM: So much for business-like. Put that champagne bottle down, Rose.

John: Settle down everyone. (Yippee!) Here's the difference from the last couple of years:

Monopoly (Milton Bradley) and Yahtzee! (Frank Thomas). Without them we score four runs in the series. The Yankees' weakness is their bullpen (and even their starting pitching isn't that solid), but you have to have hitters to exploit that weakness. Monopoly and Yahtzee! take pressure off of Chavez, Johnson, and Swisher, which will help them relax and be more productive. How many times have we agonized because we have no offense to speak of at the beginning of the season?

Saturday, April 15: Boom, Boom, Boom!

Me and Vince were at the Coliseum today, with Greg tending to an ill Christina at home. This combo had worked once before, and to make sure the planets were completely aligned, we had Harden on the hill again.

Swisher's bomb in the fifth gave us a 2–1 lead but the Rangers rallied in the sixth. After Harden fanned the first two batters, he uncharacteristically walked the next two. Normally I would have seen him through to the end of the inning, but I had to pee like you wouldn't believe. I figured if I was fast enough, I'd be back in time to see the third out. I figured right. And wrong. I was back in time to see the third out, but that was after Phil Nevin had deposited a Harden offering over the centerfield wall for a three-run jack and a 4–2 lead.

The rain had not yet begun to fall when lightning struck three times at the Coliseum....

I was barely back in my seat when Chavez led off the bottom of the inning with a first-pitch dinger, and Vince asked me if I felt a little better about the score. Big Hurt didn't give me a chance to answer; on *his* first pitch, he tied the ball game with a homer to left. There was a buzz starting to circle the stadium as Bradley strode to the plate. Once again, the first pitch became a souvenir and suddenly the A's were in front 5–4. Three pitches, three homeruns. I turned to Vince with one of those "are you fricking kidding me" looks as the fans around me high-fived and hugged each other.

Christina called but I didn't answer; there were still three innings left and I didn't want to jinx this. But I kept the message: "Hey, what the heck is going on over there? What did you do, sprinkle some fairy dust on those players or something? What the heck?"

Whatever it takes. Street threw down a road block on the Rangers in the ninth, and we had a 5–4 win. This one, I'd savor for a while.

Sunday, April 16: Egg on My Face

Baseball is cruel sometimes. There's no time to appreciate the moment or the moment will kick you in the teeth. One day after the three-homer explosion, we spent Easter Sunday at John's house. As the kids hunted for eggs, the A's went hunting for a series victory. John tuned in on the headphones and he bore good news: Chavez' two-run double had given us a 3–1 lead in the eighth, with Street coming in to close. But the Rangers staged a "resurrection" of sorts, scoring four runs off our young closer to turn a two-run deficit into a 5–3 lead.

Rotten eggs.

The A's had a chance in the bottom of the ninth, as I grabbed the headphones (Christina thought it would be good luck), but Swisher flied out with the bags full to end it. Now we're 6–7 with a day off tomorrow.

Friday, April 21: The Perfect Gift

Happy Birthday to me. 39 years. Damn, I'm old. The A's can make me feel a little younger by beating the Angels tonight. Both clubs figure to be in the hunt again come the fall. The Halos might not be the Yankees and Red Sox in terms of total salaries, but they still flaunt their money pretty well. So a win against these guys is always nice.

We took them. When I left the house for dinner we were down 3–2. But Chavez hit a two-run shot in the seventh and Kendall drove home an insurance run in the eighth for a 5–3 lead going into the last inning. The Angels, as is their custom, mounted a threat while I chowed down on prime rib at Texas Roadhouse. With men on first and third and one out in the ninth, Kiko Calero struck out rookie Jeff Mathis and as pinch-runner Robb Quinlan took off for second base, the umpire ruled that Mathis interfered with Kendall's throw, thus ending the game in a bizarre fashion that has somehow become the norm whenever these two teams face each other.

Saturday, April 29: Wedding Crashers

The A's took a proper back seat to Christina & Greg's wedding, but when one of the groomsmen flashed a "5–1" score at the reception, and Ernie III grumbled that Esteban Loaiza was a waste of money, I suddenly took interest. My phone would later flash some good news: the Kansas City rain had wiped out another poor outing by Loaiza (who would soon join Harden on the disabled list), and the A's escaped what looked to be a certain defeat. So with Mother Nature offering a helping end, I grabbed a beer and looked for someone to dance with.

Monday, May 1: Barry Good
Another nail-biter between division rivals in Anaheim. Barry was masterful (no runs on five hits in seven-plus innings), and the A's escaped too many scares for my heart's liking in a 1–0 victory. The Halos had men on first and second in the bottom of the eighth when Garrett Anderson hit a shot off Zito that everyone in the world thought was a three-run homer, but Jay Payton calmly collected the ball at the wall. Calero relieved Zito (surely because Barry needed a change of underwear after that near-miss) and got Vladamir Guerrero to line out to left, a screamer that stayed up long enough for Swisher to corral. In the ninth, Kotsay robbed Tim Salmon of a sure double, holding onto the ball as he crashed into the fence. Duchscherer then gave up a single before retiring the next two for a huge, huge win.

Tuesday, May 2: Kendall by Knockout
Break out the fighting A's!

Me and Abel kept tabs on-line, as Chavez started the day with a three-run homer in the first, and Crosby closed out a six-run ninth with his own three-run bomb. But no one was talking about homeruns after this 10–3 rout of the Angels. Instead, all the focus was on Jason Kendall who took offense to a few choice words by pitcher John Lackey in the sixth and charged the mound, starting a little scuffle between division rivals. Both players were given the heaveho, which didn't go over too well with Angel's manager Mike Scioscia. No matter. The umps had their say and the A's bats had the final word in a lovely two-game sweep down south.

We're now 14–12, still chasing the red-hot Rangers for first place.

Saturday, May 6: Winning Ugly
A win is a win is a win. Even those that are gift-wrapped by the Devil Rays. A day after a painful trip to the dentist, I watched this

one from the couch. Way back in the beginning stages of this book, I mentioned that one of the great things about baseball is the opportunity to see something new every day. This was one of those days. In the bottom half of the second, Jay Payton was at first base with two outs and Dan Johnson at the plate. Johnson received ball three from pitcher Seth McClung, but everyone—including Johnson and McClung—thought it was ball *four*. By the time any of the players realized what was happening, Payton had walked into second with one of the most bizarre "stolen bases" in history.

The right-fielder was involved in two other unusual moments in the bottom of the ninth, just minutes after Joe Kennedy had escaped a bases-loaded, one-out jam in the top of the inning. This time Payton was at second base (and Johnson at first) with no outs and the game tied at two. Scutaro, whom I assumed was going to get his usual walk-off hit because that's what he does, instead hit a soft pop fly to shortstop, Julio Lugo. Lugo let the ball drop in front of him to force Johnson at second, while Payton took off for third and then, after getting caught in a rundown, headed back for second and beat the tag—just as Scutaro pulled up to the bag! We went from first and second and no outs to a man on second—Payton, naturally—and two outs after a weird (but fitting) double play.

So up stepped Kendall, no stranger to strange plays, and he hit a slow grounder to third basemen Aubrey Huff, who let the ball go under his legs, and Payton raced home to score the winning run.

We'll take it.

Friday, May 12: State of the A's

As the A's limped into a three-game set at Yankee Stadium with a 17–17 record, I wanted to get the family's take on the season thus far. (Disclaimer: as fans, or better put, as "paying customers," we reserve the right to get frustrated every now and then, so our words can be a little harsh at times.)

DM: Any thoughts on the A's so far? Too early to take real notice? Are they gutless or just banged up?

John: The pitching has been a disappointment. Many people picked us to go to the World Series. Bobby Crosby was touted as MVP? I don't see it. Blanton has gotten rocked since his first game. Harden, like Crosby is a wimp when it comes to injuries. Zito has actually pitched better than he usually does this early in the season. Haren gives up too many homers and Loaiza has been a bust. To top it off we've got injuries in the bullpen to go along with some blow ups. Now we are starting to lose every day players.

The good news? The rest of the division is letting us hang around. Hopefully they'll all be sorry later.

Gutless? Not with Swisher, Kendall and Bradley on the team. They won't let the rest of the team be laid back any more. From what I've heard, Bradley gets in people's faces when they don't make a play that should have been made and Swisher could have played on the teams of the 70's. Kendall is the same way, which is why he's on a little "vacation" right now.

Abel: This is still May right? We just need a little more global warming and we'll play great from the beginning of a season. This division is definitely ours to lose and I don't see that happening as the weather heats up. My prediction: we clinch by Sept 15.

John: That's the same day Barry will hit number 714.

Sunday, May 14: Your Mama

I love these early-morning Sunday games when I can just lay on the couch and watch the action. The A's needed this one after scoring a total of three runs in two losses at Babe's Place. Kotsay stroked a two-run homer off Randy Johnson in the first, Payton added a solo shot in the sixth, and Dan Haren went the distance on Mother's Day, sending the Yankees to their first day-game defeat of the season, 6–1.

Wednesday, May 17: Back Where I Belong

My first game in person since April 15th and the good guys welcomed me back with a 7–2 spanking of Seattle. Barry was lights out, doing it with some help from his friends (Payton pegged a runner trying to score in the first and Chavez speared a line drive, and in one motion, doubled up the runner at first in the second.) There's a reason Chavy has all those Gold Gloves, folks. Zito also did it *despite* his fielders (Kotsay and Payton made errors behind him). The lefty left the game after seven innings with not one run to his name.

Christina and Greg took Ethan tonight and he was full of energy, clapping and cheering on the A's and giving me high-fives.

Ernie III and Mark (Kim's fiancé) joined us in the later innings for a mini-family-reunion.

Friday, May 19: Taming the Giant
Me and Vince were at the House tonight for a showdown between cross-town adversaries. Adding to the hoopla was Barry Bonds and his 713 homeruns, just one away from you-know-who.

And what a game it was; we kicked their butts! 1–0, ha!

Play was delayed by a little bit of rain but by the time we had nestled into our seats (even though our tickets were marked "Standing Room Only") it was clear that we were in for a show. Dan Haren, who has been brilliant lately (in his last outing he got the best of Randy Johnson) was at it again, keeping Bonds in the park and the Giants from crossing the plate during his eight innings of work. But the A's had a minimal amount of breathing room (our lone run being scored in the third), which set the stage for a confrontation between closer Huston Street and the Man Chasing Babe with two outs in the ninth; one swing from 714 and a tie game. The Kid against The Old Pro. Shades of a young Bobby Welch facing Reggie in the '78 Classic. Natural Ability versus The Science Project. A sell-out crowd on its feet. Would the A's walk him? Why not? For the past few years, Barry has owned moments like this.

But not tonight.

Tonight, Street had more Desire, striking out the Slugger on a nasty changeup. Ball game. That's five in a row and I'll be back tomorrow.

Saturday, May 20: Temporary Insanity
I wonder what goes on inside my head sometimes.

Before this series started I told Abel that I would "be ok" with seeing Bonds hit number 714 in Oakland so long as the A's won the game. Given the chance to use the other side of my brain, I would have quickly recanted. So naturally Barry got his blasted homer and naturally the A's lost and naturally the ball yard was half-filled with Giants' fans who all seemed to be sitting in my section, including one lady wearing one of those ridiculous half-A's, half-Giant hats. What's worse, the loss negated a ninth-inning rally that had briefly tied the game at two, only to see us give up a pair of runs in the tenth, as the bell-ringing lady with the stupid hat sitting in front of me cackled in my face. Meanwhile I was on the phone with my brother-in-law Michael (the cop) trying to see how much time I would serve for pushing the aforementioned party down the stairs. You know, being my first offense and all. This surely was a bitter pill for me to swallow; in some ways it felt like a playoff game: a tough defeat followed by taunting from opposing fans.

In fact, why am I still talking about this game?

Log off, dummy.

Wednesday, May 24: Desperately Seeking a Win

After a humbling four-game skid that included two losses each to the Giants and White Sox, I figured it was time for another family e-mail:

DM: The A's streaking ways are killing me. They're up, they're down. I've had girlfriends less moody. Seriously I feel like I'm dating a schizophrenic. No idea what each day will bring. Friday night (a 1–0 win over SF), she was massaging my feet and baking me cookies; come last night (a crushing defeat in Chicago), she was lighting my bedroom set on fire.

And since I'm comparing my baseball team to a woman, that's all you need to know about my life right about now.

Are we destined to win this division with less than 85 wins? I just don't think we strike fear into anybody, the way the Yankees and the Cardinals and the Sox teams do. I know it's early and we're banged up but come on, guys.

P.S. Christina—I would have written sooner but I just got out on bail after slapping that Giants' fan. I know I'm not supposed to hit a lady, but trust me, she was no lady. Besides, you gave me permission.

John: Dear Desperately Seeking Miss Right, you have to understand that women can be very difficult to figure out. She could be depressed by the weather, or maybe she's homesick. Maybe some new clothes would help. Maybe she's not feeling well and once she's completely healthy she'll be more open to your needs. I would give her a little more time—say after the All Star break— then see how she's acting. If all else fails you could dump her for that woman across the bay, but just remember, that lady over there will never give you a ring.

P.S. That lady could have avoided being slapped if her wheel chair didn't get stuck in the aisle.

Tonianne: If we continue on this "streak" pace, we'll win the division, lose the first two games of the divisional play-offs, win the next three, win the first game of the league playoffs, lose the next three, win the next three, lose the first three of the WS and win the last four for the championship…so what's the prob? You and your girl should be getting married just about that time.

Thursday, May 25: Going "Down" in History
And if you thought it could not get any worse, you thought wrong.…

The A's blew a seven-run lead for only the third time in *franchise* history in falling to Texas, 8–7. After Nick Swisher's two-run laser in the fifth gave his team a 7–0 lead, it looked as if the Green-and-Gold was geared to end its losing streak and get back into a first-place tie.

That is, until the hosts began to play home run derby against our pitching staff. Rod Barajas hit a three-run jack in the sixth, followed by an Ian Kinsler solo shot that made it 7–4. Mark Teixeira jumped on a Steve Karsay offering in the seventh, Kinsler went deep again in the eighth to tie it, and Phil Nevin started a wild celebration at home after his walk-off against Huston Street.

The losing streak is at six, we're 22–25, and two games out of first.

I took two Advil's and I'll write to the family in the morning.

Friday, May 26: Family Therapy
Today's e-mails went like this:

DM: I just broke up with the A's. (Actually, *they* dumped *me*; I'm just trying to maintain some sort of dignity.)

John: Last night she broke your heart. Today she'll come crawling back begging for forgiveness. If not, there's good news on the horizon. One of your old flings—KC—is coming to town, and she's feeling blue. Then again, she'll likely make you swear off women altogether after she gets through with you.

Ernie: Man, just use her. Get what you can from her, maybe a little bobble-head, and then forget about her until she is putting out again.

(Nice)

John: Looks like I picked the wrong week to stop sniffing glue.

Tonianne: Geez guys, take the good with the bad! That's why they play 162 games. Up, down, up, down. Ever hear of the June swoon? The sportswriters always had the Giants winning the Series during spring training, then June came, and everyone said, "Wait 'til next year!" So give it time, or wait 'til next year!

Abel: Don, I hope you're not planning on having *her* around at Mom & Dad's anniversary party!

DM: I already told her it was best that she stay home that day. Just because of the way she's been acting towards the whole family lately. I mean, it's not totally her fault; I should know how she gets this time of the month.

Tonight's score: Texas 5, A's 3.

Seven losses in a row.

Saturday, May 27: Finally!

The Streak is Dead! The Streak is Dead!

Barry was well, Barry, and the A's gave him some rare run support in a slide-busting 6–3 win. Zito showed why he is the true ace of our pitching staff by gutting it out over 126 pitches and this time the lead we built (6–0 after our turn in the sixth) remained standing at game's end.

Monday, May 29: How Low Can You Go?

The Kansas City Royals enter play tonight on a 1–15 skid and a 3–22 road record to their name. They are pinning their hopes on a starting pitcher (Seth Etherton) whose last victory came in May 2005—as a member of the A's. If there was ever a time for us to tee off and get back to winning baseball, tonight is it.

Instead.…

The A's stranded eight runners in scoring position and the Royals took full advantage in a 6–4 win at the Coliseum.

We have dropped nine of our last ten, and since this has to be what rock bottom feels like, I am going to bed with the comfort that this can't get any worse.

Right?

Tuesday, May 30: Royal Flush

Another game with Kansas City brought another scoop of agony. The Royals jumped out to a 4–0 lead in the first, increased it to 6–1 heading to the bottom half of the fourth, only to see the A's storm back to go ahead 7–6 after five innings.

And then depression set in.

KC used its mixture of "firsts" and "ex-A's" to win for the second straight night. *Ex-"A"* Matt Stairs ripped a two-out, a game-tying single off a struggling Street—the *first* RBI by a Royal pinch-hitter this year. Then Mike Grudzielanek drove home the winner in the tenth, the *first* extra-inning victory by Kansas City all season.

Family session tomorrow.

It *won't* be the *first* time.

Wednesday, May 31: Trouble in Paradise

DM: I know with Mom and Dad's half-century party looming, this might take a back seat, but if any of you get a moment to talk to her, it would mean a lot. Usually, I try to keep you all out of my relationships, but you all know her so well; some of you know her better than I do. I keep thinking this will boil over, but it's becoming like a disease to her and if something isn't done soon, there may be no saving us. And yeah it happens almost every May and then the summers are nice but then we do our little break-up in the fall (Abel says I should stop sneaking around with her cousin every September) before reuniting in February. Maybe a longer break is needed but I can't bring myself to do that; what would that say about me? But last night, it was so hard just being around her and Abel even threatened to hit her. It's a bad scene right now. I know we've been down this road before but if one of you wouldn't mind…you know, tell her how happy she made me back in '89, and even as recent as '03 (even though Ernie ended up consoling me at a bar after the Boston fiasco). Thanks a bunch.

John: DUMP HER!

Dump her like yesterday's newspaper. After the way she treated you last night, do it while you still have some dignity. If you don't tell her, I WILL! The fact that she's handicapped is no excuse to treat you like that. '89? That's a long time ago. You're holding on to a memory. C'mon Don! Let me give you some brotherly advice. You need a change of venue. Move to the East Coast and hook up with some Bostonian babe or New Yorker. You won't regret it. (What are the odds a gal from Boston will let you down year after year for 97 years?) And do yourself one more favor and cut the cousin loose too. (She sicker than the one you're with now.) **Adios you loonies!**

DM: And to think I was dedicating a book to her! For what? A few memories that mostly took place when I was a kid?! She has been nothing but a tease the last few years and she's cheap, too! Talk about the Big Hurt! You're right, John. Oh sure, she tried to save face last night, but in the end, she blew it. Opportunities lost! She tries to tell me that her life is just poorly managed but when will she ever accept responsibilities for her own actions? I mean, when I need a lift home, she is never there to pick me up. She's not even taking care of herself; shoot, those Texas girls are looking more attractive these days. And she's always coming up with some illness or another. Good riddance!

P.S. She just called; wants me to meet her at 12:35. Says it's *really* important.…

John: She thinks the book's about her? Hey sicko! It ain't about you! It's about *us*!

Don, don't go. It's a trap. Unless your idea of fun is a dagger in the back. Oh, she'll sweep you off your feet alright.

Rose: Do you want to know what the problem is? Your girlfriend is really a bunch of males in drag! John, *you're* the loony to suggest Don hook up with someone from Boston or New York! Don, since you haven't had any luck with women for years, stay single!

John: Thank you, Ann Landers.

Tone: Don, go meet her! Don't give up on her! Tell me who's worse, the New York woman with all her wealth and glitz (when's the last time *she* put out) or the gal from Atlanta? She's steady, maybe a little plain, but she's there year after year.

The one you're with now is young and vibrant, a little cocky perhaps and sometimes a little too loose for her own good, but she'll come around. Everyone has their ups and downs. Sometimes you just need to ride out the storm; I think there's a rainbow in your future so don't give up on her!

John: I'm just trying to save Don from being crushed again. Don, if you want to marry her, go ahead. But if you think you're going to change her, well don't come crying to me 30 years from now. If you don't like the East Coast you can always go Midwest. "I'm going to Kansas City, Kansas City here I come. They got some crazy little women there and I'm gonna get me one."

P.S. Didn't Matt Stairs play with Dwayne Murphy and Shooty Babbitt?

Tonianne: Man, just like a guy to move to the Midwest at the first little tremor (it wasn't even a 4.0). I keep trying to tell you guys that there's no such thing as a perfect marriage. You gotta take the good with the bad, or in this case, the bad with the good. It's only May. If you two are still struggling come August, then maybe you should see a marriage counselor? At least try to work out your problems before you give it all up for some "crazy little woman" from Kansas City. Remember, your girl left KC thirty-nine years ago and she's given you some of the best years of her life. So, she's lost a little something over the years; who hasn't? What have you done for her lately?

P.S. Don't give up on her cousin either. What's more important than family?

DM: What have I done for her lately? Are you kidding me? I was right there from 2000–03 when she flipped out every October. The first year I understood because she was going through a "youth phase" but after that, it became too much! And the last two years, she's done it in September!

Maybe I should wait until after October to sneak out with her cousin.

Meanwhile, the A's lead 2–0 after one inning.

Tonianne: I mean, here you guys are talking behind her back, why don't you get out there and support her? I know you've been there for her in the past but at least she's gotten you to October! Don't you think it's too soon to give up on her? It's not like she's bad; things just aren't going her way.

BTW, she's doing it again, taking the early lead (leading you on, so to speak).

Chavez' triple makes it 5–0 after seven and Blanton is cruising.

DM: OK, she just called me and said she has a pie in the oven for me. I hope it doesn't blow up in there. You know, she's not feeling well and she seems to be making an effort…wait, NO, this is what she wants. For me to get suckered in.

But I might still eat the pie.

(Should I be in a padded room for this? Oh, that's right; I already am.)

Tonianne: The pie seems to be bubbling up nicely, but it still has a few more minutes of baking time so who knows?

Jason Kendall gives the Royals a taste of their own medicine in the eighth by hitting his *first* homerun of the season—and his *first* as a member of the A's. Blanton is heading to the mound to (hopefully) close out a 7–0 win.

DM: When Kendall homers, I am not only getting a pie, I'm getting…never mind; this is a family show.

Big Joe pitches a complete-game, five-hit shutout and we say sayonara to May with a "W" next to "Oakland." The A's finish the month 12–17, not nearly as bad as last May, but bad enough. On the flip side, no one is running away with the division; even the Angels are struggling.

Thursday, June 1: Turning the Page

The A's opened last month with a stirring 1–0 win at Anaheim as Barry Zito tossed zeroes at the Angels.

Tonight, the A's opened *this* month with another shutout win, started by Barry Zito.

I love stuff like that.

Barry's counterpart, Boof Bonser (I'm not making that up) was nearly as good from the hill for the Twins, but he threw three pitches he wishes he had back; homeruns by Thomas, Kotsay, and Johnson sparked the good guys to a 4–0 win that lasted just 117 minutes.

Friday, June 2: Through Thick and Thin

Happy 50th anniversary to Mom and Dad, or as ESPN would call them, "Best. Parents. Ever." So we traded in tonight's tickets to watch the game at Carol's house, and it was during Christina's congratulatory speech that reminded me just how important the A's really are to this family.

Frank Thomas led off the second inning with his 461st career homerun and Kirk Saarloos was out-dueling 2004 Cy Young Award winner Johan Santana through seven in hopes of tossing the team's third straight shutout.

Meanwhile, Christina (Mom and Dad's oldest grandchild) paid tribute to their half-century feat. As she stood in front of the television, a few of us could see enough of the screen and we let out a groan—in the middle of her toast—as Justin Morneau took Saarloos for a two-run ride over the right-field wall. Ball game.

So they couldn't pull it out for Mom and Dad, but somehow, I don't think it really mattered to them.

Tonight, it didn't even matter to me. (Much.)

Saturday, June 3: Saving Face

If the A's are going to get back in the playoff hunt, they will surely need the services of Eric Chavez and Huston Street.

Today they got enough from both. Chavy drove in both of our runs and the reigning Rookie of the Year recorded the last six outs to preserve a 2–1 payback win.

Which brings up something I have long wondered about. Shouldn't saves be called "preservations"? To save is to rescue, and relievers don't often come to the rescue (not saying they never do, just not often), they come to preserve. In fact, in most cases, the guy coming in to "save" the ball game isn't even called a "reliever" anymore, he's called a "closer." In another words, he's called in to close it out, to preserve.

Today Street came on in the eighth inning with two men on and nobody out, so in that regard, he "saved" the game for us.

Now if only he'd save you from this discussion.

Sunday, June 4: My Family, Mi Familia

There's a party going on right here.…

Today's game took a back seat to yet another family function; this time we were in Livermore to celebrate the aforementioned fifty years of marriage between Mom and Dad. It was a good old-fashioned reunion with the extended family and many of Mom and Dad's old friends. Just an amazing event put on by the sisters (and sisters-in-law and nieces). At one point the DJ had everyone stand in a circle around the honorees on the dance floor, and then he asked us to look around at one another. That's when it hit me as to how big we really are (and only first cousins were there!) Doesn't matter that we don't see each other often enough. We're connected and we always will be. So when the DJ played "We Are Family" and had everyone clap our hands, well, if you can't get goose bumps over moments like that, you better check twice for a pulse.

The A's did their part with a 5–1 shutdown of the Twins, to take three of four in a series that saw our staff give up just three runs. Outstanding. Afterwards, a family and its baseball team crossed paths once more.

Tonianne: "When we left the party on Sunday, we went to Outback in Dublin to take Patrick and Tenny to dinner. Anyway, while we were waiting to order, this guy walks by and I say, 'Hey that looks like Jay Payton.' We sit there arguing over whether or not it was him. Tenny insists that it was him, I'm not sure and the other two are like 'no way.' So, when he comes back from the bathroom, he walks by our table, and Tenny shouts, 'Jay!' He turns, and like four complete idiots, we all wave together and say 'Hey Jay.' He says 'hey' back and walks away. Just picture us in unison saying

'Hey Jay' with our hands up like we've known him all our lives. After he walked away, we laughed so hard, we were crying. What a bunch of geek A's fans!"

Thursday, June 8: Viva Loaiza
The signing of Esteban Loaiza paid its first dividend tonight in a 4–1 victory at Cleveland. In earning his first win of the season, the Mexican native pitched seven innings of five-hit ball.

Little by little (or is it, "poco a poco"?), the pitching is starting to come around, heading into New York.

Friday, June 9: Déjà Vu in the Big Apple
Dan Haren faced Randy Johnson for the second time this year, and though he wasn't nearly as sharp, he still came away a 6–5 winner. Big Hurt homered off the Big Unit, and two other A's (Antonio Perez and Bobby Kielty) took the Livermore High grad deep, making it a Happy 42nd Birthday for my brother Abel, whose good friend Jim Wright went to school with Johnson.

Sunday, June 11: Above Water
A Yankee Sweep!

Barry labored heavily in this one, giving up five runs and seven walks in seven innings, but we took them, 6–5. So maybe the pitching isn't quite there, but now we have the bats going. Today's hero was Dan Johnson who homered twice, and for the first time since May 21, the A's (32–31) are over .500.

Tuesday, June 13: Quik Stop
I had tickets for tonight, but I have too much to do before my trip to Mexico later this week. As often happens when I miss a scheduled game, the A's played as if there was an early curfew tonight, shutting down Seattle 2–0 in two hours, six minutes.

Joe Blanton, who is either very good or very bad lately, was on the plus side for this one: eight innings, five hits, no walks. Payton homered in the fifth and that was that. That's five straight and Street has a save in all of them.

Thursday, June 15: Seventh Heaven

Tonianne sent this e-mail today: Hey little brother, your girl seems a lot happier these days! Guess you've had pie every night this week! Love ya, Tone.

And this from ESPN columnist **Jerry Crasnick:** "It was 101 degrees in Arlington, Texas on Monday when the Rangers returned from a grueling road trip to begin a four-game series against the White Sox. To add to their discomfort, they felt the familiar surge of hot Oakland Athletic breath wafting in from the West Coast. As American League West opponents have discovered, Athletics in the rearview mirror are closer than they appear."

The streak is at seven games after sweeping the Mariners out of town, 9–6, and we've moved a half game in front of Texas. Dan Johnson is on a tear right now. Hitting as low as .199 on June 3, he's now up to .249 after going 4-for-4 today.

I feel like it's been forever since I went to a game and it's going to be even longer with me leaving the country for a week. Hopefully, we'll keep this thing going while I'm away.

Sunday, June 25: Back Home

I am back in California after an amazing trip. Let's see how my A's did: we swept the Dodgers to run our winning streak to ten games, lost two of three in Colorado (including back-to-back shutouts, which is absurd), and took two out of three from the Giants. My cell phone's internet service was my only contact with the outside world while in Mexico; I could not make or take any calls. It was last night, while getting dressed for the town *fiesta*, that I checked in on the A's-Giant game. We were up 7–5 heading into the ninth, but they started a rally; a leadoff base hit, followed by a walk to Bonds. After a dozen or so anxious pushes of the "refresh" button, my worst fears came to life: Ray Durham hit a dramatic, three-run homer off of Street to win it. But the A's picked themselves off the canvas today and, behind Loaiza's third straight win (a complete-game gem), stomped San Francisco, 10–4.

Sunday, July 2: A Weak Week

I think I picked the wrong time to come home. After dropping two of three at San Diego, the A's returned to Oakland, and were swept by lowly Arizona. As we did in Colorado, we had to go extra innings just to avoid getting swept by the Padres. We had no such luck against the Diamondbacks, and now the Detroit Tigers, the team with the league's best record, come to town.

So…this slump has nothing to do with me, right?

Tuesday, July 4: Going Fourth

Quick, how do you celebrate the 4th?
With a fifth, on the 3rd.
                    (A little Bleacher Bum humor from the old days.)

After watching the A's beat the Tigers at Abel's last night (which included a televised fireworks display) I decided it was time for some live action. Been too long. So I hung out with Christina, Greg, and Ethan this afternoon. Dan Haren was awesome, seven innings of four-hit ball, plus seven strikeouts, but the good guys had to work overtime for the 2–1 win. Jay Payton singled home Bobby Crosby in the tenth and we had our second straight over the Tigers.

Thursday, July 6: Hurts so Good

The Big Hurt keeps showing why we went out and got him. Forget the batting average, which has been sitting around the .230 mark. With most of the lineup ailing or struggling or both, the presence of Thomas has been a Big Blessing. And tonight he made his presence felt again, with a walk-off, two-out, two-run homer that was crushed so hard, losing pitcher Scott Shields didn't even bother to turn around and peek.

With Anaheim, LA, whatever, riding into town on a five-game winning streak, call this 7–5, see-saw special a Big Win.

The A's led 2–0 after one, fell behind 3–2 (on three solo shots by the Halos), came back for a 5–3 advantage (yard work by Johnson and Swisher), then watched the Angels tie it at five with a fourth homerun (in the sixth) and a Vladamir Guerrero double in the seventh. The tying two-bagger came off Chad Gaudin, who had just relieved Brad Halsey, so while the tying two-bagger left Vlad glad, Chad and Brad were steaming mad. After an intentional walk loaded the bases with no outs, Chad's mission was to face the two other Angel batters that had left the building this night. Chad was downright rad, striking out Mike Napoli and getting Juan Rivera to ground into an inning-ending, game-saving double play. For the Angles, it was too bad, so sad.

And adding insult to injury was Thomas laying waste to Shield's three-and-oh offering, scoring Swisher ahead of him and starting the ritual of a happy beating at home for the mighty slugger.

Sunday, July 9: Angels in Our Outfield

Anaheim is feeling it after a 4–2 win to close out the first half and they are surely acting and talking like they've been here before. Maybe it's because they have. And why shouldn't they feel at home here? After all, they've sprayed champagne in the visitor's locker room the last two seasons. In two series at Oakland this year, they've lost the opener both times, only to win the remaining five games. They took three of four this weekend with lights-out pitching and now sit just two games behind the first-place A's, who at 45–43, are tied with Texas.

In years past, we lamented the All-Star Break; it often came as our team was heating up. Now we have to hope it derails the charging Angels from speeding past us. Everyone in the AL West is in it, but it's still ours to lose.

Isn't it?

Monday, July 10: Halftime Humor

One more e-mail for the road:

DM: Any thoughts on the first half of the baseball season so far? Lousy weekend and yet we're in first at the break for the first time since 1990. Usually we're doing the chasing at this time of year. And lastly, Tejada to the Angels? Say it ain't so, Miggy.

John: I'd trade MVP candidate Bobby "I broke my finger nail" Crosby, Rich "now my other arm hurts" Harden and a sissy to be named later for Miguel Tejada in a heartbeat.

23 / Going Steady (2006, 2nd Half)

"It's a long race
If I try I will surely finish
It's a long race
If I try I will surely win it"

—Bruce Hornsby, *The Long Race*

Wednesday, July 12: Take Me Back
The second half of the season starts tomorrow and although I have been, um, "frustrated" with the A's at times this year, I still think they have what it takes to win this thing. And I am not going to think about post-season failures and things like that. Billy Beane has always called the playoffs a crapshoot, and he says he has the data to back it up. I'm actually starting to believe him. I also believe that winning a division in baseball is one of the most difficult accomplishments in team sports. The rigors of an unbelievably long season take its toll on every ball club, and often it takes more than talent to survive. So for me, I just want to get back to the post-season, and once there, we'll take our chances. There's nothing like a playoff crowd or that indescribable buzz that filters through the stadium. I want to be a part of that again, to stand for every strike two, regardless of inning or out. To know that the nation is watching, including the fans of the teams that didn't make it this far. I guess I've gotten a little spoiled by the A's, because two seasons without the playoffs feels like twenty. I want to go back so bad I can taste it. And I am willing to go through whatever it takes to get there.

Thursday, July 13: Please Come to Boston
The A's open up Round 2 with four at Fenway, three at Camden Yards, and three at Detroit. World Cup fans would surely call this

the Group of Death. I guess it could have been tougher; there are no games against the Yankees or the champion White Sox.

Tonight we shocked the Sox in a thriller. They jumped out to a 3–1 lead after two frames, but scored only one more run the rest of the night, and fell 5–4 in eleven innings.

How did the A's do it? With a little help from their hosts. All-Star second-basemen Mark Loretta bobbled Bobby Kielty's grounder in the seventh, allowing the tying runs to score. It was only Boston's thirty-first error (and Loretta's fourth) all season.

In the eleventh Kielty's two-out single drove home Kendall with the lead run, and then he shocked everyone in the park by stealing second base. When Big Hurt singled the redhead home, we had our insurance run. And we needed it. After Ortiz and Ramirez made quick outs, the Sox rallied to within 5–4, before finally going down.

It was the A's league-leading eighteenth one-run win of the year and a great way to kick off this half.

Sunday, July 16: Leaving Town on a High Note

After whipping the Red Sox 15–3 on Friday, we fell victim to Curt Shilling on Saturday, 7–0. But if the Good Joe Blanton shows up today, we can leave Boston with an impressive series win.

Good Joe showed. He allowed just a fifth-inning, two-out, solo homerun, by which time the A's had already built a 5–0 lead, and we went on to an 8–1 win. Kendall (3-for-5, one run) and Kotsay (4-for-5, one run, three ribbies) did most of the damage.

Beating Boston is always nice, but to take three of four in their place is extra special. Especially with the Rangers and Angels hot on our heels.

Wednesday, July 19: Not for the Birds

The A's split their first two games with Baltimore, and with today's game being played early, I'll be listening in at work.

Barry was solid once more (seven innings, one run on five hits), as we won it, 5–1. Bradley homered in the third, and Chavez and Thomas went back-to-back in the sixth.

The standings remain the same since leaving Boston three days ago:

	W	L	GB
Oakland Athletics	50	45	
Texas Rangers	49	46	1.0
Anaheim Angels	48	46	1.5

Thursday, July 20: Birthday Wishes
No game today, just a birthday wish to Mom. Seventy years young and still going strong.

Wednesday, July 26: Afternoon Delight
The A's lost two of three to Detroit, and have dropped the first two back home against Boston. Today's an afternoon game, and I am leaving work early to hook up with Christina and Greg. My favorite Sox fans, Brian and Jill, will be joining us. Meanwhile, it's my first game in person since May 20. For shame.

Obviously the A's needed me today to get them back on track. Haren went seven and gave up just a run on four hits, and we cruised, 5–1. Thomas gave Boston a double dose of Hurt with a solo shot in the fourth and a three-run bomb in the fifth. Dude is something else.

Thursday, July 27: Hallmark Moment
Today is Tonianne's birthday so I decided to send her some love with a little extra mustard on it:

Happy—Green and Gold…Catfish is Perfect…Reggie's Regiment…Beep Beep Goes the Roadrunner…Vida Blue Blazer…Mustache Gang…Geno Wrecks the Reds…Final Out Land's in Joe Rudi's Glove…Finley's Heroes…Captain Sal-Reggie's Revenge…Rollie's Handlebar…Green Grounds the Dodgers…Once More In '74…Come On Claudell…Goon Squad…AmaA'sing…Billy Ball…Crazy George…Run Rickey Run…Best Outfield in Baseball…Tostadas in the Rain…Bleacher Bums…90 Feet and Take a Seat…Green Teeth…Bring Back Red Rush…Chicken Stanley…Mike Warren No-Hitter…Stewww…Bash Brothers…SWEEP THE GIANTS…The Eck…Money-ball…High Fivin' Miggy…Kendall Scores on a Missed Throw Back to the Pitcher…Chavy's Gold Gloves…Still in First Place—**Birthday!**

Friday, July 28: Tongue in Cheek

The family can be a little mean with our A's, but it's all in good fun. Blame me; I started this one.

DM: Bobby Crosby is hurt again with a "mild" back strain. Do you think the Yankees would take him and Rich Harden for A-Rod?

Tonianne: I'm unable to reply to your email at length. I have a "mild" paper cut on my right pinkie and I'll need to go home now.

DM: Hey, can one of you kidnap Loaiza so he doesn't pitch tonight?

John: When does he ever pitch?

DM: After reading how you cracked on Crosby and Loaiza, when did you two turn into Dad? I thought I was the only one! Maybe the 70's World Series warranty has worn off?

Tonianne: I AM DAD! Michael has started telling me to close my mouth—in the first inning. He makes me leave the room when the A's have the lead!

John: I'm sorry. We've had a lot of good players, a few great players and a boat load of bad players, but we've never had wimpy, fragile players. Hey if you stink, you stink, at least we know where you stand, but don't go on the DL every time you slide into a base FOR THE LOVE OF…the game!

Hehe, they're only kidding.

(Then again, maybe not.)

Tonight three generations are in attendance: Mom and Dad, Carol (with Carlos), and Nathaniel.

Loaiza leaves in the sixth after giving up four runs on eight hits. Not a terrible outing but enough to beat him on this night. A's fall 4–3, and out of first place after a forty-three day stay on top.

Saturday, July 29: Calling the Shots

Me and Hoback took in a game for the first time this year, and it didn't look good when Troy Glaus touched Zito for a first-inning grand slam. Afterwards, Hoback turned to me and said, "We'll win, 7–4." Meanwhile the Angels, who took over first place last night, went up early in Boston. Hoback calmly predicted a 7–6 win for the Sox.

So what happened?

Big Papi drove home the winning run in the eleventh to beat Anaheim, 7–6. As for the A's, they scored all their runs over the fourth through seventh innings, with Payton's two-run single in the fifth putting us up for good, in a 7–4 win.

Calling the shots.

The win puts us back in first and a repeat performance tomorrow will give us a series win over this tough Toronto team.

Sunday, July 30: Walk On, Walk Off

I figured after Hoback proved lucky yesterday that he was worthy of another game this afternoon. We were clinging to a 3–2 lead in the ninth when the Jays jumped on Street for three runs on four hits, not one of them a cheapie. As the A's came up in the bottom of the ninth, neither Hoback or I said a word. Partly because we were stunned, partly because we somehow decided at the same time that if we were going to win it, every ounce of energy needed to be directed towards the field. Crosby flied out to center. Damn. Mark Ellis singled. Kendall flied out to left. Two outs. Meanwhile, I took note of a Jays' fan a few rows in front; he kept turning around to taunt the crowd. I didn't like him very much. As Kotsay batted, Ellis took second without a throw. Kotsay got ahead in the count, three balls to one strike, and then proceeded to foul off B.J. Ryan's next seven pitches. Finally, Ryan missed with a pitch and Kotsay took first with a hard-earned walk. Just an unbelievable at-bat. I glanced towards Hoback just to make sure he was still alive. Maybe I did it just to make sure I was. On the fourth pitch to Milton Bradley, the A's were alive and kicking as he crushed a three-run homerun to deep center field for a stunning victory, while me and Hoback went crazy. What better way to head into Anaheim tomorrow night?

Monday, July 31: Just a Feeling I Get

Great game tonight. Dan Haren versus Ervin Santana, who always seems to pitch us tough. I watched this one at home. Bradley, yesterday's hero, homered with two out in the sixth to tie it up at one apiece. In the seventh Payton came up with a man on and no outs. I can't tell you why, but I just had "that feeling" that Payton was going to hit it out. And he did. Haren took it from there with a complete-game, 3–1 win.

July is in the books and the A's are still in front, but barely; by a buck-fifty over the Angels, with two more games in SoCal.

Tuesday, August 1: This Month's Forecast: HOT

In the tradition of Tonianne in the '70's, I have been marking my A's magnet schedule with "W's" and "L's" all season long. Today Abel came over to my cubicle and carefully scanned the month of August. Then he went back to his desk, grabbed a post-it, wrote on it, then came back to show me. On that little yellow square were the numbers "21–7," the won-loss record that Abel felt we'd post this month. I told him I didn't want to see or hear any of his insane predictions, and sent him back across the room. Later we came to realize that we play only twenty-seven games in August so he changed it to "either 21–6 or 20–7." Regardless, I can't stand when he does things like that.

The A's lose to the Angles tonight, 3–2, shrinking our lead back to a half game.

Monday, August 7: Texas Hold 'Em

The A's beat Anaheim on Wednesday to take the three-game series, then swept Seattle, running their winning streak over the Mariners to an astonishing twelve games. Tonight we're home, Texas is in town, and I have tickets.

It was Mark Ellis' night to shine as he stroked a two-run homer in the third and a two-RBI double in the sixth. Bradley, who has been flat-out amazing of late, crushed a solo shot in the seventh, and we won it 7–4.

Tuesday, August 8: Comeback Kids

For the second time this season, me and Hoback saw the A's go down early 4–0. And for the second time this year, we saw the A's erase that deficit on their way to victory. It was all tied up in the fourth after Swisher (a three-run job) and Payton went back-to-back, and the A's scored one in the seventh and two in the eighth to go up 7–4, before settling for a 7–6 win.

Make it five straight, the lead is three over the Angels, and we can't seem to lose when I'm in attendance. It's a nice feeling.

Tuesday, August 15: Turning it Up
After sweeping Tampa Bay over the weekend and taking the first of this three-game set with Seattle last night, me and Abel are pairing up for our first game of the season tonight.

Like Hoback, my brother likes to toss out predictions at the ball park. While watching Mariners' starter Joel Pineiro in the first, Abel says to me, "We're going to rope this guy tonight." Naturally, I cringe at such talk. But just for kicks, let's show you how Pineiro made out:

	IP	H	R	ER	BB	SO
Pineiro	3.2	12	9	9	5	1

As ugly as it gets. A's romped 11–2, and we go for another Seattle sweep tomorrow afternoon.

Wednesday, August 16: No Love
Bill Simmons is at it again. In his ranking of American League teams (and their chances of making the World Series), he lists his usual "sleepers" and "favorites." He underrates the A's at the seventh slot and labels them his "Whatever" team:

"I can't take the A's seriously—no home-field advantage, not a single dangerous bat, no Rich Harden, a 1–2 punch of starters (Zito and Haren) who seem to get shelled every three weeks (only their statistics don't reflect this for some reason), and a good bullpen that's helmed by the exceedingly hittable Huston Street (trust me, he's on my AL-only team; even when he's shaking hands after the save, you're still waiting for something bad to happen). And did I mention the legacy of playoff losses? They're like the Memphis Grizzlies of the American League. Whatever."

Someone tell me why I keep reading this guy?

Wednesday, August 23: No Jinx

My oldest brother wrote in today (rare for him) with the subject, "Will I Start a New Jinx?" Ernie cut and pasted e-mails of mine from earlier this season, when I was letting my frustrations get the best of me. Each time, the A's answered with a string of wins.

As it stands now, we have lost three of our last six games, but I'm still feeling pretty good about the state of my team.

Not that I'd ever admit that in public.

Well, you know what I mean.

Two days later, **Abel** answered Ernie with this e-mail: Magic Number is 29. That's how you do a jinx, Ern.

When no one in the family responded, he sent a second e-mail: You guys are all afraid to discuss this, aren't you?

Tonianne (finally): I was afraid to delete it, move it, or handle it in any manner whatsoever!

And they call *me* superstitious.

Monday, August 28: Hot August Nights

After winning their fifteenth straight over the Mariners back on the 16th, the A's took to the road. We struggled to salvage a four-game split with Kansas City, but then won two of three in Toronto, highlighted by a complete-game shutout by Loaiza, who gave up just four hits and no walks, while striking out seven. He's a changed pitcher since the month started. We went on to take two of three in Texas as Zito fired seven perfect innings in the series opener (we tuned in at Mom and Dad's house). Tonight, we return home to face a depleted Red Sox team, who are without Papi and Manny. Me and Hoback will join Christina and Greg for this one.

Tonight's outcome was to be expected as Loaiza once again was on the money. Seven more shutout innings in a 9–0 slaughter. Thomas and Swisher are neck-and-neck in the team homerun race; both hit Number 28 tonight.

And Abel's prediction? Well, we're 19–6 with two games left. Unreal.

Wednesday, August 30: A's Make Good, Who Cares?

The A's kiss August goodbye with a Sox sweep, an amazing 21–6 record, and a seven-and-a-half game lead over the Angels. But all ESPN is talking about is Curt Schilling, who notched his 3000th career strikeout.

Tonianne: I don't know why I do this to myself but I had to watch "Baseball (except Oakland) Tonight" knowing that we swept Boston and finished August with another great record. I just wanted to see what they would say. Anyways, forty-five minutes into the show, after they recapped the AL and NL wildcard races in painstaking detail, they finally got to our game (although I think ours was completed looong before any of the ones they'd already shown). So, of course they started with Schilling, showed the A's fans giving him an ovation for the 3000th K (but didn't mention the fans), showed Swisher's great catch, gave the score, and went on to talk about Boston's injuries and how far they are behind the Yankees.

John: The funny thing is the A's aren't surprising anyone. Many "experts" picked them to win the West and more. I think what's surprising or pissing everyone off is that they have done it without hitting much and despite a lot of injuries. I guess everyone thinks we should only be winning with a "Bash Brothers" team. We have no offensive superstar and that seems to be a problem for everyone.

As Bill Simmons would say, "Whatever."

Saturday, September 3: Most Valuable Persons

I finally got Don Jr. to attend a game with me, and we saluted Tonianne and all the other ladies that took the field for Breast Cancer Awareness Day. Christina, Greg, and Ethan were there, too.

Baltimore jumped out to a 5–0 lead, but in the bottom of the sixth, Big Hurt brought us back to within 5–4, with a three-run blast. Both Don Jr. and Greg looked at me at like I was nuts as I shouted "MVP" during Thomas' jog around the bases. Unfortunately, we left the tying run on base in the ninth, and fell to the O's, 6–5.

It's the first time I've seen the A's lose in person since May 20.

Wednesday, September 6: Panic Mode

After losing "my" second straight game last night (with Hoback, Scott, and Brittany), the A's are 2–3 to start September. Nothing a little family therapy can't fix:

DM: There is an "A" in August, but none in September, and if they're not careful, there will be no A's in October either.

Abel: Eleven days ago when we were 5-1/2 games up on the Angels (we're both 6–4 since) we couldn't be happier. Now that we've essentially "burned" ten games of the season panic is setting in. We will win the West! Relax.

DM: I just wanted Ernie to have one more negative comment to add to his collection. There is something to be said about momentum. And as an A's fan, I reserve the right to panic.

Tonianne: We don't need the E-jinx because Joe Morgan tried to impose his own on us on Sunday night. Jon Miller was saying how a 7–1/2 game lead may not be enough since we play the Angels ten more times. Morgan said that's overrated since the Angels would essentially have to sweep us to make a difference and unless we completely collapse before that (and he didn't see that happening since we have so many different guys who can win a game for us), the A's have nothing to worry about. I was like, 'Who is that talking?' Anyways, I'm with Abe—nothing to worry about!

My hour's up.

An annoying trend during this mini-slump is that we've been playing catch-up almost every night. This afternoon was no different, as the Rangers took a 6–3 lead after five innings. But the A's struck for six in the sixth and we won it, 9–6.

Tonianne: How's *that* for a comeback?

Wednesday, September 13: Haren-Raising Win

The A's are 2–3 on this trip and are one loss away from a Minnesota sweep. But we have Haren going for us this morning, and he's come up big when we've needed him to. I feel good about our chances.

Haren delivered. Boy, did he ever! Eight innings of three-hit ball. One walk, seven strikeouts. And a huge 1–0 win at the Homer Dome. Street closed it out, 1–2–3 in the ninth.

We're 5–1/2 up on the Angels with seventeen to go, including the next ten in Oakland. Our last homestand.

Friday, September 15: The Last Laugh

The World Champs are in town, and me and Scott are going.

I can't recall a bad outing by Loaiza since I ripped him back in July. Dude was just beautiful tonight: seven innings, three hits, two earned runs, a walk, and five strikeouts. Marco Scutaro had himself quite a ball game in front of his biggest fan (Scott so loves the guy that he claims he's Venezuelan); he went 4-for-4 with a run scored.

There was unintentional comedy in the stands tonight after another defensive gem by Eric Chavez. (He does it so often, I've just gotten used to it.) Chavy's throw was fielded by an outstretched Swisher at first, and as Scott mimicked the play, I thought he was reaching for a low-five from me. I swung and missed at his hand, and we sort of sat there in awkward silence until I brought it up two innings later. After that, we couldn't stop laughing about it.

Something else worthy of a chuckle: the A's won, 4–2, and the magic number is down to eleven.

Tuesday, September 19: Steph and Bob-ay

My niece Stephanie (home on military leave) turned twenty-one today, so she's my partner for tonight's game. As you surely read in Chapter 17, Bobby Kielty hit a grand-slam in her honor, and the A's rolled over Cleveland, 7–3. All of our scores came on home-runs; Chavez hit a solo shot in the fourth, and Swisher's two-run jack in the eighth put an exclamation point on the night's festivities.

Thursday, September 21: All in a Day's Work

Me and Tone skipped out of the office early today to catch some afternoon action between the A's and Indians. It was a three-hour affair, in which ten pitchers were used, but we gutted out a 7–4 win. Shades of so many summer days spent at the park in the '70's.

The Angels are in town for three, and we can clinch as early as Saturday. So I took a chance and purchased tickets for that day (I'm already scheduled to go tomorrow and Sunday.) Here's hoping.

Friday, September 22: Closing In

Another game, another birthday, another sister to attend with. This time, it's me and Tricia for Christina's big day. Ernie and John are also here tonight.

The one thing you can expect with the A's and Angels is that they'll battle to the end. Swisher put us up 2–0 with his 33rd home-run in the fifth, but Zito gave up two in the sixth. In the seventh. Howie Kendrick led off the seventh with a solo homer, but Chavez duplicated that in the bottom half to make it 3–3. With two outs in the eighth, Bradley homered off of rookie sensation Jered Weaver, and we were three outs away from victory. But, and there's always a "but" with these teams, the Angels scratched out a run off Street in the ninth. With a man on first and two outs, Maicer Izturis hit one down the left field line that—just barely—eluded a diving Payton, and the game was tied. It stayed that way until the twelfth, with Christina and Greg long gone. Christina said she wasn't feeling well, and I could relate. After Kielty led off the twelfth with a double, Swisher was walked intentionally with one out, bringing up Scutaro. How many times has this guy come through for us? Many, plus one, as his single to left brought home Kielty with the winning run, while the crowd went berserk.

Magic number is two, with two chances to clinch at home, and I have tickets to both.

Tuesday, September 26: Champs Again

After two unsuccessful attempts to clinch at home (Hoback scolded me for taking Tonianne on Saturday and Abel on Sunday), the A's blew a 9–5 lead in Seattle last night, while the Angels rallied past Texas. The lead is down to five, with seven games left. You know what that means. Yep, time for a family e-mail:

DM: If anyone has any encouraging words, now would be an excellent time to offer them. Otherwise I'll keep telling myself that I'd rather be in our shoes than in theirs.

Tonianne: I cried myself to sleep last night.

Tricia: I didn't cry, but I'm pretty sure I have an ulcer.

DM: Speaking of crying in baseball, me and Steph went to the game last Tuesday and we were mocking the drummers in left field. I told Steph, "I bet none of them have ever cried after a heart-breaking defeat" and she said, "I bet their grandmas have never cried after a loss like mine has."

And then Mom called today just to see how I was doing and we both cursed the Rangers for "losing on purpose" and it made me laugh because this might be the only time in my life that it's totally ok to hate angels.

John: Seattle was due to beat us. It's the odds, you can't defy them forever. It will be over tonight.

The A's jumped out to a 6–0 lead and this time they would hold on for a 12–3 rout. With Texas winning in Anaheim, it was only a matter of outs. When Chad Gaudin coaxed a fly ball from Rene Rivera, which was then gloved by Bradley, it was time to CELEBRATE THE CLINCH!

Immediately my phone began to ring at the house. First Hoback, then Scott. Liz and Rebecca left me and Steph behind, and we drank beer into the night.

Wednesday, September 27: Thank You Notes

DM: I want to thank everyone for standing by me and "my girl" these past few months. It was ugly there for awhile in May and June. And even in that first week of July, it looked as if it might be over. Such a dire situation it was that people were whispering that "the angels" were coming after us. She said she needed to get away, so I sent her to Pittsburgh for three days. On that Wednesday night, she called and said "meet me in Boston." I was reluctant, no fan of Beantown am I. But we hooked up and immediately I could see the change. There was a sparkle in her eye; she was full of vim and vigor. August was, well, amazing. Every day, something new. She was somewhat less glamorous than past GF's. She did not stand out in a crowd; she preferred it that way. People would talk about us—"how do they stay together"? It was her. Whenever things got hairy, she rose to the occasion to make it better again, even if it meant staying up past bedtime to work it out. It sounds cliché but she was determined not to let us go to bed angry. As the summer drew to a close, I started to withdraw some. She became worried, even thought I might have my eyes on someone else. "What is it?" she asked. "Nothing" was my reply. When she noticed that the twins from Minnesota made me especially antsy, she was convinced that my heart was not completely hers. We argued for two days but on that second night, it came out. I told her, "This is around the time of year that I get dumped. And even though it seems better, it's been awhile since I've gone this deep into September thinking that this year might be different." She replied by saying, "I know you think this is too good to be true, but I am not like the other girls. And I know that people are waiting for us to crumble but don't listen to it. I'm stronger than the others and if they want to talk crap, I will put the big hurt on them." We laughed and I realized that everything was going to be alright....We didn't have a very good weekend and things got worse Monday night, but we woke up Tuesday morning feeling pretty good about ourselves. So I took a chance last night and I popped the question and she said "I do" and well, I know this is sudden, but we might be looking at an October wedding. Meanwhile, there will be butterflies and surely more comparisons to past flings, and publicly she'll say none of it matters, but secretly she'll say she wants no part in adding to a legacy left behind the girls of yesteryear (unless, we're talking about that dreamboat from the 70's). The lesson here, of course, is that first impressions (a 15–2 stinker on Opening Night), aren't nearly as important as last ones.

P.S. I wrote this after we beat the Angels Friday night, and when Tuesday morning came, I seriously considered having one of my warehousemen drop a pallet of furniture on my head.

John: When the A's went up seven games over the Angels with ten games left, a guy at work told me it was over. I said no it's not, and that the A's were going to blow the lead. Yesterday he was starting to believe it and was calling me a jinx so I had to calm him down by telling him what I told you when you went into panic mode yesterday. 'It will end tonight.' Dad of course had gone into Tasmanian Devil mode. I didn't say anything about the A's on the way to work yesterday per Rose's request but he came into my office at the end of the day and said, 'I'm not watching those choke artists anymore! They're going to get swept by Seattle, the Angels are going to sweep Texas and then they're going to sweep the A's!' I told him that Texas would win tonight (last night) and the A's will take care of business in Seattle but he wouldn't believe me. Speaking of ladies, somewhere there is a very large one singing her heart out.

(And then like the wonderful family that we are, a little "disagreement" broke out. Hey, we do it for the holidays, why not now?)

Rose: Now I'm mad!

Dad watched the game by himself. Mom stayed in my room after she came home from a meeting. Mom was feeling guilty because we were celebrating together and he was out there by himself. I came close a few times to asking Dad why he was watching them *now*, but I knew it's because they were winning. On Monday night he had gone to bed cursing them, saying that he hated this stupid team and he didn't even read the paper Tuesday morning. Had I'd known what John just told us, I would have definitely said something. I called Mom and she said 'Now I don't feel guilty!' Believe it or not, Dad would watch an entire Giant's game before he finished an A's game.

Abel: Give me a break.

Dad has been like this his whole life. Do you really think he is going to change now? As he gets older, he'll get even worse (or better) depending on whether his teams are losing or winning.

DM: There's no true pain in watching the Giants. Unless they're winning.

John: Dad will watch the Giants until they do something good, then it's "click" cape buffaloes mating. If he's watching the Yankees and Giambi comes to the plate it's "click" Chinese Television soap opera.

DM: I must be sick because part of the joy of seeing my teams win is watching Dad curse his teams when they're down and celebrate when they win. It's just Dad being Dad. Childish, crude,

fair-weathered, that's my Dad. You might think he deserves to celebrate as much as Bonds deserves Hall-of-Fame induction, but hey
if you had popped a bottle of champagne seconds before Franco
made his Immaculate Reception, your perspective on sports might
be a little off-kilter, too.

Tonianne: If Dad didn't give up on the A's and Raiders, we
would never win. That's just the way it is, so let him celebrate today
because come next Tuesday, he'll be cursing us once again!

Ernie: Whatttt???? I thought we lost?

John: We did lose Ern. This is everyone's way of doing therapy.

After this season is over, we will surely need some. But for
now, bring on the Minnesota Twinkies and first-round curses!

24 / One For the Ages (ALDS 2006)

"Holy Toledo!"

—the late Bill King's signature phrase
(surely King would have used it in abundance in this series,
as the A's won a playoff series for the first time since 1990;
a triumph not just for today, but years gone by.)

Tuesday, October 3, ALDS Game 1 @ Minnesota

I am going to let the e-mails "call the action" for this morning's playoff game. Being that most of us are stuck at work. (Love that East Coast influence.) Barry takes the ball for us, opposite Minnesota's Johan Santana.

John: We're under way!

Tonianne: We're under where?

Frank Thomas leads off the second inning with a homerun.

John: We're in the lead! BIG HURT!

Scutaro doubles home Payton for the second run of the inning.

DM: MARCO!

Abel: SCUTAROOOOOO!

After the Twins score one in the seventh, Thomas goes yard leading off the ninth.

Tonianne: 3–1…I'm hurtin'!'

Greg: Before this season the Twins were interviewing Frank, and decided against making an offer since the turf wouldn't be good

249

on his ankle. I bet they wish now they had signed him because he's Hurtin' 'em now!

DM: I just gave Abe a one-armed bear hug while on a call with one of my installers, the phone dragging across my desk.

The A's hold on for a heart-racing 3–2 win.

Greg: That's one.

John: Ten to go. Yeah baby! Awesome!

Tonianne: You stole my line. I was just about to hit send when I got a call from Mom! I picked up the phone and the voice said, 'Go A's!' She knew we were going to beat Santana, his streak was bound to end.

Ernie: Ok, since I said I wasn't going to watch the games, and I did, and we won, what do I do tomorrow? Be careful Abe, be very careful.

John: Rose said that Joe Morgan had some great insight after the game ended, 'Oakland should go out and try to win tomorrow's game.'

Let's not forget the job Zito did. He out-pitched the Cy Young Award winner. The Twins had won twenty-three straight games that he started at home. Records were meant to be broken and streaks were meant to end.

Tonianne: Speaking of streaks, what's the record for consecutive e-mails during one work period? Not that anyone is working.

DM: Dear Trish, please do *not* turn your computer on. Trust me.

John: I sent the first one. I'll forward all 978 e-mails to Rose.

Wednesday, October 4, ALDS Game 2 @ Minnesota

The e-mail thing worked well enough yesterday, so we're going with more of the same. Only one problem: no one is writing.

Christina: What? There's not fifty e-mails waiting for me in my Inbox?

ESPN blames Loaiza's "downfall" in the bottom of the 4th to the "coffee incident." ARGH!!!! I hate ESPN. What downfall?!?! I had to mute the TV and put the radio on. (I started to think this email was pointless, but then realized the A's scored two runs while writing it.)

John: You said you didn't want us getting together so you've been cut off. Just kidding.

I think this game is more important now that we beat Santana so everyone has been nervously quiet.

DM: I was in training, and with Abel doing such a fine job with score updates, I'm thinking I should go back to the conference room.

As Christina reported, the A's take a 2–0 lead in the fifth on Scutaro's RBI double and Kendall's run-scoring single. As for the "coffee incident," Bradley spilled some on Loaiza, who had to change jerseys.

DM: I can't wait to see the headlines for this win: "Perked-up Loaiza Puts Twins to bed."

John: "Twins get wake up call"?

Minnesota hits back-to-back homers leading off the sixth inning to tie the game at two.

Meanwhile, Greg orders a latte and I order my coffee black, like my women (*Airplane* joke). Then I change "women" to "outfielders." Christina asks jokingly if I mean Kotsay. I tell her no; I am referring to the coffee spiller, Bradley, but ask her if she'd ever seen Kotsay run. And she asks if I've seen his booty, and while all this silliness is going on, Kotsay hits a shot past centerfielder Torii Hunter for an electrifying two-run inside the park homerun. Timing is everything.

The A's tack on another run and win, 5–2, to go up two games to none. Boy, have we been here before, or what?

Abel: I predicted 5–3 A's, two-run HR (by Chavez), tied at three after six innings, with Loaiza getting no decision, Calero the win and Street the save.

(He came pretty damn close.)

John: I watched ESPN news at lunch. The opening line was "What went wrong for Minnesota?"

Tonianne: They met up with the A's.

Ernie: I just got back from the Englander with my whole department. We had an "offsite meeting" that started at 10:00. I feel more stressed out than I did during that crazy week at work last week. I should have stuck to my plan and not started watching until the ALCS. FYI, I had to walk out in the ninth after Street started throwing balls.

DM: How did Dad get on these e-mails?

John: Speaking of Dad, he turned the game off when the Twins tied it. He thinks if he doesn't listen (once he gets mad) we'll win. Then he'll ask who won after he already hears us talking about the win.

The funny thing about the coffee deal was when Loaiza turned to see who did it. He looked like he was going to pound someone until he saw it was Bradley. Then his face changed to "Oh, never mind" and he just went and grabbed a new uniform.

But the bigger story is Ellis' injury, although no one in the media will make much of losing a .245 hitter. But his defense has been superb, and he and Scutaro have played together most of the season, which is important when it comes to turning two. We had been weak up the middle in years past but now with Kotsay, Scutaro, Ellis and Kendall we are one of the strongest teams in that defensive category. His broken finger is going to hurt us a lot more than it hurts him, and a lot more than people think.

Friday, October 5, ALDS Game 3 @ Oakland

The game starts at one, and I'll be there with Hoback. Abel and T have tickets, as do Uncle Dan, John, Scott, and Scott's friend, Daniel. It's overcast and gloomy, but we're all feeling a win here. We down Coronas in the parking lot and head in. Right away, you can feel the difference between today and year's past. This is our day, our time.

In the first inning, I got the first of two premonitions. The Twins had first and second with only one out, when I envisioned a ground ball to Chavez. Sure enough, the next pitch was hit his way, and Chavy turned it into a 5–4–3 double play. In the bottom of the second, I got another one. Again it involved Chavez, and the much-maligned slugger made it come true with a rope into the right-field seats for a 1–0 lead. Scutaro, who was unbelievable in this series, doubled home Payton for our second run of the inning. In the third, Kotsay reached on an error and scored on Bradley's two-run homer. That made it 4–0, and the beer kept on flowing. I had been through too much and had waited too damn long for this day to come, and I was going to enjoy it. The Twins cut it to 4–2, but in the bottom of the seventh, our Venezuelan shortstop turned out the lights.

With two outs and no men on, Big Hurt was intentionally walked. Then Chavez walked, and Payton reached first on an error to load the bases. After Swisher walked to "drive" in Thomas, Scutaro stepped up to the plate. With more than 35,000 fans screaming "Marco! Scutaro!" over and over, Marco Scutaro gave A's fans one last thrill in a season full of them. His ringing double down the right-field line drove home all three base runners, and I celebrated the 8–2 lead with a bear hug that nearly knocked over my best friend of more than twenty-five years. We have seen hundreds of games together, but that moment right there may have topped them all. Scutaro himself got caught up in it, squatting down near second base as if to say, "What have I done?" What he had done was something that the Big Three, or Giambi, or Miggy could not do. He had gotten us past the first round, and I'll never forget the way we chanted his name or how he came through for us.

Ernie: YESSSSSS!!!! Feels good doesn't it?!

John: A bunch of us were at the game. It was one of those experiences that will stay in my memory bank like being there for Joe Rudi's homerun in Game Five of the '74 World Series and being there to watch Stabler sneak into the end zone against the Patriots in the '76 playoff game. I'll never forget the crowd chanting 'Marco! Scutaro!'

Epilogue

I can go into the gory details of how the A's lost four straight to the Detroit Tigers in the American League Championship Series. I was at the first two games with Hoback, listened to Game 3 at work, and watched the finale from my couch. Alone. There's your details. Calls were made and e-mails were written. In all honesty, when it was over, I wasn't all that upset. We ran into a better team, plain and simple. It happens. End of season, end of story.

But what a wonderful ride it was!

As one of the newest members to the family looked back on the 2006 season, he found a slew of questions to ponder.

Greg: Would I remember that this was the year that Frank "Big Hurt" Thomas wore the Green and Gold, averaged .270, and hit 39 home runs? Would I remember that the A's had hoped that Thomas would be a part-time DH playing in half the games, and getting a couple hundred at bats, but then played in 137 games and went to the plate 466 times? Would I remember that Chavez FINALLY got hot early, only to disappoint at the plate with a .241 average? Would I remember that Kendall nearly got back to his career .300 average? Would I remember that Zito had an ERA of 3.83 or that Haren struck out 176 batters? I'm not much of a statistician, so probably not.

Would I remember that this was the year that key players like Crosby and Harden got hurt early, hurt often, and barely got on the field, yet we still broke our streak of getting knocked out in the first round of the playoffs? Would I remember that this was the year that young and confident Nick Swisher kept pace with "Hurt" for most of the season and knocked 35 over the fence? Would I remember that we gave Kendall and Kotsay their first taste of the post-season? Would I remember that this was the final year for Zito in Green and Gold, the last of the Big Three? Would I remember that Ellis broke his finger in Game 2 of the ALDS and had to give up his starting position to…to…what was that guy's name? Would I remember that this was the year that the A's fans really got behind Marco Scutaro, the bench player of all bench players, and gave him a cheer that will stick with him the rest of his career? Would I remember that this was the year, out of superstition, that during the ALCS I got out of my seat, went to a second deck stairwell, covered my head, and prayed to the Baseball Gods to change our mojo and get something rolling? I'm a sucker for an underdog, for superstition, and for a hard luck story, so maybe I will remember these.

But then I realized why I love being an A's fan. I'm not a fan of any particular player; it's the organization that I support. It's become a tradition for me and for my family, a very large part of our lives. It's an entire event from Game 1 to 162, whether in the stands or on TV. That's why I enjoy the A's with friends and family. That's why I insist on tailgating whenever possible. That's why we take friends to the game whenever we can. That's why we take our two-year old son, Ethan, to the games instead of leaving him with a babysitter. I'll remember days in the sun with friends and family. I'll remember the tailgates and game-day debates on who'll do what and how we'll win this one. I'll remember this was the year that Ethan, with a very limited vocabulary, would say 'A's, A's, A's' whenever we got within a mile of the stadium. I'll remember that Ethan could pick out the A's announcers on TV or the radio and could differentiate them from any other announcer. I'll remember that Ethan would watch the entire game to root on his team, a lot of patience for an eighteen-month old. I'll remember that when watching games on TV, Ethan would run around the living room, down the hall, through the kitchen, out the dining room, back to the living room, and slide into home yelling 'safe' between innings. Now that we have purchased 2007 Season Tickets, my invoice tells me that this was the last year Ethan got into the games for free. And then it hit me, and it hit me hard. What I'll remember most is that this was the last year that Ethan had the best seat in the stadium…his Daddy's lap.

Tonianne: A great year. No one but no one (except Abel) expected them to come this far. With all of the injuries, we had no business winning our division but somehow we managed to do it and there was no backing into it. We just never gave up. We finally met up with a team that simply refused to lose; they played like a team that knew everything would go their way. The A's had chances but in the end, we really didn't have a *chance*. It wasn't our time. So remember, it's only 119 days until spring training. Go A's!

To be an A's fan is to know that nothing comes easy. Not long after the season ended came the news that the team had reached an agreement to purchase acreage in Fremont, with the intent of relocating there as early as 2011. Big Sis wants to make sure it's official before shedding a tear. She's been through this before.

Tonianne: I can't count the number of times "they" had us moving (back to KC, to Denver, to Phoenix, to Florida, to D.C.). Every time I'd spend the off-season praying that we wouldn't go. At least this time (if it happens), we'll be close.

A couple days after Christmas, we learned that Barry Zito, the last of the Big Three, had done the unthinkable and unforgivable: he signed a seven-year deal with the Giants. Calls to Christina, Tricia, and Tonianne drew identical reactions: they were all going to be sick to their stomachs. Tone (who I had called during her trip to Chicago with Michael) made me laugh when she told me later that Michael brother's Greg responded not to the trade, but to how she found out about it. A phone call from her little brother, while she walked the streets of Chicago. "That's dedication, man!"

Hey, we're A's fans and we're family. It's what we do. And it will always be that way. The manner of which we spent this past season; really, how many other families interact that way…over a baseball team?

As we head into our fortieth season of A's baseball, the family that roots for them remains intact. Yes, some of them have moved on, and are sorely missed. Grandpa Abel and Grandma Toni. Uncle Don. Uncle Walt. Aunt Genie. Uncle Rick. I guarantee they'd have some stories to tell.

The Green and Gold has been passed down from one generation to the next, as if it were a secret recipe. The transformation, when seen first-hand, lends a sweet sense of déjà vu. Like when the Three Amigos (Ethan, Xavier, and Nathaniel) put their A's caps on, and "play ball," you swear you've been here before. Well, you have. Look closer: that's me and Abel in Mom's backyard. Or John and Tony Lopez at Cherry Grove. The heroes they emulate are surely different than ours from an era long forgotten, but they're still heroes.

Our devotion has stood the test of time. The means have changed, but the ideals remain the same. So while Tonianne's transistor radio has evolved into Christina's TiVo; in the end, it's still about connecting with our beloved A's.

And it is in these stories that have been told here—and the many memories left to be created—that makes me realize how truly blessed we are. The way I see it, we're part of two families, two traditions. And when those two worlds collide in April with the season's first pitch, well, that's when you know you're home.

Safe at home   ❖

The author and Don Jr. in that Wonderful Summer of 2006.